"*Nan Dòmi* is a fascinating look inside the Haitian Vodou religion. Mimerose Beaubrun provides a valuable contribution taking us along into the world of Nan Dòmi, a dream state and stage in the initiate's journey to mastery. Much in the spirit of Carlos Castaneda's Don Juan books, Beaubrun follows the teachings, at times baffling, of her guide, Aunt Tansia. In the process the reader is introduced into a world that is far more than a religious tradition. Haitian Vodou is also a way of speaking about Haiti, as Beaubrun explains, 'its language, culture, even its way of walking, of preparing food, of dressing, of making love, of communicating with unknown worlds.' The book casts its spell on the reader who persists in the journey under the tutelage of Beaubrun and her teachers. Madison Smartt Bell's excellent introduction places the religion and Beaubrun's memoir in historical context." — Julia Alvarez

"For those looking for a first-person guide — and importantly, a Haitian guide — into the ways of Vodou, Mimerose Beaubrun's Nan Dòmi is a unique, indispensable and mysterious primer." — Amy Wilentz, author of *The Rainy Season: Haiti Since Duvalier* and *Farewell, Fred Voodoo: A Letter From Haiti*

"Vodou is one of the most valuable — and misunderstood — of all New World cultural creations. Mimerose Beaubrun's remarkable work opens up for the first time the internal world of Vodou, and what emerges is a singular engagement with a system of belief that cannot fail to impress any reader with its sheer sophistication and complexity. Gradually, the author recounts the ways in which she came to know the timeless wisdom of Vodou. Absolutely essential reading for anyone interested in Haiti, or in religion and society more broadly." — Martin Munro, author and editor of *Haiti Rising: Haitian History, Culture and the Earthquake of 2010*

"This new and valuable book delves into the 'interior' experience of Vodou, as opposed to the usual outsider focus on ritual and cosmology. In telling the story of her own initiation and painstaking education in Vodou, Beaubrun takes us into the mystical dimensions of this ancient religion." — *The Guardian UK*

# Nan Dòmi

AN INITIATE'S JOURNEY INTO HAITIAN VODOU

# Nan Dòmi

AN INITIATE'S JOURNEY INTO HAITIAN VODOU

**Mimerose P. Beaubrun**

Preface by Madison Smartt Bell

Translated by D.J. Walker

City Lights Books • San Francisco

Originally published as *Nan Dòmi, le récit d'une initiation vodou* by Vents
d'ailleurs, La Roque d'Anthéron, France, 2010
Published in the United States as *Nan Dòmi: An Initiate's Journey into Haitian
Vodou* by City Lights Books in 2013

 Translation made possible with support from the Centre national du
livre: www.centrenationaldulivre.fr


Library of Congress Cataloging-in-Publication Data

Beaubrun, Mimerose P. (Mimerose Pierre)
  [Nan dòmi, le récit d'une initiation vodou. English]
  Nan dòmi, an initiate's journey into Haitian vodou / Mimerose P. Beaubrun
; preface by Madison Smartt Bell ; translated by D.J. Walker.
     pages cm
  Includes bibliographical references and index.
  ISBN 978-0-87286-574-7 (alk. paper)
  1. Beaubrun, Mimerose P. (Mimerose Pierre) 2. Anthropologists—Haiti—
Biography. 3. Vodou—Haiti. 4. Vodou—Rituals. 5. Initiation rites—
Religious aspects—Vodou. 6. Ethnology—Haiti. I. Title.

  BL2490.B3813 2013
  299.6'75097294—dc23

                          2013035055

City Lights Books are published at the City Lights Bookstore,
261 Columbus Avenue, San Francisco, CA 94133.
www.citylights.com

# Contents

# Acknowledgments

My thanks to all those who have encouraged me and to those who have given me information:

Minon (my brother), Gérard Barthélémy who made the publication of this book possible, Madison Smartt Bell, Yakini, Pierre Richard, Camp David, lakou Jean-Gilles, nan Ma (Malique), lakou Déréal, nan Balan, nan Kanpèch, lakou Palmine, Madjoro, lakou Soukri, nan Dòno, nan Badjo, anba pont Paroi, nan Lamatri, lakou Souvnans, père Bien-Aimé, man Choune, Mori Batèlmi, man Diran, man Tata, madan Jacques, Régine, Florence, Jah Lucky, Carla, Harry, T-Henry, Paul, Ted and Laura.

I particularly want to thank Aunt Tansia, Ti Carlos and Lòlò, who helped me so much throughout this apprenticeship and who know what this choice has meant.

We need
Dance, poetry,
Sounds, music,
Dreaming to nourish
Our bond of communication
With the Unknown.

Anacaona
(Transposed by Aunt Tansia)

# Note to Readers

In order to facilitate reading, words and terms in Kreyòl that are repeated throughout the text are italicized and asterisked on first appearance and followed by a concise translation in parentheses. These words and terms are subsequently presented in roman type.

A Lexicon of Kreyòl words and terms is provided at the end of the book, often with expanded translations.

# Preface

*by Madison Smartt Bell*

Since Europe (and later the United States) first became acquainted with it, Haitian Vodou has been known and popularized only through its darkest, most sinister side. The misperception is very severe; it is as if one were to promulgate a definition of Christianity based entirely on a description of Satanism. Like so many false images of its kind, this spooky picture of Vodou is based on incomprehension and fear.

The spectacular outward manifestations of Vodou observance—hypnotic drumming and chanting, which drive frenetic dancing, which itself is likely (and intended) to culminate in violent-seeming fits of spirit possession—are off-putting to the European mind and its descendants. Since Europe first began to penetrate Africa, white explorers and reporters have described such scenes under the rubric of "savage rites"—spiced with hints or outright accusations of cannibalism, the latter seldom justified by any facts whatsoever. It is a very common human habit to take alarm at anything which seems alien, and then, using rules of spiritual polarization that are by no means unique to Christianity, repel it by defining it as diabolical.

And, to be sure, these diabolical definitions have always had their political motives. The ideology of conquest and colonialism requires that the conquered and colonized be depicted as unenlightened and uncivilized and, if possible, even somewhat less than human. To justify the slave trade it is helpful to see those who are to be enslaved as unfortunate heathens in desperate need of redemption by a militant Christianity, equipped with whips and chains. For centuries, Europe used these rhetorical devices to put itself at a safe distance from Africa. Therefore, whenever a *blanc* (in Haitian nomenclature all non-Haitians are defined as *blanc*, whatever the color of their skin) encounters Vodou for the first time, the psychological reflexes of his reaction are already in place . . . and have been there for centuries.

We have been well instructed to fear the strange. And yet, if Vodou is disturbing to the European mind, that is partly because, after all, it is *not* so strange. The tremor that Vodou makes us feel down in the older deeper roots of our brain is a pulse of atavistic memory—a response to ancient, original religious impulses which are better called "primary" than "primitive." So when the *misik rasin* group Boukan Ginen sings

> *Lafrik, Lafrik maman nou*
> *Lafrik, Lafrik papa nou*
> *Lafrika, se ou ki wa. . . .*[1]

they are singing to those of us of European descent as much as to themselves. *Lafrik se lakay tou nèg.* In Haitian parlance, *nèg* means not "black" but "human being"; the "*blanc*" is distanced as a potentially monstrous alien. Since all humankind originally evolved out of Africa, then inevitably, *Africa is the home of all human beings.*

The Spanish priest Bartolomé de Las Casas, who was among many other things a sort of *ur*–liberation theologian, was not alone in suggesting that Africans be transported to Hispaniola,[2] to replace the native Taino[3] people whom the conquistadors had almost completely exterminated by slave labor. Las Casas had seen a population of over a million Taino reduced—in a mere thirty years—to less than ten thousand. He was wrong to

---

1 Africa, Africa is our mother
Africa, Africa, is our father
Africa it's you who are king. . . .
2 Hispaniola is the name Christopher Colombus gave the island when he landed in what is now the Bay of Saint-Nicolas in 1492. The inhabitants called it Ayiti, "mountainous land." [Translator's note.]
3 An Indian tribe (from America), inhabitants of the island of Ayiti before the colonial period, all but decimated by the Spaniards.

hope that the substitution of Africans for Indians might save the remnant of the latter, who after all did not survive. But his disappointed hope helped turn the trickle of African slaves toward the New World into a flood.

Today's Haiti, the western third of the island of Hispaniola, was ceded by Spain to France in the Treaty of Ryswick in 1697. French Saint Domingue, as the colony was known, soon became the most important producer of sugar and coffee in the whole Western Hemisphere—France's richest overseas possession by far. The wealth was created by African slaves; when the French Revolution erupted in 1789, they numbered about half a million. The conditions of slavery in Saint Domingue were extraordinarily harsh—slaves who were not literally worked to death were inclined to commit suicide—to the point that the slave population came nowhere near reproducing itself. Between 1784 and 1790 some *two hundred and twenty thousand* slaves were imported to the colony—merely to maintain a stable workforce. In 1791, when the Haitian Revolution broke out, two-thirds of Saint Domingue's slaves had in fact been born in Africa.

Most were shipped from the West African coast, out of the kingdoms of Benin and Dahomey. They came from many different cultures and tribes: Senegalese, Yolof, Bambara, Mandingo, Arada, Ibo, Nago and Kongo—to mention only a few. The languages of these different groups were for the most part mutually unintelligible. Their religions, though different in detail, shared common fundamentals. The white land- and slave-owners, outnumbered by their chattel by a factor of twelve to one, made some effort to jumble slaves from different tribes, to make it more difficult for them to whisper among themselves or plot against their masters. At the same time, some means of communicating with all the slaves was necessary. The lingua franca of the colony was a patois described by a twentieth-century manual as what one would expect to evolve from requiring half a million Africans to learn French by listening to it but without being told any of the rules.

In theory, the French colonists were meant to bring their slaves into the fold of the Catholic Church, but in fact the evangelical program was fairly weak, especially after the Jesuit order was expelled from Saint Domingue on suspicion of excessive sympathy for the slaves. The slaves did have some exposure to Catholicism, however, and incorporated many aspects of the cult of the saints into their own beliefs and practices—which were prohibited more in theory than in fact. Slaveholders tolerated gatherings of slaves for the purpose of drumming, singing and dancing—these *Calenda*, as they were called, were seen as useful to release tensions that might otherwise be expressed in the slave rebellion that all the white colonists quite reasonably feared. These assemblies were officially understood as entirely secular "country dances," though contemporary descriptions by whites reveal that at least some of the colonists knew very well that they had a religious dimension.

On August 14, 1791, a secret gathering (secret from the whites) took place in a forest called Bois Caïman[4] on the border of the Plaine du Nord, Saint Domingue's richest sugar-producing region. The written historical record (set down, of course by Europeans) establishes that at this meeting a general insurrection of the slaves was planned—whose outbreak, the first explosion of the Revolution that ten years later would make Haiti independent, reduced the plantations of the Plaine du Nord to ashes within the first few days. The Haitian oral tradition holds, with equal if not superior conviction, that the centerpiece of the meeting at Bois Caïman was a great Vodou ceremony in which the entire pantheon of immortal spirits was called to assist and inspire the Revolution.

Understanding of the meeting at Bois Caïman tends to split on a sharp racial and cultural fault line. For Europeans and their descendants, the most significant thing about it is the diabolical plot to raze the plantations and massacre the white population—in its entirety if possible—a plot sealed by a blood sacrifice and perhaps abetted by actual devils summoned to the scene by the powers of African sorcery. For Haitians, however the slaughter of the *blancs* (whom the slaves had small reason to regard as human beings like themselves) is a relatively insignifi-

---

4 During the ceremony at Bois Caïman on the night of August 14, 1891, the call to the struggle for liberty was given by Boukman Dutty, the chief of the rebels.

cant byproduct of the event, whose real purpose was to create a Haitian national identity, complete not only with a shared revolutionary purpose but also with a common language—Haitian Kreyòl—and a common religion—Vodou. In historical reality the evolution of Kreyòl from the contact of numerous African languages with French and the coalescence of Vodou from various African religions with a common exposure to Catholicism must have taken a great deal longer to happen, but (like the Creation story from Genesis) the legend of Bois Caïman *makes* it happen in one instantaneous flash of an enormous spiritual power. Given the massacres that were part of the immediate practical result, it's understandable that *blancs* should find this story frightening—but to Haitians, what it most resembles is the Sermon on the Mount.

The African slaves of Saint Domingue inhabited a world of death. For most, the ancestral religion was in fact a system of ancestor worship. Many different African religions share the belief that the souls of the dead, instead of departing to a far distant Heaven or Hell, as in the Christian tradition, are translated into a parallel universe quite close to our own—close enough to touch, though normally we cannot see it. These are Les Invisibles, Les Morts et Les Mystères, who yield the individual identities they owned when incorporated into human bodies, and pool into a vast reservoir of spiritual energy, reminiscent of the Emersonian Over-soul.[5] This parallel universe is to be found on the dark side of any mirror, or beneath the surface of any pool, and especially below the surface of the ocean, where we must find *Ginen anba dlo*—Africa beneath the waters. When slaves said that by drowning themselves in the ocean they would return to Africa, this is what they meant.

The brutality of the slave trade, the horrors of the Middle Passage, and the horrendous conditions of slavery in Saint Domingue tremendously accelerated the passage of souls from the world of the living to the Island Below Sea. An estimate

_____
5 Ralph Waldo Emerson (1803–1882) defined the notion of the *Over-soul*: That unity, that Over-soul, within which every man's particular being is contained and made one with all others. . . . Mind is the only reality. [Translator's note.]

of twenty-five thousand deaths per year would be conservative; thus, by the time the ceremony at Bois Caïman took place, at least two and a half *million* African souls must have passed beneath the waters. No wonder the eruption was volcanic when it came.

The practice of Haitian Vodou involves penetrating the barrier between the visible and the invisible worlds, opening passages, gateways and crossroads. The Kreyòl word for crossroads is *kalfou*. Such *kalfou* may be found in many places and represented in many ways, and they have a slight numinosity wherever they may be found. Most *vèvè*—the elaborate designs drawn on the ground as maps to guide the spirits where to come—incorporate the image of the crossroads, especially the *vèvè* specialized for Attibon Legba or Maît' Kalfou. The same image of intersection can be seen in the crossbar of a sword hilt and is easy enough to perceive in any variation of the Christian cross. Material meetings of the ways, roads or streets or mountain pathways are apt to carry the same spiritual charge, and are often seen as powerful locations for the placement of charms. It is well to remember that Hispaniola is one of the most important historical crossroads in the entire Western world—the *kalfou* where American Indians, Europeans and Africans came together for the first time. Out of the fiery violence of that meeting, a new religion was forged.

A formally organized Vodou peristyle will usually erect a *poto mitan*—post in the middle. The *poto mitan* creates a *kalfou* where it enters the ground—implying the lower half of the cross pattern invisible beneath the surface of the earth, as the extension of a tree's roots is equal, symmetrical to that of its branches. Often enough a tree may fulfill the function of a *poto mitan*, at the same time that it serves as a *reposwa*, or resting place for spirits. Or, priest or practitioner may simply stick the point of a blade into the ground, creating a *kalfou* image that stresses the piercing of the membrane between the invisible and material worlds. The image of a sword so placed is part of the most common *vèvè* for Attibon Legba.

Legba has points of similarity with the Greek Hermes; like Hermes he may find a *reposwa* in cairns of stone, and his actions resemble Hermes's message-bearing transits between the different spheres of gods and mortals. Haitian Vodouisants identify Legba with Saint Peter, the guardian of the gates to Paradise, and particularly with Catholic icons in which Saint Peter displays a key. Legba must be invoked first in all ceremonies, for he is the spirit with the power to open the gate, the door, the crossroads between our world and *Ginen anba dlo*; only with Legba's permission and blessing can the *lwa*[6] form themselves out of the great well of Les Invisibles, Les Morts et Les Mystères, and surge up the channel of the *poto mitan* to enter the world of the living.

"Legba, then," writes Maya Deren in *The Divine Horsemen*, "is guardian of the sacred gateway, of the *Grand Chemin*, the great road leading from the mortal to the divine world. It is he who grants contact with the loa, and he who must first be saluted if this is to be achieved. 'Papa Legba, open the gate, Attibon Legba, open the gates that we may pass through, Papa; when I have passed, I will thank the loa[7].'"

Deren goes onto explain that the Grand Chemin, as an image of the road of a person's life, follows the "celestial arc of the sun's path," and the person walking that road enacts the stages of the famous riddle of the Sphinx, first crawling on all fours as an infant, then striding on two feet as an adult, and finally in old age stooping to the point of adopting a cane as a third leg. Legba is most often seen in the last condition, limping with his staff and weighed down by a big straw sack, while Vodouisants encourage him with song: "Try to walk now, Alegba; We will carry Attibon Legba: We will carry his Poteau mitan. . . . When we're tired we'll set it down. This post we carry on our back."[8]

Following this sunset curve toward the horizon, Deren goes on: "It is as if in coming westwards, the Africans had left behind the morning and noon of their own destiny, the promise and power of their own history. The God of the Cross-roads himself approaches the Cross-roads, and already in the dark mir-

---

6 In general, the lwa is a divinized ancestor drawing its power from its earthly life. The lwa is a family asset. It is an enlightened spiritual being.
7 Maya Deren, *The Divine Horsemen*. New York: Chelsea House Publishers, 1970, 98.
8 Ibid., 99.

ror of the nether regions appear the first dim outlines of his inverted reflection, as the sun setting into dark waters, might there appear as a new darkly rising moon. Already Legba, who is the tree stretching skywards, also carries the name Grand Bois, master of the island below the waters, of its submerged forests. Already his omniscience, which was the result of his central, supreme position in the center, from which all could be seen, becomes the omniscience of one who, being below earth, is of all parts of it. Already he is linked to Carrefour,[9] whose other hand holds firmly that of Ghede, Lord of the Underworld, God of the Dead."[10]

Deren's description captures how, in the Vodouisant master vision, the world we normally can't see (the parallel universe, in Mimerose Beaubrun's term) tends to be a symmetrical reflection of the world that our bodies live in and that our senses perceive. The passage also shows how the spirits are mutable rather than fixed; instead of remaining rigidly separate, they tend to flow one into another as they rise out of or drain back into the great lake of Soul from which they were formed. Most spirits have more than one aspect, and many have several. Even the beneficent Attibon Legba has his inverted reflection on the dark side of the mirror: Maît' Kalfou, potentially much more deceptive, sinister and dangerous. Ogou Feray is the warlike aspect of a *lwa* analogous to the Greek Ares—a spirit of iron, blood and fire—but he has numerous other less martial aspects, like Ogou Balendjo, the friend and protector of travelers. Erzulie, in one respect a Vodou Aphrodite, may appear as Erzulie Fréda, a compassionate apparition, represented by the Catholic icon of Our Lady of Sorrows, her heart laid open by a sword. But in her jealousy and rage she manifests as Erzulie Jé Rouj, the Red-Eyed Erzulie—and there is also Erzulie Dantòr, associated with war, revolution, and the sacrifice of a black pig at Bois Caïman.

One finds in the panoply of Haitian Vodou spirits the same wide range and similar universal personalities as are found in any polytheistic pantheon—or, if one prefers the model of depth

---

9 More commonly, Maît' Kalfou
10 Deren, op. cit., 100.

psychology, in the archetypes of the collective unconscious (the latter phrase works as a secular synonym for *Ginen anba dlo*). As Roman Catholics position God the Father, the Son, and the Holy Ghost well above the hierarchy of Catholic saints, so Vodouisants place God the Creator—Bondye, Bon Dieu or Gran Mêt Ki Bay Lavi (Great Master Who Gives Life) above their individuated spirits—whose relationship with their *serviteurs*, or human servants, tends to be more direct and more personal. The relationship may also be double-edged.

In the north of Haiti, especially, Vodouisants tend to distinguish between *lwa* and *zanj*. The former are spirits more apt to be called upon to provide material assistance to the people who do the calling: money, power, successes in love or in war or revenge. The more sinister aspects of the *lwa* are more likely to take part in such affairs; if one wants to settle an issue of jealousy, one will more probably seek Erzulie Jé Rouj for help, not Erzulie Fréda. These transactions do tend to involve harm to others, an exercise of force and constraint on the assisting *lwa*, and a resemblance to deals with the Devil as they appear in the Judeo-Christian tradition.

By contrast *zanj*, or angels, are more likely to manifest themselves spontaneously, or in response to prayer and song—in response to an effort on the part of believers to purify their body and brain as a temple for the *zanj* in question. The appearance of *zanj* is inspiration in its purest and most beneficent form. Those who court relations with *zanj* are more likely to be seeking spiritual betterment than furthering personal and material ambitions. In this atmosphere, the highest values are very similar to those of charismatic Christianity: nearness to divinity, detachment from the material world and the passions it engenders in the individual, an abrogation of the individual self in favor of uniting with a higher power, and a mystical sense of union with the community of fellow practitioners, which union is mediated by the presiding *zanj*. This unselfish way of serving the spirits is usually called Ginen.

In the seminal song "Kalfou Danjere," the *misik rasin* group Boukman Eksperyans puts these two different ways of serving the spirits into diametrical opposition with the fierce refrain,

*Tuyé, nou pa tuyé*
*Tuyé, nou pa tuyé,non*
*Tuyé, nou pa tuyé*
*Ginen pa Bizango!*[11]

In actual practice, the separation is seldom quite so absolute. It is very common for a *houmfò* (Vodou temple) to practice Ginen wholeheartedly at the same time that it harbors a Bizango secret society. The arrangement may be expressed by the maintenance of a separate *kay mistè* (chamber of mysteries) for each practice. Moreover, most *houngans* and *mambos* (Vodou priests and priestesses) are understood to "work with both hands"—the beneficent right hand is applied to good works in the spirit of Ginen, while the sinister left hand works to enable the more culpable human desires: lust, avarice, envy and wrath. Right-handed actions in Vodou are usually about purification and healing—physical, psychological and spiritual—and involve the partaking of gifts freely given, in the manner of communion in the Christian church. The left hand, when it is not overtly violent, still uses force as it may be expressed and embodied in the iron of chains and the gold of coins.

A *pwen*, in the Vodouisant lexicon, is a point of spiritual power, which may be used to do magical work in the material world. A *pwen* is a point in the spiritual world where spirit energy has fixed itself, or been fixed, in a material object: a jar, a bottle, a stone, a carving, or even a bundle of cloth. *Houngan* balanced more toward the left are called *bòkòr*—they are apt to traffic in *pwen achté*, or bought points. The spirit caught in a *pwen achté* resembles the genie shut up in the lamp—the owner of the object can compel the spirit to do work, and so the spirit is best understood as having been captured and sold into slavery. This situation is expressed by the chains or ropes or cord or thread that are used to tie up and bind the typical *pwen achté*. Since the

---

11 Kill, we don't kill
Kill, we don't kill, no
Kill, we don't kill
Ginen is not Bizango!
*Bizango* denotes a Vodou sect, a kind of secret society. It is also a state of being.

spirits trapped in them labor under duress and resentment, *pwen achté* are notorious for turning on their purchasers.

At the right-handed, Ginen end of this spiritual spectrum, practitioners may have the use of *pwen* freely. These *pwen* are sometimes called *pwen herityé*—inherited as opposed to purchased points—they may include *pyè tonnè*, the thunderstones which come down to today's Haitians from the extinguished Arawak[12] Indians, or the *canari* jars in which an aspect of an ancestor's soul has been preserved and protected. Powers that a Ginen practitioner may deploy through the focus of such *pwen* come freely out of the goodwill of the spirit which exercises itself through the *pwen*.

Zombification is the ultimate expression of the idea of enslavement implicit in the *pwen achté*. Like so many elements of Haitian culture, zombification turns out to be both metaphorical and literal at one and the same time. For decades, if not centuries, observers assumed that the legend of dead bodies being physically resuscitated and forced, while deprived of their souls and their consciousness, to labor, was no more than mythological. The rapport of this metaphor with Haitian history was apparent: The *zombi*, whose will and identity have been destroyed to force him to work for another's purpose, bears a very close resemblance to an 18th-century plantation slave, if not to a twenty-first-century cane cutter laboring for practically nothing in cane fields across the Dominican border. But in the 1980s, the ethnobiologist Wade Davis[13] discovered that what was so effective metaphorically also did exist as an actual fact: Certain *bòkòr* did have knowledge of a toxin that would stop all life signs long enough for an apparently dead body to be buried and resuscitated a couple of days later—brain damage and sheer terror would be enough to produce the classic subhuman characteristics of zombidom. Yet when Davis first went looking for *zombis*, he was presented not the *zombi cadavre* (the resuscitated corpse) but what was to the Haitian mind just as

---

12 One of the Indian tribes living in Ayiti before colonization.
13 See Wade Davis, *Passage of Darkness. The Ethnobiology of the Haitian Zombie*. Chapel Hill: University of North Carolina Press, 1988.

powerful but infinitely more convenient: the *zombi astrale*, the soul shut up in a bottle.

Of course magical work is by no means unknown in the Judeo-Christian tradition (no more than in others of the world's great religions) nor is it always necessarily associated with witchcraft, Satanism and diabolical deal-making. Consider the Catholic practice of saying novenas, or praying for the intercession of a particular saint to solve some particular problem. But these are always private acts, sheltered and hidden from the adjacent public sphere of outward observance, ritual and worship.

At the outer perimeter, a Vodou ceremony looks a lot like a neighborhood party. And to a degree that's just what it is. Of course, some ceremonies are secret and can only be entered by high-level initiates, but many are at one level community festivals. On the outskirts, everything is quite worldly. Women are selling food and drink. People come to see their friends and enjoy the entertainment of drumming and dancing. A good deal of secular business gets taken care of, as it does, for example, on American golf courses, if not so much in American churches anymore.

The closer one approaches the center, though, the more this ordinariness falls away. The center is among the drums, or more precisely in the space immediately before the drums, the focal point where the most intense dancing takes place. Here too, possession is most likely to occur, as the observers become celebrants the closer they come to the inner circle. The dancers are not merely amusing themselves but dancing their way to an altered state. Under the pressure of tightening of bodies around them and the compression of drumming and chant, one or another will give way to the crisis of possession—from the outside it may look like a convulsive seizure, but sometimes possessions happen very quietly, on the perimeter of the event, to celebrants who don't seem to be dancing or singing at all. Sometimes the possessed look as if they know exactly what they are doing and how they are doing it. Sometimes they seem to be taken completely by surprise.

Very few people have tried to describe the experience from the inside, but Maya Deren does a beautiful job:

"I did not even mark the moment when this ceased to be difficult and I cannot say whether it was sudden or gradual but only that my awareness of it was a sudden thing, as if the pace which had seemed unbearably demanding had slipped down a notch into a slow-motion, so that my mind had time, now, to wander, to observe at leisure, what a splendid thing it was, indeed, to hear the drums, to move like this, to be able to do all this so easily, to do even more if it pleased one. . . .

"As sometimes in dreams, so here I can observe myself, can note with pleasure how the full hem of my skirt plays with the rhythms, can watch, as if in a mirror, how the smile begins with the softening of the lips, spreads imperceptibly into a radiance which, surely, is lovelier than any I have ever seen. It is when I turn, as if to say to a neighbor: "Look! See how lovely that is!" and see that the others are removed to a distance, withdrawn to a circle which is already watching, that I realize, like a shaft of terror struck through me, that is no longer myself whom I watch. Yet it *is* myself, for as that terror strikes, we two are made one again, joined by and upon the point of the left leg which is as if rooted to the earth. Now there is only terror. . . . Resting on that leg I feel a strange numbness enter it from the earth itself and mount, within the very marrow of the bone, as slowly and richly as sap might mount the trunk of a tree.[14] I say numbness, but that is inaccurate. To be precise, I must say what, even to me, is pure recollection, but not otherwise conceivable: I must call it a white darkness, its whiteness a glory and its darkness, terror. It is the terror which has the greater force, and with a supreme effort I wrench the leg loose—I must keep moving! Must keep moving!—and pick up the dancing rhythm of the drums as something to grasp at, something to keep my feet from resting on the dangerous earth. No sooner do I settle into the succor of this support than my sense of self doubles again, as in a mirror,[15]

14 Deren's body thus becomes itself the *poto mitan* for the passage of the *lwa* into her world.
15 This sense of doubling of the self is sometimes called *marassa*, after the twin or sometimes triplet Marasa spirits of the Vodou pantheon. Terror and pain come from the power of the experience of splitting and shredding as the ego clings to its seat in the brain, loath to let go of the person—and the person is astonished and often frightened to learn that after all the ego is not the whole person, or even the whole

separates to both sides of an invisible threshold, except that now the vision of the one who watches flickers, the lids flutter, the gaps between moments of sight growing greater, wider.[16] I see the dancing one here, and next in a different place, facing another direction, and whatever lay between these moments is lost, utterly lost.... With a great blow the drum unites us once more upon the point of the left leg. The white darkness seems to shoot up; I wrench my foot free but the effort catapults me across what seems a vast, vast distance.... My skull is a drum; each great beat drives that leg, like the point of a stake, into the ground. The singing is at my very ear, inside my head.... I am caught inside this cylinder, this well of sound. There is nothing anywhere except this.... The white darkness moves up the veins of my legs like a swift tide rising, rising; is a great force which I cannot sustain or contain, which, surely, will burst my skin. It is too much, too bright, too white for me: this is its darkness. "Mercy!" I scream within me. I hear it echoed by the voices, shrill and unearthly: "*Erzulie!*" The bright darkness floods upward through my body, reaches my head, engulfs me. I am sucked down and exploded upward at once. That is all."[17]

The induction of a trance state by whatever means necessary is common to many religions. Sometimes the means is even more flamboyant than the dancing and drumming of Haitian Vodou. The North African Jilali urge themselves into crisis by slashing each other with knives as they dance, and something similar is found among the kriss dancers of Bali.[18] Sufi dancing is a calmer, more apparently controlled exercise than these self-mutilating frenzies—but the goal of the whirling dervish exercise is certainly an altered state. "What typically happens if you enter the Hayy at any depth is that you see the forms of the

of consciousness.

16 These are classic symptoms of entry into a hypnotic trance.

17 Deren, op.cit., 258–260.

18 The dance of the barong or kriss (from the name of a Balinese sword with a wavy blade) pits the barong (symbol of the positive forces in the Universe) against the sorcerer Rangda, who impels the disciples of the barong to turn the kriss against themselves. In the course of this dance, the participants enter into a trance. [Translator's note.]

world, your own not excluded, overwhelmed and annihilated in the singleness that animates them, their outlines obliterated by a tidal signature of primary light. . . . Later on, the Turn may become many things, sometimes a mill wheel grinding off the chaff around the hearts [of] native grain, sometimes a downpour of grace, sometimes only a crucifying pain in your shoulders as you struggle to keep your arms up."[19] Monastic ritual also has such purposes, with its taxing, intentionally exhausting routines of wakefulness and ceaseless prayer; consider the intense contemplative method of Saint Ignatius of Loyola. The extreme effort and privation of the North American Indian vision quest leads to much the same goal. And in a completely secular context we have seen excitable young women "falling out" at Beatles concerts and the like, though their experience, which seems to lead no further, is apt to be put down to hysteria.

What sets Haitian Vodou apart from many otherwise similar practices is what happens when the trance state is achieved. Where once was Maya Deren now appears the great *lwa* Erzulie. It is said: It is a fearful thing to fall into the hand of the Living God.

Psychologists examining the phenomenon of possession in Haitian Vodou have found themselves perplexed. A mental illness model becomes ridiculous when so applied. Practically any Haitian may sometimes be susceptible to possession and it is absurd to believe that an *entire* population (of more than eight million people) suffers from schizophrenia, epilepsy or any other psychopathology.[20]

However, a wholly material explanation for possession can be found in hypnosis and in the role played by hypnosis in multiple personality syndrome. The rhythms of Vodou drumming and chant have all the characteristics of hypnotic induction. One explanation proposed for multiple personality syndrome as a First World psychopathology is that an auto-hypnotic state

19 Rafi Zabor, "The Turn: Inside the Secret Dervish Orders of Istanbul," *Harper's Magazine*, June 2004, 56.
20 See Steve Mizrach, "Neuropsychological and Psychological Approaches to Spirit Possession in Haiti," www.clas.ufl.edu/anthro/scholarly/spiritpos.html.

facilitates the suppression of a the core personality and permits its replacement by a different identity and a different consciousness—and also the successive apparition of many different personalities which are likely to be perfectly unaware of each other.[21] This mundane and reductive scheme transfers reasonably well to the experience of possession in Vodou. The religious interpretation of the experience can then be explained in terms of "set and setting"; i.e., the *lwa* materialize because they are expected to—both by the possessed individual and by the surrounding, supporting culture.

But most who experience such transformations prefer expansive to reductive explanations. At what would seem to be the absolutely opposite pole from Haitian Vodou, among the most extreme Pentecostal sects in the United States, one finds an amazing similarity in the subjective experience. Pentecostal snake-handlers would almost certainly consider Vodou to be Devil-worship—a pure expression of Satan's power in the world. But this first-hand description of the snake-handling practice shows how closely related the two experiences really are:

The look in Carl's eyes seemed to change as he approached me. He was embarrassed. The snake was all he had, his eyes seemed to say. But as low as it was, as repulsive, if I took it, I'd be possessing the sacred. Nothing was required except obedience. Nothing had to be given up except my own will. This was the moment. I didn't stop to think about it. I just gave in. I stepped forward and took the snake with both hands. Carl released it to me. I turned to face the congregation and lifted the rattlesnake up toward the light. It was moving like it wanted to get up even higher, to climb out of that church and into the air. And it was exactly as the handlers had told me. I felt no fear. The snake seemed to be an extension of myself. And suddenly there seemed to be nothing in the room but me and the snake. Everything else had disappeared. Carl, the congregation, Jim—all gone, all faded to white. And I could not hear the earsplitting music. The air was

21 See Eugene Bliss, *Multiple Personality, Allied Disorders and Hypnosis,* New York: Oxford University Press, 1986.

silent and still and filled with that strong even light. And I realized that I, too, was fading into the white. I was losing myself by degrees, like the incredible shrinking man. The snake would be the last to go, and all I could see was the way its scales shimmered one last time in the light, and the way its head moved from side to side, searching for a way out. I knew then why the handlers took up serpents. There is power in the act of disappearing; there is victory in the loss of self. It must be close to our conception of paradise, what it's like before you're born or after you die.[22]

Possession frees the soul from the self. Practically all religions and mystical practices of the world seek this release—by whatever means necessary. What Vodou has in common with the other great religions of the world is the voluntary surrender of the egoistic element of self—if not the entire individual self—in favor of a divine power. One must lose one's life to find it. This insight is beautifully expressed in another song by Boukman Eksperyans, "Sa'm Pèdi."

*Pèdi lavi-ou*
*W'ap jwen lavi ki pa janm fini*
*(jan Kris di. . . .)*
*Sa'm pèdi pou sa!*
*M pa pèdi anyen, non* [23]

Or, as Saint Paul put it in Galatians 2:20,[24] *It is no longer I who live, but the Christ who lives in me.*

Mimerose "Manzè" Pierre Beaubrun is a founding member of Boukman Eksperyans, which, with her husband Theodore "Lòlò" Beaubrun, she continues to lead. From the start the group

22 Dennis Covington, *Salvation on Sand Mountain: Snake-Handling and Redemption in Southern Appalachia.* New York: Penguin, 1996, 169-170.
23 Lose your life
You will find the life that never ends
(as Christ said. . . .)
What do I lose in this?
I don't lose anything, no
24 *Epistle to the Galatians* II, 20.

has been politically, as well as artistically and spiritually, engaged. With other *misik rasin* groups like Boukan Ginen and RAM, Boukman Eksperyans wrote and performed the soundtrack for the Lavalas populist movement and the first landslide election of President Jean-Bertrand Aristide in 1990. After the coup d'état against Aristide in 1991, the group was threatened with assassination by the ruling military junta and went into exile until the restoration of the democratic government in 1995. In a sad irony, the Beaubruns and other members of Boukman Eksperyans had to flee Haiti again in the winter of 2003–2004, this time under death threats from the Lavalas regime. Since then they have returned to their country, where they continue to be active in the pro-democracy movement. The members of Boukman Eksperyans were named Peace and Goodwill Ambassadors by the United Nations in the summer of 2002.

Like her husband, Mimerose Beaubrun is a member of Haiti's small but significant educated minority. At its early levels, the Haitian educational system preserves, as if in amber, the entire corpus of the French Enlightenment inherited from the colonial period. One graduates from a Haitian *lycée* with a title of *philosophe*, speaking the French of Voltaire and conversant with most of the knowledge accrued by the other eighteenth-century French *Lumières*. Grafting a modern university education onto this very solid base has produced some of the most formidable intellectuals to be found anywhere in the world.

Mimerose Beaubrun topped off her conventional education at Les Frères du Sacré Coeur de Turgeau with a degree in Social Anthropology from the Faculté d'Ethnologie in Port-au-Prince. She made her first conscious entry into the world of Vodou as an anthropologist/ethnologist—with a project to study the social structure of the Vodouisant/familial communities called *lakou*. At the same time both she and her husband were beginning to collect Vodou drum rhythms and traditional songs to incorporate into the repertory of the fledgling Boukman Eksperyans. In that process, both Manzè and Lòlò made profound reconnections with their own ancestral *lakou*: his in the mountains above Port au Prince and hers near the border town of Ouanaminthe near the frontier of the Dominican Republic in Haiti's North-East

Department. This renewal of living roots in Vodou brought a strong religious current into the music of Boukman Eksperyans, a current that runs under the songs' overt political messages and furnishes them a deeper, more eternal power. Among her own forebears, Manzè discovered her ultimate teacher and guide to the mysteries: Aunt Tansia, whose knowledge, wisdom and spiritual power govern the text of *Nan Dòmi*.[25]

Since Haiti has spent 200 years as a pariah state, the African roots are much better preserved in Haitan Vodou than in other religions of similar origin elsewhere in the Caribbean and in Latin America. For that reason, Haitian Vodou is especially beloved of anthropologists and has been much more exhaustively studied than other related religions of the region, whose traditions have been more diluted by greater contact with the outside world. But practically all scholarly reports on Vodou are outsider accounts, and practically all outsider accounts are arrested in descriptions of external rituals and practices, which means that they are stopped on the threshold.

Most anthropological studies of Vodou are also hampered by their effort to determine and describe some universal orthodoxy analogous to Judeo-Christian orthodoxies . . . but no such orthodoxy exists in Vodou. As anthropologist Gérard Barthélemy has put it, Vodou offers plenty of rite, but next to no dogma. Because the presiding spirits have their origin in the souls of dead ancestors, Vodou makes plenty of room for idiosyncratic variations between one *lakou* and the next. Paradoxically for a religion that insists on uprooting the ego on a regular basis, Vodou, because it offers anyone the possibility of incarnating a divine spirit, is unusually empowering to the individual at the same time.

Like all the great religions of the world Vodou has an external, public practice of rituals and ceremonies—and also an internal, mystical dimension which is more likely to be practiced in extreme privacy, though it would be somewhat inaccurate to call it personal. Before *Nan Dòmi*, works about Vodou have con-

25 Nan Dòmi: a concept that defines the second stage of attention. One enters into a state that permits one to see abstract things unknown until then. It is a state of lucid dreaming.

centrated on the former—on the public, external dimension of the religion and its surrounding manners and mores. Mimerose Beaubrun set out, originally, to write another such work. But after a couple of decades of study and collection, all her notes, tapes, photos and drafts were washed away in a flood. Nothing remained but the essential core of what she had learned and internalized in a place where neither fire nor flood could destroy it.

*Nan Dòmi* is the only account of Vodou's private, mystical, interior practice that has been offered to the public so far. Its content stands in the same relation to ceremonial Vodou as Zen to conventional Buddhism, Sufism to conventional Islam, the practice of the desert saints to conventional Christianity. Mimerose Beaubrun has been a *student* of Vodou for half her life, but she is also an adept, and in this uniquely valuable work, she divests herself of all scholarly apparatus to speak from Vodou's purest heart.

# Prologue

For nearly ten years I have been interested in the *lakou,* "a kind of vital space, a place of multidimensional life where several families or, rather, an extended family shares all aspects of life (spiritual, economic, cultural)." In fact, the lakou has three functions: preservation, protection and renewal. At first, my aim was to write an academic thesis on the dynamics of its economic structure, and I set out to visit different lakou in order to better understand their inhabitants' way of life. In this sense, I was bound to be a participant—I lived in a lakou—and thus was in a position to render an account of what I had seen and understood, a sense of what I had experienced. At times my research seemed to be leading me toward discoveries; nonetheless, I often felt powerless, and my efforts remained fruitless. Like a child changing school five times in a year, my sources of information changed from one moment to another.

At the end of five years I had learned nothing, and all my efforts had been in vain: I could say nothing concrete about the lakou. But I didn't suspend my research. On the contrary, I steadily continued to explore its history, oral as well as written. I gave myself body and soul to my research, immersing myself in all aspects of the lakou. Little by little the forces internal to this system ended up transforming me, causing me to evolve in another direction.

I have experienced states of soul engendered by the system of beliefs rooted in the very foundation of the lakou. Although I would have preferred not to become attached to any particular belief, in spite of myself, I ended up obsessed by my research, with the sole intention of continuing and moving forward. In the beginning, I acted this way out of self-interest, moved by the desire to finish my anthropology thesis whatever the cost. But as time passed, my thoughts and actions changed. These changes determined the course of my work, and I witnessed the dismantling of what formerly constituted the structure of my intellectual development. My work, situated within the framework of cultural anthropology, drew closer to mythology.

What happened to me in those five years led me to put aside all my plans: "I am dreaming." I have no other words to explain this sentiment. All I can do is gather as best I can the whole of my experiences such as I have lived them, from the day I began my research in the field. I have promised myself to represent everything I saw and all that happened to me during that time. I cannot give any tangible guarantee of the veracity of the stories I was told during my dream states. I also know that my experience is beyond my comprehension. What I have tried to do, in truth, is attempt to give the best of myself. Judging by what I feel now, I have entered little by little into the heart of a mystery that will help me penetrate other mysteries. I can no longer go back. I remain profoundly moved.

From the moment when I began to enter Nan Dòmi, I discovered inner resources that I did not know I possessed. Driven by a force I could not identify, I was compelled to concentrate on everything that I "saw" in my dream states. Little by little, I developed a second mode of "paying attention": Dreaming became an art. That art combines the attitudes which, guided by a particular kind of control, can make you tumble into another mode of consciousness.

Of course, I did not begin my experiences alone. There were two of us, Lòlò and me, and we had a guide. We did not want to undertake this research without the help and supervision of a *Danti*★ (elder). At the outset of my research, Lòlò warned: "This is a road for which we have no map. We risk getting lost if we don't have a safeguard, and above all a true guide."

So it was that Lòlò, my husband, accompanied me everywhere. He was the scout who led me into several lakou that he visited well before I did. Though we had both been initiated already by Aunt Tansia, we wanted to verify the knowledge we had gained, not for lack of confidence in our master, but simply in order to better orient ourselves in connection with other teachings we had received. Thus for many years I frequented Lakou Nan Jisou, on the Lori property at Haut-du-Cap, in the home of *man*★ Choune ("man" is the diminutive of "maman," a term of respect for elderly women); Lakou Beaubrun de Malique nan Ma, located about four kilometers northeast of Pétion-Ville; Lakou Lamatrie, in Haiti's North-East Department near Ouanaminthe, on the Dominican border; Lakou Souvnans, near Gonaïves, the third-largest city in Haiti; Lakou Palmine à Lamontagne at Jacmel, in the home of man Tata; Lakou Nan Madjoro to the east of Pétion-Ville, in the home of madan Jacques; Lakou Nan Balan at Mornes-Rouges, in the home of *Mori*★ (Vodou priest) Batélmi; Lakou Nan Kanpèche at Haut-Cap, in the home of man Diran; Lakou Déréal in the north, near Quartier Morin, in the home of Yaya; Lakou Jean-Gilles at Puits Blain, where I was accepted and where I have resided for nearly eighteen years. The people whose names I have cited marked me. They practice the ancient science of Ginen with such mastery that I ended up adopting their principles, concepts and methods. In each lakou I always had to wait before at last being accepted into the intimacy of the *Fanmi Ginen*★ (the family of initiates belonging to the same discipline) and its wisdom.

If Aunt Tansia, my first master, gave me life, these others have nourished me. When I began to accept their teaching, I understood that the lakou was quite different from what it had appeared to be.

I remember my first conversation with father (a term of respect for elderly men) Bien-Aimé, *sèvitè*★ (spiritual head) of Lakou Souvnans: As he addressed Lòlò, he looked me straight in the eye and repeated many times, "*Ginen pa Bizango.* (Ginen is not Bizango.)"

In his honor, our musical group Boukman Eksperyans took up this theme in 1992 in a *chante pwent* (satirical song)[26] directed

---

26 During Carnaval (the popular celebration that precedes Lent), all the musical

33

against the dictators of that period. Although my times with father Bien-Aimé were all too brief, I retain his vivid lessons. To explain the concept of Ginen to us, he carefully pointed out the difference between *moun òdinè*★ (ordinary mortals) and *moun Ginen*★ (initiates who follow the rule of Ginen). He explained that the ordinary man, in fact, believes in nothing and thinks he can mix everything up. Thus what constitutes mystery escapes him. The ordinary man is incapable of attending to Ginen because he squanders his energy in the Bizango world. That is why he lives in a state of confusion. It is thus important, father Bien-Aimé explained, to attend to both worlds at once. The moun Ginen can do it because he has *Je*★ (literally "eye," or "opening," can refer to a supernatural power of seeing, clairvoyance) and the energy. He always economizes his energy, whereas in the ordinary man there is a kind of leak through which energy is lost. I have always been struck by the self-assurance evident in the elderly man's words. I asked him, "What is Ginen?" He answered, "*Se sa w pa wè a.* (It is the Invisible.)"

After another meeting, father Bien-Aimé seemed annoyed that Hérard Simon, the *Lanpère*★ (the Emperor, a title given to the second person in charge, responsible for the lakou), was insisting on bringing about modifications in the structure of their lakou. He told us in confidence that his own son leaned toward this change. "But they will never convince me to do what is proposed," he said. "For everything having to do with Lakou Souvnans was seen in a dream and later recounted by Nèg Ginen.[27] It took this man forty years to be able to recall all the directives that the *Mistè*★ (Mystery, in this case referring to a lwa) had revealed to him regarding the proper functioning of the lakou. He also went *anba dlo*★ (beneath the waters) in order to complete his knowledge, accompanied to the riverbank by *Gran Bwa*★ (a lwa who inhabits the forest). "I, who am only his disciple, do not have the right either to add to or take away from whatever is suggested," father Bien-Aimé said. He went silent for five minutes, and I was left hanging on his words as if

---

groups (rara, bande à pied, rasin) compose satirical songs.
27 The name of the founder of Lakou Souvnans.

I were hypnotized. Then he continued, placing one finger on his mouth and the other hand on his forehead, "*Ti moun*★ (my children), I am going to tell you a secret that is not a secret. That is what I call it because it contains a lesson whose meaning few people have grasped."

I looked at his eyes, his gaze was intense. I wanted to grasp his message. He continued, "Let those who have ears with which to hear, hear. Lakou Souvnans was revealed to Nèg Ginen in a dream. No one knows who his mother or father were, nor how he died. Certain people say that he *Janbe*★ (to die, and to travel underwater to Africa) to Guinea. As for me, I believe it to be so, for all those who have received the rule of the lakou, without exception have subsequently been received into the world of our ancestors. *Abobo*★ *pou Nèg Ginen!* (Welcome to Nèg Ginen!)"

We responded in chorus, "Abobo! (Welcome! So be it!)"

"*Ti moun, mpa lwen pou ale* (My children, I am not long for this world)," he said. "I have dreamed about that. I haven't said anything to anybody." He smiled. "I would like for your group to come dance *Lamatinik*[28] with me. I have dreamed about having a wonderful celebration. This dream is beautiful."

"What have you seen in your dream, father?" I asked.

"Nothing specific. However, I was very happy and I saw you playing beneath the tree of *Ogou*★ (lwa of fire, iron, blood, and war). It is there that you will play."

"*Mèsi pè a* (thank you, father), it's an honor for us."

"*Se Ginen-an*★ (it is the Spirit) who should be thanked. My duty is to receive you when the Spirit leads you to the living root. Ginen-an is a great medicinal tree; its leaves and branches serve to replenish our energy. Energy is the only thing we really need. The ordinary man runs about in search of material things to fill up the space around him so that he will feel surrounded and protected. The ordinary man is afraid of emptiness. He has only one vision, that of appearing in the guise of one of the flattering images that his *Gwo Bonnanj*★[29] has invented. He uses up all his energy to accumulate titles and material wealth. Often,

---

28 Ritual dance; a ball organized for the lwa and the lakou's dead.
29 Gwo Bonnanj, or Landwat (the Place), or Sèmèdo: intellect or physical body, depending on the context in which the term is used.

death surprises him as he toils without his having had the time to enjoy the sought-after glory." He was silent for a long time. Then he resumed: "An ordinary person is unformed and has no information. He even interprets his dreams with the goal of acquiring money. In effect, he doesn't even know how to distinguish dreams from what is imaginary, he doesn't observe, his dream is a reproduction of this world. He lies to himself. *Ala de gagòt, papa!* (How disgusting!)"

I never saw father Bien-Aimé again. He departed this world when I was in the United States. I was not exposed to his teaching long enough to allow me to understand his methods very well, but I knew that he defended the rule of Ginen.

Later I met man Choune in the region of Haut-du-Cap. She is the sèvitè of Lakou Nan Jisou, which was originally entrusted to her mother. One day when we were at the *kay mistè*★ (house or room reserved for Vodou ceremonies), she invited me to salute the spirit of the *Kay*★ (dwelling), Papa Pyè.[30] She handed me a jug of water. I began to *Jete*★ (ritual to attract and greet the arrival of a lwa) when she suddenly came up to me, face to face. She touched my forehead, and I instantly felt a warmth that went from my head to my feet. She told me to turn clockwise, then counterclockwise three times. As my head turned I felt my cranium open at the place where the soft spot on a baby's head is. I felt a puff of air escape as when a tire is deflated.

"Voilà, it is necessary to center your *pwen*★ (magical power) over the pwen of the Kay, she informed me.

"Isn't there a general way of saluting Papa Pyè?" I asked humbly.

"Yes and no," she replied. "Each time the sèvitè of a lakou permits you to salute the spirit of a Kay, an act for which the sèvitè is responsible, if you do not have the line of the pwen of this Kay, there will be no communication."

"I'm confused," I confessed. "I do not really know what I'm supposed to do."

"It's as if I lent you a phone and asked you to call a friend

---

30 A Vodou divinity. Supreme manager of the rules of the group. The master of Intention, the mediator.

of mine whose number you don't know, and I alone can give it to you."

"Ah good! I didn't know," I replied.

"Nobody knows anything, my child. One never stops learning. Ginen-an is clever. It never reveals everything, not all at once. It doles it out *ti gout pa ti gout* (in small drops). It is necessary to be patient. *Kabwèt Ginen mache dousman men li toujou pote bon konmisyon.* (The Ginen cart makes its appearance gradually, but it comes without fail.)"

I asked what she meant. She answered: "*Ginen se Lèsprit* (Ginen is the Spirit). You cannot know where it comes from or where it is going. You cannot capture it to enlist it in your service. Certain people think that Ginen-an is a synonym for a prosperous life. They are deceiving themselves: Ginen-an is inexplicable. It does as it wishes, it draws to itself whomever it wishes, no one can choose it for his own Ginen. It alone chooses you and takes hold of you, and will never let you go! No one can resist it." She was silent for a moment. She handed me the jug again and urged me to Jete. I performed all the gestures appropriately. Then she invited us to sit down.

"My mother experienced all the misery life has to offer as a result of her desire to resist Ginen. She did not want to *sèvi*★ (serve) because she was young and beautiful. When *Mistè l'a reklame* (when a Mystery called her to be initiated), she refused. She preferred an ordinary life to the humiliation and wounding irony of so-called Christians (enemies of Ginen)." She was silent for a moment and then began again. Her voice had changed, "She suffered from many complicated maladies before she accepted the *lave-tèt*★ (ritual of initiation into Vodou). The night of her initiation, she had a dream. In her dream, the Spirit showed her the layout of this lakou. Then, it showed her the pwen and the place where the kay mistè should be built. She also learned the gestures you must make to enter into communication with *Mistè-yo* (the Mysteries).

"Then you are saying that it is not easy to set up a lakou?"

"*Non monfi, sa pa fasil. Se Ginen-an ki chwazi moun li vle. Bra a li long; ata menm lonbraj a li gen pouvwa fè ak defèt, se li ki deside anplasman pou monte yon lakou.* (No, my child, it is not easy. It is the

Invisible who must choose you. Its arm is long. Even its shadow has the power to create and destroy. It chooses the geographical location on which to place a lakou.)"[31]

"But there are certain shared features in the architecture of the kay mistè?"

"Yes and no. No, because there are many *angles* and many *chambers: Kongo, Rada, Gede*[32] *Petwo, Simbi,*[33] *Sinigal,*[34] and the like, above the *veil*. You find the same symbols but *chak kay mistè gen pwòp Je pa li. Direksyon Je a chak, fikse nan ang ke yo plase y la. Men, tout lakou Ginen chita sou yon sèl prinsip: nou sèvi Lèspri, Sa-nou-pa-wè-a*. (Each kay mistè has its own way of *seeing*. Each one is placed on a mystic space and is able to *see* by following the rules governing its construction. However, all the lakou Ginen have one thing in common: We serve the Spirit, the Invisible.)"

She saw that I didn't understand entirely, so she explained: "The Vodou pantheon is like a veil that covers all the mysteries of Vodou. You find there the *Pe★* (altar) Rada and the corresponding lwa; the Pe Kongo and the corresponding lwa; the Pe Petwo—called Bantou Lenba in the north—and the corresponding lwa. The three of them form the perfect triangle, with each Pe representing one angle. Each angle is the meeting of two lines—the vertical and the horizontal—and the meeting *point* of the two lines is an opening, that is to say, a Je. A kay mistè is established according to the vision of its founder. It is also necessary to mention the Pe of the Gedes (a small grave or pile of stones with a cross on top), not at all well known in the north, which is guarded by *Brav★* (Bon Être, one of the Mysteries) or

---

31 In this sense: It controls the world of emanations.

32 An African tribe—ancient inhabitants of Dahomey—conquered by the Fon, deported to Saint Domingue in colonial times. The Gedes: Mysteries of cemeteries, a family of lwa who rule the world of the dead.

33 Master of sources, of rivers. Traditionally, there are three fundamental Simbi: Simbi yandezo, Simbi yanpaka, Simbi yanpola. The Simbi are movers of souls, that is, conductors of the souls of the dead. They are also very accomplished herbalists, called "leaf doctors" in Haiti.

34 The Sinigal (Senegal) are slaves of Wolof, Fula and Mandingo origin who were taken to Saint Domingue in the colonial period. Some of them spoke Arabic and were Muslims. Lwa Sinigal: one of the families of lwa who march in the same retinue as the Simbi, to the Petwo rhythm.

by Baron Samedi (lord of the cemetery and the crossroads) and Grann Brigitte (a Mystery). A ceremony always begins with the appearance of a Gede—in the north it is Ti Jean (a Mystery) instead—and ends with the dance of the Gedes. They play the role of cleaners and are generally very jovial. They are arrayed in a Rada mask but retain all of their individuality in regard to the ritual.

"After everything that you have just told me, I gather that Ginen is quite complicated. I have a hard time understanding it," I said.

"*Men, se senp li ye.* (It is simplicity itself.) There is nothing to understand or learn, that's how it is. With neither beginning nor end, Ginen is wisdom. *Pèson pa ka wè bout a li, ni ki kote li sòti.* (No one is able to see where it comes from nor where it is going. Thus no one can sound the depths of Ginen or see its roots.)"

"In that case," I replied, "can you become a Ginen if it's a state of being? Can you acquire that state of being, just as you can acquire wisdom?"

"Everyone is called to enter that state, my daughter. Nonetheless, many are called and few are chosen. *Moun se mistè.* (The human being is a mystery.) You cannot judge or know who is Ginen. One person may have the appearance of a wise man but possess no personal power. Another may know the magic of plants and for that reason believes himself to be Ginen. Now, a Ginen is a person who has found the mystery of his being and knows how to manage it. For we are Mysteries and we are surrounded by mysteries. But few people are aware of that. Because after he is born, we teach a child to be a kind of solid block—objective, reasonable and prideful. Yet we are nothing but an abstraction. *Adje pitit! Se yon ti souf ki kenbe nou. Epi, nou santi nou yon pakèt afè, n ap gonfle tankou balon yo bay van, adje! Wa pa kouzen-nou.* (We are poor devils! We are held up by a breath. But we are too big for our boots. We are swollen with pride just as a balloon is filled with air. The king is not our cousin.)"

"Man Choune, I love to hear you speak."

"It is not man Choune who speaks to you, my daughter."

At that point I became quiet, and then I suddenly noticed a flame was coming out of her left eye. A living light radiated all around it. I was trembling. I had perceived something inexplicable. I thought about one of Aunt Tansia's lessons about the ways to defend myself against the lures of this world. I had promised myself to speak to her about the "mystery of the Incarnation," which an elderly man had explained to me—I had known what I wanted to say then, but the words hadn't come. I stammered, and she gazed at me for a long time, a long time without saying anything. I was ashamed. Finally, she said, "You concern yourself too much with the affairs of this world, my child. You do not have enough energy to find the words to explain what you want to say." In fact, she was right. I was incapable of explaining myself.

Once again, the words did not come to me. In the face of this sudden transformation of man Choune, I experienced the same frustration.

On another occasion we paid a visit of condolence to man Choune. She was very sad. As she slapped her hands together, she kept repeating: "I ought to have 'listened' to my dream. If I had, Ti Son would not be dead."

We tried to console her, "Man Choune, do not be sad, it is the will of God."

"No, dying depends on the will of men. The Spirit gives us the power to disobey death. Christ did so, and so have many others. If I am sad, it is because I was negligent in a way that cost my son his life. I feel something like remorse. I ought to have warned Ti Son that the shadow of death awaited him on the road, at least he would have known. Even if he had to die, I wouldn't feel guilty and consider myself an accomplice, because he would have been aware of the danger."

We talked until night fell. I listened without speaking, for I had nothing to say. Everything in that house was sad; even the plants seemed faded. We spent the night at her house as proof of our friendship. I didn't close my eyes. What captured my attention that night was that the histories of all the lakou that I had visited were linked to a dream someone had had.

I noticed the same thing when man Diran recounted

to us the story of Dede Magrit,[35] Nan Kanpèch: "She was an extraordinary woman. She went on a pilgrimage that lasted nine years in search of higher levels of consciousnesss. She traveled the Mornes-Rouges, the Bonnet-à-l'Evêque and the Piccoli to finally settle in Coupe-à-David at Camp David. She was initiated into Nan Dòmi and received the gift of clairvoyance. She subsequently became one of the most important mambos in the north of Haiti. She was also a great healer; her methods went beyond medical practice, and her prescriptions worked without fail. People who were ailing, above all, those who suffered from *malkadi** (epilepsy) came from all parts of the country to be healed by Dede Magrit. She was called the 'woman with the divine hand.' She used a calabash as a tool for consultation. She also knew how to read the leaves of the malanga—whose roots we eat—for recipes and prescriptions for the treatment of maladies. She nourished herself with *kabich* (unleavened bread), or *pen dou* (a biscuit made from manioc flour), and coffee, sugar cane juice and water. She did her work under the direction of *Ogou Badagri* (lwa often associated with St. James the Greater) and *Ogou Feray* (lwa of war whose element is fire)."

She also recounted for us, with great passion, the history of her "dream" of the lakou, of her walks near Mistè Nan Pikoli, and her long visit of eleven years anba dlo.

Aunt Tansia had always told us that she was able to enter Nan Dòmi completely. She even knew the world of the dead. I fell into a mental muddle. Dreaming, in my view, consisted of an imaginary world of hidden memories. The *Petit Larousse* dictionary defines dreaming this way, and so do many other books. But for Aunt Tansia, dreaming was a state of the unknown world that had no connection to the imagination. "It is real," she taught me.

She then provided me with an explanation of dreaming: "Due to a whim of Ginen, we are made of two compartments separated by a line, which is the will. This line of separation is itself controlled by Intention. In order for the will to be able to impose its orders, it requires the support of Intention, which itself

---

35 A famous servant of the lwa born at Coupe-à-David, a lakou situated on the outskirts of Cap-Haïtien, the second-largest city in Haiti.

obeys the orders of Perception. Will and Intention go together and are indistinguishable. The compartment placed on the left side is set in reverse. It is summoned and directed by *Ti Bonnanj*★, *Lanvè,* or *Selidò* (the spiritual body, a portion of God). It cannot be described; you know it, that is all. The other compartment, the one on the right side, is called *Gwo Bonnanj, Landwat,* or *Sèmèdò*. It is there where we find the mental world and the intellect with all their compartments. It is our Gwo Bonnanj who teaches us all the things in the known world and helps us to distinguish among them by means of *Bon-konprann*★ (reason). When you are in a dream state, you are automatically under the control of Ti Bonnanj. He it is who rules the unknown world. He is the master there. That is because he has his own rules. Entering into the unknown world is not without danger, just as a child cannot set out alone on a highway. We are on the brink of madness in the unknown world. Madness is the unforgiving, unforeseen event."

I trembled with fear as I heard these words.

"What are you afraid of?" Aunt Tansia asked.

I knew she could read my mind. She had seen my fear and reassured me by explaining that madness is a state in which you question things without waiting for solutions. The impatient searcher gets stuck by scrambling things without being able to put them back in place. Whenever the seeker confronts discoveries, he is obliged to ask his Gwo Bonnanj to interpret them for him, lest he fall into *bouyaj* (the world of confusion). Madness is a form of conflict between references, memory and the new codes perceived in the Unknown.

"Do not be afraid," she told me. "Do you know that fear is the principal enemy blocking our intelligence? The unknown world is within our reach. We have only to change our perception in order to enter it. Entry into this world is like a rebirth. Whoever wants to see *sekrè bragèt a Pas la* (the secret of passage or the opening of the passage, the crevice, the line) must by necessity learn the rules and the methods of Ti Bonnanj. To enter into the unknown world it is obligatory for you to learn the codes and discover the borders that separate the two worlds. They look like a line of light."

It was Aunt Tansia who initiated us into Vodou. She taught

us that there was a traditional *lave-tèt*, which is the order of the ancients, but there is also a new order. The lave-tèt of this new order is as effective as the old one. It is only that the rituals of each one are different.

This *granmoun**⁎* (elderly woman) charmed me with her youthfulness, her generosity and her great knowledge. She was about 118 years old when she undertook our education (Lòlò's and mine). She kept repeating that she was waiting on us to finish our instruction before Janbe, which was her last *sèvis Ginen*⁎[36] (ritual belonging to the last stage for the initiate). She was the first one to speak to us of Vodou in terms of consciousness. I was a Catholic, born to Catholic parents who were horrified by Vodou; my husband was born into a Protestant family, fierce enemies of Vodou.

She often used to calmly repeat, "Don't fall into the word trap. You only know a thing when you have full consciousness of it. Consciousness itself is holy. There is no good or bad consciousness: There is nothing but Consciousness."

Her teachings lasted two years, after which she underwent Janbe into the other world. It would take me years to absorb everything that she taught me. Even today, there are things that I am unable to penetrate. I put them to the side and wait. Moreover, I only retain a few bits and pieces due to lack of practice. But I am certain that they are buried somewhere in my memory, in my Consciousness.

Her instruction was delivered orally. Aunt Tansia's method was rigorous. She was a disciplined and stern teacher, but at the same time, she was full of humor and possessed an extraordinary intelligence. She insisted that we apply everything we claimed to understand: "*Apranti kòdonie se yon kòdonye k ap pran fòm ti pa ti pa. Sa w pratike a se sa w ye.* (The apprentice cobbler is a future cobbler. You are what you do.)"

---

36 Ginen service entails the master's commitment to celebrate diverse ceremonies (about thirteen) with the unique goal of proving his faith (the material realization of his will), of visibly manifesting his mental strength to his disciples before transmitting his powers to the new generation. The last ceremony must be the most trying, for the officiant who is also the master must reveal the day and the hour and his own way of Janbe.

She recounted stories about other Ginen she had worked with in order to stimulate our desire for conciousness. I delighted in the story of Abodourine, the *negresse* who astounded the entire town of Ouanaminthe by vanishing into thin air thanks to her knowledge of magic. And that of Vivil, who was able to undo his point of assemblage through his power; he was the most effective courier of the *Cacos*,[37] and turned himself into his double as easily as he changed clothes. Of Zanna, who awakened from death *"ti moun kou granmoun"* (both young and old). And even Beke, a *lougarou*★ (sorcerer) who sucked the blood of newborns. The practices of these Ginen fascinated me.

"My god! It is unimaginable. I would love to be worthy of using their methods. But unluckily they are no longer a part of this world," I told myself.

"*Podjab, pitit an mwen!* (You poor devil, my child!)," Aunt Tansia exclaimed ironically. She burst out laughing. Then her voice took on a serious tone again. "Why do you regret their absence from this world?"

"I would have asked them to teach me."

"There is nothing to learn, my child. No one has need of anyone else to know Ginen. For, in reality, Ginen is not something you learn by heart. It is not the same as with the rituals: Ginen cannot be explained. You only need something to stimulate your need to know, for example, the witness of a *grandèt*★ (elder) to convince us that this power is within our reach. Each living being is a warrior and he is alone in combat. Depending on his magical force, *si li gen dèyè a li* (how much energy he has) to undertake battles, he will be the victor or the loser."

At present there are things that remain hidden to me. I do not dare approach them. Nevertheless, I have learned three series of mysteries of the *san en nanchon*[38] which form the roof held up by the seven *poto*★ (pillars) of the structure of the lakou. These

---

37 At the time of the U.S. occupation (1915-1934), the term *Cacos* was used to refer to rebel Haitian peasant armies whose leader, Charlemagne Péralte, was assassinated in 1919.

38 Literally "one hundred one nations." A concept that defines the whole of the Mysteries and nations that form the pantheon of Haitian Vodou.

three series are the *twa wòch dife* [39] which form the base. In the first series, we find Nan Dòmi, the manifestations of the spirit and the service of Ginen. Here I aim to deal with Nan Dòmi by placing before the reader's eyes all the experiences I have lived through from the day when I was able to enter into this state and master it.

---

39 A concept that defines the architectural scheme of the kay mistè, signifying the three foundational rules that support the mysteries of Vodou. A tri-unitary formula that produces the miracle.

## CHAPTER 1

# The Teaching of Perception
# with Aunt Tansia

We were at Lakou Beaubrun de Malique Nan Ma (four kilo-meters east of Pétion-Ville) with friends. Lòlò and I had been invited to attend a ceremony of *replasman bòn*★ (replacement of boundary markers). It was midnight when the prayers and lam-entations ended. Everyone then gathered under an arbor impro-vised for the occasion to sing and assist in the descent of the lwa, to dance and enjoy themselves. I sat down on the north side of the arbor, leaning my chair against the wall of the kay mistè.

I observed the people, the décor enhanced by the *tèt gridap* (handcrafted lamps), and I listened, emptied of all thought. I sa-vored the songs. I relaxed and let my body vibrate to the sound of the drums, when suddenly my eyelids became heavy: I was sleepy. I tried to resist, throwing some cool water on my face, but my eyes closed of their own accord. I fell into a deep sleep with a jug of water clasped in my hands. Yet I was not completely asleep. I could hear everything that was happening under the arbor. I had the strange sensation that my hands and legs were swaying. I wanted to see them. I put my left arm close to my face; I couldn't see it. It was very, very dark. I tried harder. Even-tually I saw saffron yellow, then white. When I focused my eyes I realized that I was on my feet dancing before the drummers, still holding the water jug in my hands. Then I stopped paying attention, and let myself go in the dance. At one moment, I said to myself, "My God, how will I be able to stop?" But I couldn't retain this thought. The dance, the sound, the rhythm were all too strong. They led my body to move in a circle, crazily. I could hear everything despite the deafening noise of the drums. I was unable to talk. I was incapable of pronouncing a word, overcome by a leaden drowsiness—while, at the same time, awake. I experienced pleasure in that state between two waters: profoundly asleep and fully conscious of myself.

A resident of the lakou, Mme. Raynold, asked me to go honor the Pe (altar) of the Kay. She took me inside the kay mistè, presented me with an egg on a white plate, manioc flour (which I do not like) and barley water syrup. I ate the egg whole (that is, including the shell). Then I ate a bit of the flour and drank the syrup. I thanked the woman without saying a word—that is, in a mental language. She understood and thanked me politely, "I am at your service." I took her hand, led her to a certain spot and told her that in that place there had been a *Ma*★ (pond) that had dried up to portend the dearth of people thirsting for consciousness. She answered that in fact, there really had been a pond there, but she had not realized it until now.

I touched her and her whole body trembled. She fell to the ground and I awoke in a pond a few meters southwest of the kay mistè. I was surrounded by people looking at me. I didn't understand why I was getting so much attention. I didn't even try to understand. Lòlò took me by the hand and whispered in my ear, "A lwa possessed you." It didn't matter to me at all. I was neither content nor annoyed. I only knew that I was in the process of dreaming.

Lòlò covered me with his shirt. He kept asking me questions, such as, "How do you feel? Are you cold? Do you want to change your dress, is it damp?" I didn't respond. I felt a kind of indifference, a sentiment of non-pity (that state that neither tolerates pity for oneself or for anything else, because nothing is important in itself).

Later, in the course of my analyses, I would conclude that, as with an ontological process, people can come to know different levels of consciousness and experience many states of being simultaneously. I would place my experience within that category. Because my experience was out of the ordinary—that is to say, it did not appear to have been lived in the everyday world—I understood it as having taken place in the unknown world. I recalled Aunt Tansia's teaching of the two aspects within our reach: the known world where everything is solid and reasonable, and the unknown world, which comprises the states of Nan Dòmi—dreaming, for example. I also recalled the methods she employed to train us and familiarize us with the unknown world. She used to tell us in a joking way, "*Pa bobo kole ake ankenn bagay. Vire Je an nou chak fwa ke nou santi yon atirans.* (Don't become attached to anything. Avert your gaze every time you feel attracted by something.) In that way you will gain mastery of the Je. This work must also be accompanied by the force of will." That was her way of introducing the teaching of perception.

One Saturday afternoon we were in our courtyard, waiting for Aunt Tansia. For two days she had been telling us that, on this Saturday, she would begin to employ special measures in regard to our physical bodies, which supposedly lacked suppleness and were too attached to trivial things. She arrived at three o'clock, bent over her cane, a casserole in her hand. She gave us the casserole and asked us to drink all its contents, which she called "*bon bouyon*" (delicious soup). But the dish did not have the consistency of a traditional broth: It had no meat or *donbrèy* (flour paste), or bananas, yams or malangas; only two small crayfish swimming in an ocean of green water and a few leaves of *mouton zenzen*★ (a kind of legume, a power plant), she told me when I asked what they were. I tasted it first; the liquid was bitter. I was somewhat vexed because she had urged us to fast and wait for her "famous" repast. But Lòlò didn't hesitate. He drank half of the "broth" and handed me the rest. It was hard for me to swallow. She asked me not to leave a drop in the casserole. Reluctantly, and out of respect for her, I finished the rest. When I gave the empty casserole back to her, she stood straight up and began to dance and sing, "*Papa Loko,*[40] *Zany misyonè, Ago*★ *e!* (Papa Loko, missionary angel, listen!)" She asked us to learn the

---

40 Master of the temple, conservator of tradition, he is in principle the treasurer of the ritual accessories in the kay mistè.

song. We obeyed and, after repeating it three times, I sang, my heart joyful. I forgot the bitter broth.

Before leaving, she solemnly announced that she would be there the next day at the same hour with the same intention: that is, to continue her favorable treatment. She had the audacity to ask us to fast once again.

The next day, to our great astonishment, we were not at all hungry and our bodies avidly awaited the broth. She returned at the same hour and we repeated the same scenario. Only the song had changed. She sang for *Agwe-t-Awoyo*[41]: *Agwe-si, o! Agwe-la, nan lanmè mwen te ye. . . .* (Agwe-si, o! Agwe-la, I was amid the waves of the sea. . . .)"

In all, the treatment lasted for twenty-one days. Lòlò and I did not go out; every day, from morning on, we were absorbed and motivated by a single goal: to see Aunt Tansia again.

On the evening of the last day, she asked us, "How do you feel?"

"Very well," I answered without hesitation. I felt light and strong at the same time. I told her so. She laughed good-heartedly. "You feel light because after three weeks, you are no longer concerned with your body. You have let the chains of your worries fall away." She fell silent for a moment, then spoke again. "The body, this solid part of our being, forces us to weave bonds of attachment with this world around us. The worst part is that we find it reasonable to assume these cares."

She tickled my ribs. I was startled, since I was deep in thought: *Cares are the lot of human beings; to be rid of them is to enter the realm of the gods.* Aunt Tansia understood my thought and said, "Of course you are gods; it is not I who say it, it is the prophet himself, *se vre wi* (in truth). You yourself know it, and that's why you feel yourself to be so strong. Your concentration during the last twenty-one days has helped you become conscious of your strength. Since then you have entered into a different world. The door of consciousness is open to you." She asked me, "Have you by chance noticed anything? I suggest that you look at Lòlò's hands." Without turning my head, I saw rays of light. I told him

---

41 Lwa of the seas and the oceans.

so. At the time, Ouanaminthe had no electricity and we were sitting in the dark.

"This light was always there," she continued. "You saw it today because you have altered your perception. Didn't you learn in your catechism that all, all of us are Light? However, some of the lights are brighter than others."

"Aunt, is what I am seeing real?"

"It is completely real, *pitit an mwen*. You now have a different perception of this part of the body that we call the hand."

It took me some time to recognize that this part of the teaching would unfold based on perception, which necessarily leads us to give a definition to things.

"*Tou sa nou wè, nou ba yo yon non, nan monn sa* (We give a name to everything we see in this world)," Aunt Tansia said to me. "By social consensus, we have decided to give a name to everything. We have described this world as we do because we perceive it as such. *Nou eksplike chak bagay daprè jan nou wè-y.* (We explain each thing according to our perception of it.)"

Still following an ontological process of thinking things through, I told myself that man is a mysterious being, possessing infinite possibilities that have not been exploited. Aunt Tansia was sighing throughout our dialogue. Then, suddenly, she became quiet. A moment later, she spoke again as if taking a breath. "All is well. I think that you are ready. The veil is finally torn away. Soon it will be necessary for me to go away."

At that time I understood nothing. I only knew that I was living through special moments with Aunt Tansia and I savored them. I would have liked for her to remain by my side for the rest of my life.

One afternoon, Aunt Tansia had a boy summon Lòlò on the pretext that an important visitor wanted to see him. Lòlò rushed to her house. After half an hour Lòlò returned, accompanied by a young man, the sacristan of the Catholic Church. As this man approached to grasp my hand, I felt a wave of warmth all around as if someone had just lit a big wood fire. He looked me straight in the eyes and I knew he was reading my mind. I didn't lower my eyes; on the contrary I let myself open up. My eyes were the portals of my being. I let myself be looked at. And where could I have hidden? He would have seen me—that, I knew. We were still face to face when my father approached, accompanied by a friend. They were having a discussion on the subject of faith. Suddenly the visitor asked for silence and for someone to bring him a Bible. My father gave him one. He thanked him, and opened it directly to the page where it was written: "The Kingdom of Heaven is like a grain of mustard seed." He read it aloud with perfect diction. When he finished, he handed the Bible to my father, opened to the same page. My father read the same verse and expressed aloud his surprise because he knew that the sacristan was illiterate. Then the visitor handed me a packet of leaves, which I had not noticed in his hands, and said, addressing everyone, "Do you know the name of this plant?" No one knew. He said, "It is called *twa pawòl*.★ This plant is the very symbol of faith. Consider it carefully: Faith is like this point that unites the three leaves into one. Faith is the union of thought, of the word and of the act. It is perfection."

"Do you mean to say, without sin?" I asked him.

He answered, "I don't know what 'without sin' means to you. I am talking about that state in which you find yourself in perfect harmony with your whole being." He spoke with so much self-assurance that I no longer knew whether I was convinced or not. I contented myself with acquiescing to his words.

A few weeks later, Aunt Tansia had summoned Lòlò because she wanted to introduce him to a very good friend. When Lòlò arrived at her house, he thought it was a joke—the only person with Aunt Tansia was Ton De, an old man the whole town knew. He was the janitor and bell-ringer at the Catholic church. Lòlò greeted them both, but Ton De introduced himself to Lòlò, grasping both his hands and calling himself "Kalfou." Aunt Tansia explained to Lòlò that Ton De/Kalfou had important things to teach us. She insisted that our meetings take place at her house. So it was for two weeks.

During that period, Ton De/Kalfou taught us. The lessons amounted to what follows: *Ginen-an se tankou yon gwo pyebwa.*

(Ginen-an is like a giant tree.) All the birds can build their nests there. Despite wind and storms, the birds will have nothing to fear. They will be protected by the branches. The birds will not fall unless the tree itself falls. The roots of the Ginen tree go deep. It is an ancient science.

"Don't be afraid," he exhorted, "of obstacles that you will find along your path. You will be called all kinds of names; don't let go of the branch that holds you up. You will be criticized for good as for ill, but don't let go. You will be the object of all kinds of flattery; don't let go. Efface your personal history, cut yourself off from the world and its snares. Like the bird that takes flight after the storm, you also will fly toward toward total liberty after your trials."

We saw Ton De after that, but he never referred again to his use of the name "Kalfou." When we tried to talk to him about it, he always answered, "*Ma pa konnen de ki sa n ap pale a.* (I don't know what you are talking about.)"

Aunt Tansia was radiant when we gave her a complete account of our meetings. She hummed a chante pwent throughout our conversation. She didn't stop laughing to herself and chanting: "*Bòkò ki bezwen se li ki ranmase.* (The *bòkò*★ in need is the one who collects.)"

One Sunday morning a song awakened us. It was Aunt Tansia's voice, "*Loko, m bezwen yon layo pou m ale ranmase vye fanmi-an m yo* (Loko, I need a cart to go get my family.)" She brought us some *mabi,*★[42] and had us drink it on an empty stomach. Then she told us the story of the priest who was officiating that morning. "*Ti moun yo, Père Charpentier te transfòme maten-an.* (My children, Father Charpentier was transformed this morning.) He came down from the altar to greet and embrace all the faithful. That very priest, who is so racist and so haughty. No doubt he was in his Ti Bonnanj."

We laughed heartily. I knew the priest. He never greeted anyone. Even when someone bade him good day, he would act as though he hadn't heard them. He always walked looking straight ahead, ignoring everyone around him.

---

42 A drink made of fermented cane syrup and orange juice.

Aunt Tansia left after many pleasantries and promised us to return later in the afternoon.

Indeed, she did return. As she sat down she went on, " I'm here to bear witness. First of all, previously I told you that you will meet many other personages, be it in Nan Dòmi, be it that they present themselves to you *Je klè\** (while you are conscious)." She was silent for a moment and resumed, "I want to say something to you. Up to now, you have not been able to establish a point of reference. Ti moun, learn this: There are twenty-one important knots in the Ginen. Each knot is a pwen. You must find these knots and find out which one of them you can undo and tie again at will.[43] This knot will be yours. No one can do it for you. There are people who out of laziness or ambition prefer to buy a pwen (here, 'pwen' refers to a Vodou charm). What they don't know is that each pwen has its own rules. The seller will never hand over all the rules to the buyer. His pwen constitutes his force; he knows that he will never give away all his force for whatever he may be offered. *Ti moun, sèvi Ginen pa achte pwen, tande. Alòs, yonn di yonn konprann. Pa fè kòr-an nou lezi, Travay, ti moun, travay dur.* (My children, instead of buying a pwen, follow Ginen teaching. Greetings to the good listener! No laziness. You must enter into it seriously, my children.)"

While she was speaking her face was transformed; her features became those of a young woman. She was very, very beautiful. She unfastened her chignon. Her hair was the color of honey. She was agile, at ease, and moved coquettishly. If this change in her physical appearance was surprising, her changed mood was even more so. I was astounded. I couldn't believe my eyes. She saw my surprise and said, "Why are you looking at me like that? This isn't the first time I have visited you." Suddenly something in my mind clicked and a memory surfaced: I remembered having seen a similar woman, this very woman I was looking at in front of me. It was in a dream when I was very young (only nine or ten years old). I was climbing up some stairs and this woman was perched on the topmost step. Hypnotized by her beauty, I did not stop looking at her as I mounted the stairs. But once

---

43 An expression that may be translated as "to pierce the mystery."

I got to the top there was no one there, only total darkness all around me. I was seized with panic and called out, "Jesus!" just as my mother taught me to do any time I was in danger. This recollection prompted me to cry, "Ah! Is it you? You?"

"Yes, it is I," she answered. Then she sang a song:

> *O! Tansia, ki sa w ape fè la a?*
> *—Se pase mwen t ape pase.*
> *O! Tansia Balendjo!*
> *—M sonje nan tan mwen.*

> O! Tansia, what are you doing there?
> —I'm passing, I'm just passing along
> O! Tansia Balendjo!
> —I'm dreaming of my old times.

I wanted to understand this scene better, but instead I thought about everything and nothing until I finally dozed off, and in a half-sleep I heard her recount her story:

"Tansia was very beautiful. She was the most beautiful woman in the country. Her skin was the color of a peach, her hair thick and wavy, her teeth white, eyes a clear brown, and she was five feet seven inches tall. She loved life, dancing and love. Among her many lovers she counted men of state, Haitians as well as Dominicans and Cubans. She was sure of herself and proud of her beauty. She was also very intelligent and loved politics. She was an active member of the Cacos. She exploited her important contacts in order to discover the plans of the enemy camp and then thwart them. She had an only son whom she loved a lot and spoiled. She had everything and asked nothing more from life. It was then that Ginen caught her in its nets. The Invisible always chooses the moment to appear when the apprentice isn't expecting anything, when his self-importance is excessive. It always chooses its hour and its moment. But Tansia didn't know that the Spirit was lying in wait for her. It chose death to manifest itself. It happened when her favorite lover, the father of her son, was denounced along with her adored child.

They were arrested and imprisoned in the national penitentiary. The boy was sixteen. They were taken to Port-au-Prince, betrayed by one of their own and mistreated along the way, following their departure from Mont-Organisé (a municipality in the Nord-Est Department of Haiti). When Tansia learned about this misfortune, she assembled her things—horses, servants and provisions—and set out for Port-au-Prince with the intention of seeing her lover, the President, and pleading his innocence. They spent fifteen days on the road, and it rained during the whole of the trip, making travel difficult. She had a high fever when they reached Port-au-Prince. At Pont-Rouge[44] she stopped at a friend's house, washed, combed her long hair and attended to her appearance before rushing to the National Palace. Suddenly, she heard an uproar in the distance. She experienced a moment of anguish, but she mastered it. Her mission was too important to pay attention to rumors, even though Port-au-Prince is, by definition, a city of rumors.

"She went first to the prison and there, in front of the prison door, were hundreds of cadavers. She fell on the body of her lover. Then on her son's corpse. She saw something like a black cloud. Thinking that she was living a nightmare, she sank face down to the ground and cried, 'My God, what have I done to you?'

"Then a great light covered her. She stood up, no longer feeling anything, either pain or anger, and in control of the situation. Tansia gathered her dead, helped by the *majò prezon*.[45] She went to the cemetery, where she buried them herself. Then she spent the whole night dancing with the frenzied crowd in the streets of Port-au-Prince. The crowd chanted words of vengeance while brandishing a lopped-off head and penis. She went up to the man who was holding them and snatched the head from his hand. She recognized the head of the President, her lover. At that moment she saw Death, who said to her, 'Tansia, what do you want? What are you looking for? What are you doing

---

44 A historic place north of Port-au-Prince where Jean-Jacques Dessalines, the first Haitian head of State, was assassinated in 1807.
45 A longtime, trusted prisoner who benefits from certain privileges, among them that of working as a guard.

there? Get out of that crowd and go away! Leave my kingdom!'

"So she left and walked without any destination in mind, without stopping anywhere for at least three months before she found herself at last in her birthplace. What energy this woman Tansia possessed, capable of withstanding the blows that come from life as well as from death!

"From that day on, she always wore a dress of *syam*★ (a cloth made of cream-colored, raw cotton) and resolved to dedicate herself to the welfare of orphans and prisoners. She buried her life as a woman of the world, renounced all her worldly goods, distributed them to others, and chose to serve Ginen-an. Death had abruptly put an end to her interest in a life of prosperity. She flattened all obstacles. So it was that Tansia lost her former self, leaving me a place to become a candidate for the rank of grand master.

"That is why I wanted to dance in her, with her: to give her life. I wanted her to live, to follow me without going back. Tansia became extremely thin, she fell ill, struck down by tuberculosis, a shameful illness at that time. I cured her in fifteen days and she became more beautiful than ever. Men who had been wary of her began again to gather around her, captivated and filled with desire. I used Tansia to attract and set a trap for all those I wanted: Vivil, Èmilien, Pasteur Marc, and even Zann the servant."

I listened carefully. She ended by embracing us and introducing herself, "My name is *Erzulie Pierre*, daughter of *Loko Atissou*[46] and *Mètrès Dantòr* (Mistress Dantòr)." I wept copiously during her story, without being able to stop. My body shook with spasms. Tears moistened my face and my blouse. Nevertheless, I was not sad. She wrapped me in her long dress and blew into my hair. I trembled. Her breath caused a shiver down my spine. I was cold; like a baby, I curled up in a ball. She blew again and it was then that Lòlò let out a cry and the house shook. Suddenly I fell asleep. I saw a beautiful river in my dream, clear and limpid. I was thirsty and bent down to drink. I was beginning to quench my thirst when I perceived a shadow above

---

46 Name of a lwa messenger.

me. I raised my head and saw a snake as big as a boa (like one I had seen in the movies). My eyes met hers and I was afraid. I ran, and she pursued me. All of a sudden an enormous flame appeared in front of me. I couldn't go on. Then I jumped to get through the flame and ended up on a red horse waiting on the other side. I turned to look behind me. There was no fire, no snake, no forest, no river—nothing. It was all black. I opened my eyes wide; at one moment I saw saffron yellow, then white, and I awoke nestled in Aunt Tansia's skirt. My body trembled, seized by spasms. She had me drink some water, pouring it over my face. I was hot.

"You are in your Ti Bonnanj, you have been dreaming, you have just seen your *allié*,"[47] she said to me. And before she left, she advised me not to take off the white headscarf she had put on my head.

After this experience, I went to see my mother, who questioned me about my state of mind. She found me too calm, as if something in me had changed; she noted my eyes were not the same. She was uneasy. My father too. He wanted to know more about the people I had seen recently. "Have you seen Aunt Tansia?" he asked mistrustfully. I did not answer.

I had nothing to say to them. All communication was cut off between us. An unfamiliar way out was offered to me; it was now or never to exit from the "educational and intellectual mechanism" to which I had been exposed. I was now face to face with another dimension. A new synthesis was born in me. I lost the entire vision of the world that I had had since childhood. I understood something profound and important: that I would have to fight hard against the necessities and certitudes that up to then had demanded so much of my energy. I was confronted with a new situation, related to these activities that were not part of the heritage of my own personal culture. I sensed the beginning of a great desire for consciousness. What my mother and father said no longer had any importance. The

---

47 The alliés are luminous, vibrant beings who live in the hollows of the earth and who exchange knowledge and savoir-faire with the inhabitants of the earth. In Vodou tradition, each human being has an allié to help him perfect his mystic baggage (initiatory).

only thing that counted for me was the instant when I had the courage to accept the slow toppling over of what had been my whole culture.

I saw Aunt Tansia again three days later. I began to feel a kind of warmth in my head. I was sweating heavily. She had me pour a lot of water over my head, rubbed my temples with oil from the *Koko Ginen*★ (an oleaginous tropical plant), and placed a compress of orange petals on the *pòtay-mistè*★ (points of opening in the body). She traced a triangle with her fingers on the hair at the back of my head and shaped the hair into the corresponding design. The next day at noon, Lòlò started to suffer violent headaches. His pain lasted three days, beginning each day at midday. Aunt Tansia washed his scalp for three days during each crisis. After that the pain went away.

Aunt Tansia had us drink mabi, then asked me to tell her the dream I had about the snake. When I finished, she sighed. "I can interpret your dream in two ways: The first is to see in the snake a presage of great wealth. Not only material wealth. It's up to you to choose. In the second interpretation, the fact that you saved yourself provides proof that you are not ready to undertake the struggle with your allié. Now, regardless of cost, you must conquer it: only then will it consent to serve you and open the door of its mystery. You will go in and discover your knot. All that presupposes that your head be *fixée* as soon as possible. That is to say, your *Mèt tèt*★ (the 'master-head'; this is the lwa chosen during initiation whom the adept has agreed to serve) must be firmly in place. The reason for this is that there is nothing more dangerous than the botched setting of the *Selidò* (another term for Ti Bonnanj). The dreamer may, as a first option, use his dream to acquire many material goods, achieve political power, or dominate others. In this latter case, he becomes a ghoul and sucks up everything that passes by his door. The dreamer will then remain attached only to the attractions of this world. That is what happens with the lougarou. Nevertheless, there is another possibility: The dreamer may set off as an adventurer into the world of the Unknown. It is not easy to get there, but if you succeed, it will lead you to liberty."

I understood what she meant to tell me, but all the same I

asked her, "Aunt, how do you explain my experience, did I have a *Zany*★ (angel)?"

"Non, *pitit an mwen*, not yet, you have only dreamed. Yet this state is very close to that of the Zany."

The explanation was clear, but I wanted to know a little more about this state in which everything transpired simultaneously in the same context. I also knew that fasting had played a role in the Aunt Tansia's methods, as well as the famous "bouillon," the mabi, and the lave-tèt. I was sure of it. But one particular thought nonetheless led me to pose the question: How had I been able on this occasion to pass beyond the threshold of logical thought where everything is real and objective? The only answer I got from Aunt Tansia was the promise that she would soon undertake another step on my behalf, one that would help me to manage the placement of the Mèt tèt.

This time, I asked her no more questions. I set about to await that day.

## CHAPTER 2

# Placement of the Head

## *Plasman Mèt tèt oubyen Fikse tèt*

I didn't see Aunt Tansia again until two months later. Lòlò and I returned to Port-au-Prince to see relatives and friends we missed. All of them thought that we seemed changed. The biggest teaser among them said: "*Gen lè, andèyo a pa pi mal pou nou.* (It seems that the country agrees with you more than the city.)" In a sense it was true, for I was bursting with energy. I was happy to see everyone again, but I did not want to stay in Port-au-Prince for long. I missed Aunt Tansia. Lòlò shared my feelings in this regard. After discussing it, we decided to return to Ouanaminthe despite the disappointment of our friends who wanted us to stay with them a little longer. The decision was really made for us: We needed to return to Aunt Tansia.

As soon as we disembarked from the bus that took us to Ouanaminthe we headed for Aunt Tansia's house. We met her on the road, and she was heading for our place: "*Abobo! Pitit zantray an mwen yo!* (Welcome, children of my flesh and bone!) Let's begin by going to my house. I have prepared two long sticks of sugar cane for you."

"We were just on our way to your house."

"Thank you for thinking of me."

That is how the conversation began; she told us that she had seen us Nan Dòmi. She had dreamed of the three of us together. The vision showed her our bodies close together and walking as we were at that moment. I asked her to interpret the dream for me. She appeared to ignore my request. She seemed happy to see us again. Once we reached her house, she had us bring two chairs and turned away to get the sticks of sugar cane. When she came back, she held only one stick of sugar cane and seemed angry.

"Where is Azurène?" she cried in a loud voice like the rumble of thunder. "Zann, Zann!"

That was Azurène's nickname. Everyone called her that. Zann was Aunt Tansia's female companion. She performed certain services, such as washing clothes and dishware. She also took care of household duties at the primary school run by the Christian Brothers when Aunt Tansia was not able to do so. She had a round, unwrinkled face, prominent cheekbones, thick, long hair she wore in two tresses that encircled her head like a headband, clear skin, and almond-shaped eyes. She was short: scarcely four feet one inch tall. Plump, her buttocks resembled two little pillows that moved up and down when she walked. Seen from behind, one would have taken her for a young girl, yet she was eighty years old. Zann only smiled when someone gave her money, and she spoke very little.

"Yes, Tansia," a voice answered.

"Azurène, *vini mwen pale w tousuit* (Come here, I want to talk to you right now)." Azurène appeared. "Where is the other stick of cane?"

"I sold it," Azurène answered.

"You dared to sell it? It's not true, it isn't possible!"

Aunt Tansia was so furious her whole body shook. She raised herself up on her toes like a ballerina and cried: "You are a *guigne* (bad luck) Azurène, you are wicked and dishonest. Why did you do it? Why?"

"But Tansia," Azurène responded, "I sold it for a gourde while everywhere else a stick of cane sells at *ven kòb* (twenty centimes).[48] Is it wrong that I struck a bargain for you? There is always sugar cane in the house. I don't know why you're getting so angry over a simple stick of sugar cane."

"You know why very well, you witch! I was very careful to

---

48 The kòb is old Haitian currency. One hundred kòb equaled one gourde. A euro is worth sixty gourds.

tell you to watch those two sticks of sugar cane for me and not exchange them. You betrayed me. Never do a thing like that to me again. If you do. . . ."

"Forgive me, Tansia, I didn't know," Azurène hastened to say, so as to calm down Aunt Tansia.

"Be still, filthy hypocrite."

It was the first time I had seen Aunt Tansia in that state. She seemed to be carved out of stone, a monolith. Her head touched the top of the entry door. For ten minutes, she stood on her toes, with one hand lifting a part of her skirt to her waist. I thought she was magnificent! Grace and power emanated from her features. Her eyes flamed red, like embers, a wind arisen from who-knows-where blew through her hair. It was a sublime sight!

A minute later she became the Aunt Tansia I knew, calm and tender. I was fascinated to see how easily she passed from one state to the other. She approached us, embraced us and excused herself: "The gift is gone but I will replace it with a surprise, a good surprise. While you are waiting, share this single stick of sugar cane."

It was about eleven o'clock when we left her. The next day she came to see us very early, bringing mabi. We drank it on an empty stomach. Since we were still in bed, she came to us, entering into our bedroom. She complimented us on the décor and the placement of the furniture.

"Your bed is well positioned. The east side is the best position for the head; the north is also good. Did you know that the head is considered the center of command?" Suddenly she changed the subject: "May I have a little water?"

"Of course," Lòlò said, "I'll get it for you." He got up and returned with a big tumbler full of fresh water.

Aunt Tansia drank it all and thanked Lòlò. I watched her while she drank. She drank so slowly and so gracefully that I felt thirsty too. I asked Lòlò to bring me some water. Aunt Tansia frowned, surprised. "What? You have no water in your room?"

I told her I didn't.

"My child, water is indispensable."

"Yes, I know."

"Really? Explain it to me; how do you know that?"

"Well, just the way everyone normally knows it," I answered her.

"That is a good answer. In any case, I know it, but not as everyone else does."

I asked her what she meant.

"I know water as a necessity. I know it also as energy. It has great power. One can perform all known magic in a single drop of water."

She paused a moment and resumed: "At night, before going to bed, drink a big glass of water and don't forget to wash certain parts of your body: face, teeth, *bouboun*\* (pubis), hands and feet."

I burst out in wild laughter. "Aunt, I have known about this lesson in hygiene for twenty-two years." But she was serious, her face inscrutable. One glance at her and I stopped laughing. She blew her nose and took out a little tobacco from her pretty *poban*\* (small jar); then she began:

"These recommendations resemble a lesson in hygiene, it's true. Nevertheless, I am making them with a specific goal in mind. A genuine use of energy demands seriousness, cleanliness and simplicity."

"I understand," I replied, "but I would like to know the other faculties of water, apart from those I already know."

"You will acquire this knowledge all by yourself, you only need to get a bit closer to water."

"How?"

"Begin by placing water everywhere in your house and above all in your bedroom. Put a pitcher of water at the head of your bed."

"That's enough to open up the mystery of water to me?"

"Yes," she responded categorically.

The next day I went to the market and bought a pitcher. To make it more attractive I painted it white and covered it with designs of leaves and flowers. It was very beautiful. I filled it with water and followed all Aunt Tansia's recommendations to the letter. Then I waited. A month passed. . . . Nothing. Two months . . . still nothing. I told Aunt Tansia. She said: "I can't do anything for you."

I was perplexed. I didn't expect that response. Without paying any attention to my confusion, she began an explanation: "Water is a symbol. It is also a vehicle. Now, every vehicle lets itself be driven by whoever knows its codes."

"Water has codes?" I asked her.

"Yes, my child: Fluidity and humidity are its codes. Humidity is felt. Fluidity is seen."

I was pensive for a long time, but unfortunately I still didn't understand anything. She saw it and said nothing more. She hastened to leave and promised to return in two weeks.

I spent ten days thinking about water. Every night before going to bed I observed the water rituals, as I had done for two and a half months, without becoming discouraged even once. Finally one night I had a dream. I saw myself looking at a forest. I wanted to enter it but I was stopped by the idea of chancing upon a snake. At the moment I evoked the idea of a snake, an expanse of water spread out at my feet. It was very clear. I began to moisten my face. I washed my hands and feet, as well as my teeth, then I bent down to wash my bouboun. I looked at the water and saw the image of my vagina. I opened my eyes wide to better understand what I was seeing: It was a long passageway. I came closer and saw a long red carpet. I wanted to go forward, but I hesitated to step on it. Then, remembering that I had washed my feet, I put my feet carefully on the carpet. It was soft. The wall of the passageway was white, whiter than anything I had seen before. I walked for a long, long time. I moved like a happy child. I didn't look behind me. The passageway did not come to an end, and I was not tired. On the contrary, I would have liked to walk in that place for the rest of my life—if Lòlò were with me, I said to myself. At that instant I was projected into another place and I saw Lòlò talking with a woman. I approached them but I couldn't hear their conversation. I was not jealous, but the fact that Lòlò was having an intimate relationship and was not sharing that moment with me left me with the feeling of being abandoned. I experienced the coldness of solitude as well as suffering. That feeling made my throat dry. Terribly thirsty, I thought about the river. I wanted to go back in order to quench my thirst, but I couldn't find the way. I woke up in front of a full bowl of water in the dining room, my hands reaching for something in the water. When I saw Aunt Tansia again I told her my dream. She shook her head and said that it was not finished.

"The first time," she said, "you didn't continue with your dream because you were afraid. This time, it is because you lack confidence in your power. Your fear comes from your self-pity. Self-pity and fear have blocked your energy. The only chance you have now is to try to catch yourself in the trap."

"But I don't know how to catch myself in the trap."

"That requires will power and a lot of good humor. The only way to achieve it is to begin by vanquishing your reason."

That made me feel ill at ease. She appeared not to acknowledge my discomfort. In fact, she seemed quite determined to emphasize this aspect of my temperament. "You take everything seriously. The worst of it is that you take yourself too seriously."

I was shocked to hear her judge me. She saw that and narrowed her eyes. She was thoughtful for a moment. Then she came over to me and whispered in my ear, "Who are you?"

I didn't know what to say. I mumbled, "I don't know."

"What bothers me about you is that you are too *solid*. Despite all the manifestations of Ginen-an, you always go back to your inner reflections, which does not make my work easy."

"What are you reproaching me for, Aunt Tansia?"

"Your lack of spontaneity."

"What you say makes me sad."

"You are not sad because of what I am saying but because you cling to your personality, to your 'I.'"

I felt the air fill my chest. I had trouble breathing.

"Let out the *move-zè* (bad air). Do it quickly, you understand me, if not '*sonje byen, krapo-gonfle mouri pete epi san bounda.*'" This is an expression meaning that by getting all worked up we become so grandiose that essential things escape us. At that point I couldn't hold back any longer and I began to cry. She fixed her gaze on me: "Weep for your death, my girl."

Her irony hurt me. I sobbed for at least an hour. Then I experienced a sensation of calm, as if I had lost track of time. I recognized that I was capable of seeing myself with all my prejudices and complexes. I was frozen into immobility by it all.

I had completely forgotten Aunt Tansia's lesson, which explained that to bring the dream to completion, the dreamer must profit from all his "voyages" so as to mobilize the totality of his being. To accomplish that, the dreamer does not have the right to either think or imagine, for he risks falling back into the world of reason. To be "fully realized" the dreamer must liberate himself from this world. The dreamer must be in a position to see beyond the limits of this world and of this personality, which it has invented for us.

For Aunt Tansia, the purpose of dreaming was not only to develop the ability to see the known world, but also to be a witness to the Unknown. She used to say: "That takes a lot of energy. Our personality does not give us energy. Rather, on the contrary, it absorbs what energy we have. For the dreamer, everything is consistent; there is nothing but energies. The dreamer experiences no hesitation; he considers all living beings as energies. He has no need for idols and doesn't fabricate any. He is detached, impersonal. That is why he feels neither superior nor inferior. The idea of superiority or inferiority is erased in him. It is the very absence of this idea that is going to transform the dreamer and help him bring his dream to maturity. It is his humility that allows him to realize that nothing is important.

"To enter into the dream state," Aunt Tansia repeated to me, "it is necessary to silence oneself. One must silence all thoughts."

As she said this she was facing me, looking straight at me. I looked at her too. She smiled and asked sweetly: "Bring me your pitcher of water. We are going to drink together." I smiled at her—that reminded me of the joke about the complicity of *tafyatè*★ (drinking companions). I felt relieved, light on my feet. I went into my bedroom to get my pitcher. I took it to her. She took it from my hands, looking offended. I was taken aback.

"Why did you paint your pitcher? she asked me.

"To make it beautiful," I responded.

"It is stupid to think that terra-cotta is less beautiful than this trashy glaze. You have removed all the energy of the pitcher. Whether you make it a decorative pot or something else, it will never serve as a means of communication between you and the Spirit."

"I didn't know. I'm so stupid."

"You must know that everyone does stupid things when they are not guided by Ginen-an."

"What is Ginen, *Bondje-manman-mwen*⋆ (Holy Mother)? The truth is that I will never know what it is unless I get a firm and clear explanation."

"One can never explain it, one can only experience it."

"But what are the attitudes one must adopt to be able to experience it?"

"The first is to undergo initiation with the goal of discovering its nature. The second is to undergo Mèt tèt in order to be able to master the world of Ti Bonnanj. The third, finally, is to be receptive to the manifestation of the Spirit."

I listened to her without really understanding, but I registered it all. I had such a need to know in order to be able to reorganize all my memories. To do so, I had to organize my experiences, synthesize them, and then set out on this new path, filled with self-assurance. I decided to make a unified whole of what I had learned and experienced—be it in the known world or in the unknown world. I told this to Aunt Tansia.

"That is right," she replied. "To be able to find the totality of yourself, it is imperative to bring out this need to connect the two forms of perception. To begin with, turn inward and be still."

Aunt Tansia's method of helping me bring my dream to maturity thus consisted in training me to impose silence on myself. "Don't judge anyone or yourself. Silence all your thoughts in yourself," she ordered me.

She had me practice some rituals utilizing the corresponding aids such as the *kwiy*⋆ (half-calabash), the *bale wouze*⋆ (a sacred plant used to bless altars and the tables where the food for the lwa are arranged), basil, water, the pitcher and the hygienic lesson I had received. And she gave other recommendations such as never putting one's hands under one's head when sleeping, never sleeping with a pillow at the back, not turning around quickly after having a dream, completely recounting one's dream to oneself before divulging it, never leaving shoes under the bed, eating before eight at night, placing a jug of water at the head of the bed before retiring, performing *jete dlo*★ (sprinkling water ritually on the floor) every morning, executing the gesture of benediction of the *twa gout dlo*★ (three drops of water; a concept that defines the authority of the initiate), to drink water on an empty stomach, not to play with one's shadow, never to *mache pa bak* (walk backwards), to put the pitcher in the sun, to *limen*★ (light the candles and pray) every full moon, to wash oneself that day at noon with water warmed in the sun and rub one's whole body with the leaves of *lachòy*★ (sage) and basil and marigold flowers, not to cross one's legs when praying.

"Dreaming is a process that requires will. However, you must not force yourself or abandon yourself. A door is already open for you; only try to see clearly what is about to be shown to you."

"I would like to be able to change. I feel blocked."

"You already have the chance to be able to reenter the dream state; your only problem is that of equilibrium."

"Help me."

"Only your allié can help you. Look for him and confront him. Once you have proved yourself, he will place himself at your service."

"Good God!" I cried, but she cut me off.

"There is no cause for discouragement. It's up to you to exploit your gift or let it rot. As for me, I advise you to go deeper. How many are there who would give whatever it takes to possess this gift? *Yo pran 'beny chans,' yo achte mouchwa tout koulè, yo monte Pe* (They take lucky baths, they buy all kinds of headscarves of all colors, they dress altars), but the spirit doesn't descend."

"What is the connection between luck and power?"

"Luck is power, my child. Reason cannot comprehend that."

"How can a bath give power or luck to someone?"

"*Sa se Mistè* (That is a Mystery.). What I know is that we have a connection with all forms of life. Plants, among other things, can deliver many secrets."

She got up to leave, but I held her back by her skirt.

"Speak to me some more. I need to know. I am still afraid of one thing. Help me, Aunt."

"You are afraid of many things because you yourself have not made the move to enter the trap."

"I shall apply myself to this. But tell me, how and why does the dreamer become a lougarou?"

"That happens when the head of the dreamer has not been placed—the head being considered the center of command—when the dreamer only works in the heart of competition in the inmost part of the known world. In that case, he remains blocked in a repetitious cycle of desires. He does nothing but waste all his energy and can only replenish it by sucking the energy of another dreamer. That is why he prefers a newborn babe who is a dreamer *par excellence*."

I sighed deeply, I took her hands, and she enveloped me in her long dress. That was a gesture of affection I loved very much. I thanked her and she left without saying a word. After she left, I stayed in the courtyard to admire the full moon. Lòlò was lying on a mat, under the *kénépier* tree. We didn't speak. There was no need to. Only silence mattered. Like two condemned prisoners enchained by the same fate, we awaited the verdict of this silence, the only sign that would announce our Liberation.

## CHAPTER 3

# *Lwa* or a State of Lucid Dreaming?

Aunt Tansia advised me to be resolute in everything I did, so as to be in control of my entry into Nan Dòmi—into the dream state. To dream is to see, she kept repeating. A dreamer is a medium, a witness to the unknown. Therefore, as a precondition he must distinguish the state of dreams from the state of the lwa.

"These are neighboring states," she explained to me.

"What are the signs of each, then? How do I recognize them?"

"The dreamer enters into the unknown world. The lwa comes out of the unknown world and visits the known world through a medium (his *chwal*)★. The dreamer, in the course of his journeys, meets some entities and carries on dialogues with them. Or he might meet other dreamers in the form of energy. He can go back and forth quickly between the known and the unknown worlds, which always gives him the impression of being outside of time. The dreamer communicates beyond sound, while the lwa speaks the language of humans."

Aunt Tansia explained that one can call upon a lwa directly by means of prescribed ritual acts such as the benediction of *twa gout dlo*, songs addressed to the lwa in which one requests its presence; or with the sounds of drums, *tchatcha*★ (maracas) and the like. On the other hand, one enters into a dream at a sign. The lwa comes by means of an injunction.

I was not satisfied. What troubled me most was that my body was being occupied and I was losing all control over it. I didn't like that.

She advised me to let my body manage itself, because "the body has information that cannot be discerned through logic."

I needed several lessons from Aunt Tansia in order to understand what she wanted to teach me. My confidence in her did not prevent a heaviness of spirit. I trusted her, but the weight still pushed down on me. I still clung to ways of thinking that hindered my progress.

"Certain things I experience when I begin to dream terrify me. Sometimes I have trouble breathing."

"All that is because of your obstinacy in dragging logical thoughts along with you."

I explained to her that often I felt *peze* (a sensation of swelling in the limbs) caused by something stronger than I was. I was afraid. Sometimes, I told her, I would call for help, but no sound would come from my throat. I would see people pass by again and again without heeding me. She called this state *Pase pa filyè★ Lesprit* (passing through the Spirit).

Aunt Tansia ordered me to attach a *kakòn-je-bourik★* (a kind of dried fruit) to my navel. She said that I would soon begin to hear new sounds. She brought us two kakòn, but I failed to do as instructed. As if she were aware of this, she would ask me from time to time if there was anything new. Each time I answered her: "I haven't done it yet." But one morning she arrived with a resolute air and greeted me with a nod of her head. For a moment I thought my negligence annoyed her. I knew I was not observing the rituals. I was too rational to bend to practices that in my view seemed banal.

"You are too full of yourself. As you are now you will never come to control the state of dreams. Sooner or later, if you don't strive to free yourself of your reason, you will find yourself depressed."

I asked her what I should do.

"Dance my child, dance. Only dance can create an emptiness inside of you."

"I don't know how to dance. I am afraid of dancing."

"Because you are holding on too much to the known world. Let your body vibrate to the rhythms. Space is rhythmic.

Time is rhythmic. Everything dances. The entire universe and everything it contains, the energies dance."

I was convinced and I asked her to help me. "Teach me to dance, Aunt."

"As for me, I can't teach you. Besides, my role here is coming to an end very soon." Hearing her speak like this made me very melancholy. It was her way of getting me used to the idea of her departure for the unknown world. As if to console me, she enveloped me in her long dress.

"You need a *konèsè* (expert teacher) to teach you to feel your body. Listen carefully to me—dance is not logical, even though it is a discipline. Dance is madness, but it is controlled madness. Only a teacher who is knowledgeable has the capacity to lead you to the madness that is dance."

"Tell me, are there 'expert teachers'? What does that mean?"

"The expert teacher is the one who can see the outer shell containing the energies. You, for example, are enclosed in turtle's shell. It will take a lot of strength to break it.

"I want to find this teacher."

"Look for him."

"But how will I recognize him?"

"He will appear to you rolling his body in a movement that will remind you of the snake in your dream."

"Why so many mysteries?"

"Because everything is a mystery. You are a mystery surrounded by mysteries."

"Will this teacher be available to me?"

"He will, because breaking open your shell will be a challenge for him. It will be enough to encourage patience and cunning on his part so as to end with the complete gushing forth of your energy."

"Will it take time?"

"Why do you speak of time? Don't cling to time. Live in the *kounye a-la-a*★ (the present moment)."

She left that day, leaving me with another problem:

From that day forward, Aunt Tansia began a new phase of instruction. She taught me how to do the *woule vant*★ (belly dance) in two directions. The dance consisted of rolling my stomach from my pelvis up, then doing the same thing in the opposite direction. She advised me to perform this movement until I felt a sensation similar to an orgasm. Her plan was to lead me to become aware of the belly dance in my womb.

"The womb," she said, "contains all our frustrations, our fears, our complexes, and the like."

She suggested that I practice that exercise often, which would bring me relief and allow me to rid myself of fear. I agreed to exercise seriously.

"When you go shopping, for example, do the woule vant. It doesn't matter where, or at what time, do your belly dance."

One day I finally succeeded in experiencing the sensation she spoke about. I was in Pétion-Ville at a pharmacy. I had given my prescription to the clerk. As I waited for my medicine, I began the belly dance, and suddenly I heard a whirring in my ears. Concentrating, I realized that it was a noise like that made by the waves of the sea. The more I concentrated, the more I became aware that the noise was coming from my womb. There was a strange sensation in my navel. I felt a trembling at the level of my Fallopian tubes. I reacted by shaking my buttocks. The pharmacy delivery boy, who had just walked in, looked at me, wide-eyed.

"Do you have a fever with the shakes?" he asked me, anxiously.

"No, I am fine. I'm not ill," I answered him calmly.

"Excuse me. Just now I thought I saw your body shake."

"I am dancing."

As if he understood, he burst out in laughter. I was observing myself as I danced. The dance released a certain suppleness in my movements. I set off experiencing the euphoria of my new dance. I was happy! On the way home, I composed a poem addressed to Aunt Tansia:

> Ô Tansia!
> I owe
> My new birth to you
> I want
> To always love you

Only a mother
Has the patience
To give birth:
You did not lie
When you told me:
"Dance is the most
Beautiful ritual
That foments harmony
Between the body and the Spirit,
Dance is
One of the most beautiful languages.

Aunt Tansia loved to dance the Yanvalou. But she said she preferred the Kongo.

"A dance can make one laugh, cry, change a human being, many things. For dance is sacred," she would say.

Six months later, when I saw Aunt Tansia again, I told her about the experience in the pharmacy.

"Keep it up," she said. "You are going to be able to become conscious of another dimension through your movements."

"You are right, *tante*. Dance has led me to another dimension."

"Dance is a passport that permits you to take long journeys into the unknown."

"I am going to enroll in a dance school. I have discovered that I love dance."

"You must also enroll in space, in the world of mysteries. It is only through dancing that your allié will come to you. Your dance will attract him. He will see you and he will show himself to you. Then you will confront him with movements of the head, hands, hips, stomach, whatever you wish. I guarantee you will conquer him. Because, intoxicated by your movements, he will submit, stretched out at your feet. He will be your *gad*★ (protector) and your counselor."

"Does he have a set role? If he does, what prevents him from doing his work right now, helping me to find my balance?"

"Nothing or nobody. He only needs your consent."

"But I agree that he should come to help me."

"It isn't enough to tell him so, one must be truly disposed to have him come."

"I am, on condition that he executes all my commands."

"He is not a slave but a protector guide who will take you wherever you wish, '*san li pa eskize konesans a ou.*'"

"What does '*eskize konesans*' mean?"

"There are people who from birth have been chosen to fulfill the role of chwal. As they grow older, the pact is buried in their subconscious. But the Spirit will continue to dance on its chwal even when the chwal is not conscious of what is happening. That is called, '*eskize konesans chwal la.*' It manifests itself whenever conditions are right. The Spirit *se filyè*★ (communicating spirit) acts unexpectedly. However, it can mount its chwal after having asked its permission beforehand. In that case, one says: '*San li pa eskize-konesans-chwal-la.*'"

Then she began a song:

> *M ape mande sa ka resevwa-mwen?*
> *Ala m sòti nan peyi nan Ginen*★,
> *Tou sele ak gwo lwa nan tèt an m la,*
> *M ape mande sa ka resevwa-mwen?*
> *Ala mpa moun isit, o!*

> I'm asking, who is going to take me in?
> I'm coming out of the land of Ginen
> Saddled with a great Loa inside my head,
> I wonder, who can take me in?
> I'm not anybody from around here, no!

The song was beautiful and appropriate. I understood what she was teaching me. I was amazed. Aunt Tansia arose and stood face to face with me; she smiled. Her eyes were shining.

"Look at me, look how I dance. Do you want to sing, and I, should I dance? Sing while you do a belly dance. Breathe from the stomach, bring your breath up to the throat and expel the notes forcefully."

I began to sing timidly; "*M ape mande sa ka resevwa-mwen....*"

But she cried out: "Sing with your guts! My allié is there and he wants to meet you. At least sing for him."

I sang louder, louder. You could say that the sound that came out of my throat had no limits. All I wanted was to feel movement at the level of my womb and to see myself dancing with Aunt Tansia.

She had her arms raised, mimicking the form of a bowl or some other round object. She thrust out her chest, stood up straight on the heel of her right foot, and on the toes of her left foot. She began to gesture. A moment came when I no longer recognized her. Her eyes were big and beautiful like two jets of light. An instant later I glanced at myself and I saw myself. I had also changed. Suddenly I felt a cramp in my neck, but I only saw balls of light. Some of them came toward me. I eluded them. They asked me for my news. I told them that everything was going well for the moment but that my body had certain failings that led to illnesses. One of them suggested that I correct these defects. I said that I did not know the secret to be able to do so.

"A massage with oil of *palma-kristi*★ (castor oil) and of papaya leaves heated in *clairin*★ (unrefined rum distilled from cane sugar) will help you."

I thanked it.

"But where is Aunt Tansia?" I asked.

"Here," a voice answered.

She had taken on the form of a ball of bright light. By her side was a smaller light, which was slightly pink. I sensed that she was smiling at me. Something in my body affirmed it. I responded with a smile to her smile.

She made a sign for me to look to my left. I looked and I saw a ball of light the color of indigo blue. I loved it immediately. I wanted to get a bit closer, the better to admire it. It leaped up right before my eyes. I drew back. It advanced, I drew back again, but all around I felt immense balls of light brush against me. Their contact burned me. Aunt Tansia approached and asked them to retreat. They obeyed. She took my hand and ordered me to stop dancing. But I didn't want to stop.

"Why," I asked her, "why should I stop dancing?"

"Because you are going to find yourself *gonmen*★ (trapped) then *gobe*★ (eaten)!" she cried.

I stopped reluctantly and let myself slide down to the ground. She stood me up, passed her hand over my face and made me drink a large glass of water. At the same moment, all the balls of light disappeared. I sat down right on the ground, regretting the end of my vision.

"It is absolutely necessary for you to develop your energy," Aunt Tansia said.

"What should I do for that to happen?"

"You must try to maintain a relationship with the Zany of your family, with *Djètò a*★ (the ancestral soul)."

"I don't understand what you mean to say."

"The group of fields of energy that you have just seen constitutes your family. You followed me into the world of the lwa. You have communicated with the lwa of your family. You lacked vigilance, one moment more and you would have been trapped, because you are not balanced."

I stood up and sat on the big above-ground root of the *kénépier* tree (which is located on the east side of the house). She followed and sat alongside me.

"I think it's stupid that I am trapped, as you say. What have I done to displease them?"

"You love words too much. You only feel safe when you have explanations."

We continued sitting on the root without saying a word. Suddenly, she began again: "Can words account for the living bond that joins you to the Zany of your family? Can words sound the depth of a Djètò or the intentions of the *Djehoun*★ (Mystery of the Word)?"

I told her that the state I had found myself in just before had pleased me, but that now I was beginning to be afraid of it. She looked into my eyes and I was unable to sustain the force of her stare. I lowered my head.

"You are too inclined to obsession. That is why these energies could have trapped you and eaten you afterwards."

She explained to me that when one sets out on the road to

consciousness one must free oneself of all obsessions, whatever the cost.

"In order to rid oneself of obsession, it is necessary to have clear communication with Ginen-an. And in order to have that communication one must pass through filyè."

She explained to me that some dreamers have been able to establish a line of communication with their lwa. These dreamers are storytellers. The fact that they can recount stories shows them the road to perfection, to liberty. She told me that the Ginen of the old order recounted stories—oral tales like *Bouki ak Ti Malis*.[49]

"However, with the new order, there are going to be new stories. They will originate through the leadership of the Mysteries and under the auspices of the Ginen. The storytellers of the new order will know how to manipulate their bond of communication with the Mistè. The goal of these storytellers is to transcend their own stories."

"What bothers me," I asked her, "is how do I develop this bond of communication with the mysteries?"

"By developing your personal power. Without that there are neither dreams nor Zany."

"But how can I attain that? Tell me," I insisted.

"Begin by traveling with your Ti Bonnanj. Let yourself go."

"Let myself go where?"

"To Ginen," she answered dryly.

"But where do I leave from to be sure that I am on the Ginen way?"

"Ginen is present everywhere. All you need is to want to go."

I knew all that, but I had forgotten it. I was agitated. I wanted to know more. Aunt Tansia's departure for the other world, the unknown world, was drawing near. The idea that she was going to leave me created a kind of impatience. I wanted to understand everything at once. My intellect took the upper hand: I felt caught in the trap of a myth. I asked Aunt Tansia to tell me how she had been able to remain faithful to her obligations,

---

49 Allegorical figures in Haitian stories.

retain the rules and methods, and to teach me. She responded that she had to do nothing other than take advantage of what she found already accomplished: "The Ginen who preceded me did an immense amount of work. After many trials and under the efficacious direction of the Ginen, I was able to learn."

She didn't have time to finish. Suddenly I felt something grab me from behind, obliging me to stand up. Aunt Tansia ordered me to relax. I don't know how I was able to do so, but I relaxed.

"Concentrate on your womb," she advised.

I was aware of my belly, but all of a sudden I began to see lights: red, white, then indigo blue. From that moment forward, I felt light and strong at the same time. Someone I could not see was on my right. Its voice spoke to me: "I am going to show you something."

I was held up under my left arm, and the two of us started to fly through the air. I was happy. We traveled for a long time. "Look down below!" The voice had me view a construction made from columns of light. It was beautiful, sublime, spectacular!

"It is the future civilization," the Unknown one confided to me before disappearing.

I returned to my normal state an instant later. I wanted to recount my vision to Aunt Tansia. But she made a sign for me to be quiet and gave me water to drink. I understood what she wanted me to do. I drank and proceeded on to the Jete.

"I dreamed, Aunt."

"Rather, you were *sele*★ (saddled)."

"What do you mean?"

"*Yon Zany sot danse nan tèt a ou* (A Zany was just dancing in your head)," she said.

"I saw things. How do you know that it was a Zany? I was conscious."

"It spoke to me and made me see what you were seeing. The explanation is that '*eskize konesans a ou.*' I was saddled just as you were by the same Zany."

I did not understand this practice. But, the fact was that I was in the midst of living the experience. I asked, "How does one sense the approach of a Zany? I am completely confused. I thought I was dreaming."

"Don't concern yourself with this. One senses the arrival of a Zany in different ways. You may feel a vibration inside your head, a blow perhaps, on the back or the neck. It is a Zany knocking on your door to discuss with you the location of the place where your corporeal shell is to be found. That has no price, my child. Don't haggle. Let it come in. For it has come no doubt to work or to bring an important message."

I said no more, but I rejoiced in my inner being that Aunt Tansia was a great master.

She asked me, "If I come one day to knock on your door, will you open it to me?"

Aunt Tansia made Janbe into the other world in 1981, leaving me a weighty inheritance to carry and above all to manage.

CHAPTER 4

# The Double and the Dream Body

*Nannan ak nannan-rèv*

On December 24, 1980, Aunt Tansia invited Lolò and me to take a stroll with her before going to church to attend midnight Mass. After walking a little more than a mile I began to feel fatigue. She proposed that we go to the big public plaza in front of the cathedral to rest a bit. Despite the darkness, Aunt Tansia recognized a man she knew. "Hello, Jeantilus," she greeted him. "Tonight is the big gathering, isn't it?"

" Unfortunately, this is not my night," the passerby answered.

"Why did you say that to him?" I asked her.

"I just wanted to tease him a little. He is one of the biggest *galipòt*★ (sorcerers) in the region. Anyway, he should have a celebration tonight for the members of his society. Especially because tonight there is a *dekou*★ (new moon). This would be the best time for it."

It was eight o'clock, and we were seated on a bench in the public plaza. We were chatting about this and that when suddenly a bird's piercing cry traversed the space, going from north to south and back again three times. Aunt Tansia got up and stood in the middle of the plaza. She cleared her throat three times and spat. Then she put her arms around our shoulders and laughed softly.

"It is Beke taking her stroll," she assured us.

"Do you mean that the cry of that bird *symbolizes* Beke's stroll?"

She did not answer my question, but went on:. "This woman is extraordinary. She is very audacious. Yesterday evening, she flew off. She passed quite close to me. She danced, flying in circles, around the church's clock tower."

"How can she fly? Does she actually fly, like a bird?"

I had scarcely finished my sentence when the bird's cry began again. I started and drew nearer to Aunt Tansia.

"Look," she said. "She is perched on the *anakayit*★ (a tree) right next to us."

I looked at the tree, but couldn't see anything. It was the night of the new moon and there was no electricity in the region. The darkness was too dense. I was very disappointed not to witness that scene, and I wanted to mock Aunt Tansia in order to seem logical. At the same time, I felt a kind of doubt that obliged me to mask my weakness; I didn't want her to realize I didn't understand.

"Aunt Tansia, you have perfect vision."

"*Pe, non!* (Be quiet!)" she said, silencing me. Concentrate instead on the color of your entry into dreaming and you will see that darkness is nothing but a thin envelope that one can tear apart."

She had hardly finished speaking when the cries began again. I felt a shudder go down my back. I tried to think about the color white, but I couldn't concentrate. The bird's cries obsessed me. I raised my head in their direction. My eyes looked for the source of the sound. I wanted to see. All my attention was focused on the bird's cry. My intention was to see it. My will to see was so intense that I was able to locate it in my body. I felt a kind of warmth coming from my belly, a bit lower than my navel, like an urge to *pipi cho* (pressing need to urinate) held back for too long. I was on edge. Then I let out a cry of relief and suddenly saw a black mass moving from branch to branch, emitting cries. And I saw its eyes. They resembled the flash from a flashlight. I grabbed Aunt Tansia's hand and shook it nervously.

"Aunt, I see it."

"Who?"

"The bird."

"Ah, good! What is it like?"

I said that I had not seen a bird, but rather a black mass and two flashes.

"Very good."

"What is it doing there?"

"I don't know. Ask it yourself."

But I knew. I quickly realized that Aunt Tansia wanted us to be witnesses of a fact. But my rational mind didn't want to accept the fact. It was too much for my little head. I asked Aunt Tansia to explain it to me. I wanted to uncover this mystery whatever the cost.

"Aunt?" I murmured.

"Shh! Listen now."

Then she began to sing:

> *Tako! Tako! Tako!*
> *M pa vin isit*
> *Pou m manje moun, o!*
> *Tako! Tako! Tako!*
> *Malfini pase, li ban m zèl*
> *Zòtolan pase, li ban m zèl*
> *Frize pase, li ban m zèl*

Tako! Tako! Tako!★ (bird of prey)
I'm not coming here
To eat people, O!
Tako! Tako! Tako!
The chicken-hawk passes; he gives me wings.
The ortolan passes, he gives me wings.
The screech-owl passes, he gives me wings.

She finished her song as quickly as she had begun.

"That was beautiful," I said.

She ordered us to be quiet: "*Chut, pe!* (Hush, be quiet!)" We didn't speak for a time. It seemed like we were simply contemplating the darkness. I understood what she wanted: silence and our attention. I easily became silent. But I was in suspense, awaiting Aunt Tansia's explanation.

Our silence didn't last long. A few minutes later, the cries began again, this time without stopping. Aunt Tansia told us that Beke wanted to leave, that we must take care not to follow her last cry. To do so would be dangerous, because Beke was trying to draw us into her territory. Aunt Tansia ordered us again to be quiet, while she directed our attention to something else.

We fell silent. A thousand thoughts jostled in my head. Then a long and terrifying cry sounded. This time I trembled from fear. My heart raced. I could hear the sound of my heart beating like a *tanbou kata*★ (a type of drum) against my eardrums. It seemed that Aunt Tansia heard them too. She placed her hand under my elbow. Her gesture brought me a kind of peace. I thanked her, and in a low voice asked, "What does all that mean?"

"You have just met Beke."

"You are joking, Aunt Tansia, I have known Beke for a long time."

She laughed heartily. Her voice resonated strangely, like an echo.

"In a way, yes. But this is the first time that you have seen the *other* part of Beke."

"What does that mean?"

"That you have altered your level of consciousness enough so as to see her other body, her *nannan*★ (her double), and her *nannan-rev*★ (dream body)."

"How many bodies does she have then?" I joked.

"My child, everyone has three bodies: the *kadav kò*★ (physical body), the nannan and the nannan-rèv. The kadav kò is the envelope of the nannan. However, in a dream state, the physical body, which represents the Gwo Bonnanj, is enveloped by the nannan. It does so to protect the dreamer by giving him a sense of solidity so that he won't lose himself in the world of Ti Bonnanj for lack of preparation."

I understood everything she was saying to me but I lacked concrete details. I still wanted to question her on the subject of nannan-rèv, but something was blocking me. I had a strong sensation, which came from a pocket of gas moving up and down from my solar plexus to my colon. It made me nervous.

"You are anxious," Aunt Tansia said.

"Yes, I am."

"Let's go. That's all for today."

She got up quickly and advised us to return home directly and above all to *vire rad an nou lanvè*★ (to turn our clothes inside-out), before going inside the house. She embraced us. We walked all the way with her.

She went into her house without turning around. Lòlò and I walked side-by-side up to the entrance of our house. We followed Aunt Tansia's advice to the letter. It was very dark and no one could see us as we maneuvered to disrobe and dress again. By doing so, we reintegrated the corporeal shell.

That night I slept very little. I was thinking of Beke. I didn't want to doubt what Aunt Tansia said, but the story of Beke's flight intrigued me.

Beke had been my neighbor when I was a child. I had known her for years. She was petite, with a round face, almond-shaped eyes and long, silky hair—what we call a *marabou*.[50] She was always smiling. However, I did not consider her beautiful. I did not like her odor, which reminded me of the *pois pian* (a plant that gives off an unpleasant smell), nor the way she looked at me. She also had an odd habit of tickling any child who crossed her path under their armpits. I hated that game. Her fingernails hurt. The children complained. We considered her a mildly nasty person. I tried to avoid her when I saw her on the street. But that didn't prevent me from being attracted to her in a way. She sold fried food and made her living from her *fritay*★ (fried food) stall. But she was not poor. She had a very pretty little house. She lived alone. Everything in her house was beautiful. Above all, her dishware and her cotton sheets embroidered with silk thread.

Every afternoon at four o'clock, she would prepare *griyo*★ (grilled pork) and *bananes peseés* (fried plantains), in a place near the fence that separated my parents' house from hers. The smell of griyo would waft into my room, reach my nose and stimulate my appetite. So, every afternoon I hastened to a rendezvous with Beke. All I had to do to escape my mother's vigilance was to tell her I was going to the latrines at the foot of the courtyard.

---

50 A Haitian whose features are thought to resemble those of some populations in India.

I squatted, pretending to urinate. And very quickly I squeezed under the bottom row of wire and was within reach of the fritay, although my parents and above all my mother had forbidden me to go to Beke's house to eat anything prepared by her hands. But I never obeyed them. I crossed the fence at the slightest invitation from Beke: I loved her fried food, and she knew it.

However, I stopped going there and took my parents' warnings seriously after the death of a little boy named Prosper who used to go to Beke's house *frite*★ (as a freeloader), like me. We both loved the *kaka griyo*★ (leavings of grilled pork) with *pen manchèt*★ (a long loaf of wheat bread) that Beke always gave us. The entire town accused Beke of having killed little Prosper. She never defended herself. On the contrary, one might say she seemed to be proud of being accused, if only because of her way of looking at people so arrogantly. One afternoon I leaned longingly against the *lonturay* (fence made of wire or cactus) to look at the big *chodiè* (pot) of griyo on a stove heated with charcoal. I admired the griyo and the fire. I was also listening to the conversation between Beke and man Kao (another neighbor). Beke was saying, "*Ti kabrit ki san gadò se vyann pou lèpasan* (A little goat without a herdsman is meat for the hunters.)."

It should be said in passing that she was referring to me. Then, man Kao, who was sitting on a small chair on her doorstep, got up and said to her,: *ðYon jou gen yon zo ki pou pase an travè nan gògèt a ou*. (A misfortune will befall you one day: a bone will stick in your throat.)"

Then she turned angrily to me and warned in a severe tone, "Listen to me, *Pyang*"—that's what she called me—"*jou mwen bare ou devan pòt Kay a Beke, se filange m ap filange fès a ou pou manman a ou, ou tande?* (I'm warning you that the next time I see you at Beke's house, I'll give you such a hiding that even your mother would be pleased, you understand me?)" I understood her message, despite my young age—I was eight at the time.

After that day, I never set foot in Beke's house again.

I recounted all that to Aunt Tansia the next day, when I went very early to her house. I asked her about Beke's flight: Was it really Beke or just an illusion? Was the flight real? How was she able to recognize Beke?

Calmly, and without looking at me, she explained that at present I couldn't see things except from the outside. However, it was an important event and I ought to consider it carefully.

"If you want to progress, you must see things as much on the outside as on the inside. That is what constitutes the *eritaj-a-lafanmi Ginen* (the heritage of the Ginen family). It is necessary that you go to your *Bitasyon*★⁵¹ *a ou, nan demanbre*★ *a ou.*"

I listened to her for a long time without saying a word. Deep inside, I was waiting for answers to my questions. She knew it, but she was not in a hurry. I was obliged to wait. Then, to fill in the time, I pretended to be patient by playing with my hair. I said to myself, "I'm holding her to the obligation to give me a just and clear response. I don't want anything approximate, otherwise I'm going to catch her out. . . . I had no time to formulate the thought before she shook me vigorously and said, "Stop your scheming! If not, you won't understand anything."

I started. The accuracy of her insight threw me off course. I didn't dare think anymore. I began to listen with full attention.

She resumed speaking: "Beke possesses the level of consciousness that enables flight, and so do I. Beke is a dreamer. You and I are dreamers also. However, Beke has perfected her art, as I have mine. But you have not yet perfected yours."

"Can you tell me how she acquired this consciousness?"

"By practicing the method that imparts the power of transforming oneself into whatever one wishes."

"What is this method that grants the power of flying like a plane, like a bird?"

"It is a science."

"I can't believe that our bodies can do that."

"Nonetheless, you have seen it."

"I don't know what I have seen. Please explain it to me."

I knew that I was lying when I said that. My body gave the lie to my reason. But I held to my insistence that Aunt Tansia should explain all this to me in words my intellect could comprehend. In a word, I wanted logical and precise answers.

---

51 The site reserved for lwa or spirits; a family domain where trees that serve as altars (or holy *pye bwa sèvi*) are located; the family patrimony where the powers are transmitted from one generation to the another.

"There are things one cannot explain. One can only experience them."

"I would like to experience flight."

"You can if you wish."

"That is not enough. Isn't a certain apprenticeship required?"

"That is correct. The first thing to know is that our being constitutes a field of energy. If you don't believe that, you have not risen to a teachable level. Even secular science recognizes this. Apparently, the skeptics who are dependent on laboratories to prove to them that a human being can transform his field of energy at will are the majority in this world."

She was silent for a moment and catching her breath, exclaimed: "*Adje pou yo!* (So much the worse for them!) For they will remain prisoners of the world of reason, of what is objective, and they will die without attaining consciousness."

"I also depend on my reason," I told her.

"You are lying. You are a dreamer, my child. You know how to travel in the two worlds. You know the difference between them. That proves your independence."

"Nevertheless, I am blocked. It is very difficult for me to accept the fact that a human being can transform himself into an animal."

"The animal that you think you perceive is nothing but a symbol. In our culture, in particular, symbols retain their subtle nature. That is the strength of our culture. This animal, as you have called it, provides the occasion for Beke's experience. She has managed to manipulate her field of energy; that is all."

"How did you know that it was Beke?" I asked.

"I saw Beke. I saw her because I know her as energy. I can recognize whoever it might be as such, as energy. It is not a guess. It is consciousness."

"Was Beke exercising her consciousness?"

"Yes, if you like. She likes to do it at eight o'clock at night. It is her favorite hour."

"So she was just amusing herself?"

"Perhaps she was, perhaps not. It is true that there may be a certain pleasure in transforming oneself into something else. But a lougarou does not enjoy itself. Its actions are inspired by necessity."

"What kind of necessity, Bondje-manman-mwen?" I asked, exasperated.

"Defiance of death."

I was left open-mouthed for a long time. I tried to grasp the meaning of that phrase. I had never thought that one could defy death; or, even more incredibly, that there were methods for doing it.

Perplexed, I asked, "Then Beke will not die?"

"Living beings are made of particles of dust that cohere in a large point that we may call *moun*★ (human being), or *zannimo* (animal or plant)."

She closed her eyes and repeated as if she were praying. "Being dust, we are attached to the earth. *Nan tè a gen leman, ô Lèmis! O!! O'Batala*★[52]! (In the earth there is a lodestone, ô Lèmis, Oh!! O'Batala!)"

With her left hand, she struck the ground, then her chest, then her forehead three times. Then she continued: "Nevertheless, whoever succeeds in detaching himself enough to separate the particles of dust that form our physical body and reorganizing them into another body is a *Konnen*★ (wise man), a granmoun. Still, that does not mean that he won't die. To know how to disobey death is an art. That is why, when the dreamer learns how to manage his field of energy, he must be able to protect himself at the same time. He must store up the necessary surplus of energy that will permit him to Janbe to the Unknown, without risking great danger."

Once again, I felt paralyzed by her words. I was afraid of the Unknown and I confided my fear to Aunt Tansia.

"It's not so grave a matter for you to be afraid of the Unknown," she laughed.

I sensed the irony in her gesture. She blew on my eyes, and I laughed too.

"All dreamers have the same reactions at first, because the dreamer is a sedentary type, a traditionalist and a hard-headed conservative who doesn't like to disturb the way he lives."

---

52 O'Batala is the ensemble of biological ancestors who constitute the priestly corps and transmit the wisdom of the past.

She was describing me perfectly. But I wanted her to keep talking, so I asked, "How do you know that?"

"I know it because I was also like that, and many others are as well. Still, what is harmful is to concentrate part of oneself on material things. The Gwo Bonnanj always needs the adhesion of the Ti Bonnanj to be able to act. In a word, I'm telling you that the mental faculty must have intuition to be confident about the acts undertaken. Yet, when one abuses oneself by running after material things in order to attain a certain self-assurance, one abuses one's vital force at the same time. If Beke doesn't transcend all that, death will take her. That is the big difference with Abodourine."

Abodourine! From the moment I heard this name I was carried away with enthusiasm. I asked her to tell me the story of that woman for the umpteenth time. She did, with pleasure. She loved Abodourine. She was Aunt Tansia's spiritual mother. Her story sounded like a fairy tale. I always closed my eyes when I heard it. It transported me into another, unimaginable world.

Aunt Tansia said, "Abodourine knew how to master the four elements—water, earth, fire, and air. She was able to go through air and fire, walk on water and descend anba dlo. She entered grottos to converse with Arawak spirits, and the like."

"Aunt Tansia, were there witnesses?"

"Of course there were, I was one. However, in spite of all her feats, Abodourine did not allow herself to be trapped by her power."

"How can one be trapped by power?"

"Because power engenders pride and self-satisfaction. Abodourine knew how to maintain her equilibrium. When she had achieved mastery of her art and succeeded in coalescing the totality of her being, she decided to Janbe. One morning, she gathered all her neighbors and announced her departure. She placed herself in a *layo*★ (large winnowing basket or tray) readied for the occasion.

"Why did she do that?" I asked.

"It was a ritual signifying her disintegration. According to her, the particles of dust that formed her kadav kò would be winnowed, scattered, and distributed, as well as her consciousness."

She became silent, closed her eyes, placed one hand over her left ear, and raised the other in the air. She crossed herself three times, then resumed speaking. "She unrolled a bobbin of red thread as she taught her last lesson. . . ."

I interrupted: "What did the bobbin represent?"

"This bobbin of thread was all that she possessed. It represented her link with the world. It was with her from the day of her initiation. It served as her calendar."

"How?" I asked, astonished.

"It marked historical dates."

"I don't understand. How could she write on thread?"

"She made knots. Each knot represented an important fact."

"What an imagination!" I exclaimed.

"What simplicity," Aunt Tansia corrected.

I asked her to go on, enthused.

"You love words too much. You become dependent on them. That is what causes blockage in poets. Prisoners of words, they remain eternally nostalgic for a world that they have perceived, but never truly been able to describe."

"Nonetheless, words are useful," I protested.

"Clearly, we have invented them to be able to explain what we believe we know. But there are things that we can't explain."

"For example?"

"Abodourine unrolled the bobbin's red thread and said, 'I'm leaving you the store of my consciousness. When I reach the end of the thread there will be nothing left of me.'"

I didn't understand. "That's not an example."

Aunt Tansia went on without looking at me. "She transformed herself at first into a white substance, like a kind of vapor, then disappeared before our eyes. All the doors were closed. I was a witness to it all."

"What grandeur!"

"What energy!" she corrected. "What do you see in this story?"

"I understand something, but I can't explain it."

"Oh! You can't find the words to communicate your thought? Find another way to do it, there are other possibilities, I guarantee it."

We fell silent. I was stymied. After a long pause, I said, "Do you realize, Aunt, that at the very mention of Abodourine's name I am no longer myself? I am fascinated by the power of this woman. How was she able to do all that?"

"Without any doubt, Abodourine's self-discipline was the engine of her success in the world of magic." She described Abodourine's methods for conquering envy and desire, the last enemies she would eliminate. "For Abodourine, material objects were not of primary importance. It was she who taught me that envy and desire are concealed behind material things and become an impediment for the dreamer. Right at the beginning of her apprenticeship, Abodourine shed all her goods. She traversed the country for eight consecutive years. She went to all the cemeteries and places where blood had been spilled in order to deposit small pine baskets. She lit them after each invocation. She did it for the sanctification of all those who died to give birth to the new Fatherland of Haiti."

Though I loved Abodourine's story, it disturbed me, above all when Aunt Tansia told me how Abodourine detached herself from all her material goods.

"She no longer ate on plates. All her food was served to her on a banana frond or a leaf of palma-kristi."

"It is horrible to think of doing that," I replied. "I don't see how that could lead to anyone's purification or spiritual evolution." To me, that was *"manje dwèt pou zong"*—biting off one's finger tips instead of one's nails. Abodourine's actions seemed like masochism to me.

"It was her choice. Each person employs his own tactic for monitoring himself. Abodourine was a dreamer. She knew that she did not have the right to attend to material things. She monitored herself in order to be able to defeat her pride."

"That was very rigorous."

"But efficacious. What is essential is to get to the point of *dechouke*★ (uprooting) the roots that attach us deep down."

Abodourine, Aunt Tansia told me, was Peul (or Foulani),[53]

---

53 The Peuls, also known as the Foulbés, Fula, and Foulanis, are a people living in West Africa (Upper Dahomey).

and related by birth to a royal family of Africa. Proud and wealthy, she was indignant that her brothers had been kidnapped and reduced to slavery. When she left in search of them, she had hatred in her heart. Vengeance was her banner. She came to Haiti with the sole objective of assuaging her hatred. But at the very moment she set foot at the port now known as Fort-Liberté (administrative center of the North-East Department of Haiti), the Spirit seized her and from then on, her personal history came to an end. The Spirit revealed to her then that malicious acts committed for personal benefit were to be avoided. Then she was transported by the Spirit to the mountains of Mont-Organisé and there she received the "Ginen order." She accepted the discipline imposed on her and became *Adja*. *[54]

"It was she who taught me how to get rid of the desire for vengeance that drove me mad after the killing of my son and Philomé, my lover," Aunt Tansia confessed.

"Tell me, Aunt, what is the harm in possessing the things one needs?"

"The harm lies not in the things but in the attachment one has to things, which becomes an act of possession. The dreamer does not have the right to pay attention to material things—for if he does, he falls into the trap of competition and he will lose, in one blow, a part of himself. The dreamer needs all his concentration to be able to find his other body, which is his double, in order to work toward attaining the totality of his being."

"That somewhat resembles religious stories I've heard."

"Why not? All religions have only one objective. They just use different methods."

She became silent and smiled wryly. She made a gesture with her head and began again. "I will only say in passing that Catholicism and Protestantism do not truly honor the teaching of their master. Just imagine: A few days ago Zanna brought a child of eight back to life, thanks to her magic powers. The Baptist preacher was very displeased. He visited Zanna with the

---

54 A Fon word that means "to dance to enter a trance state." In Vodou tradition, dance is the choreographic portrait of a family of lwa. The great initiates are excellent dancers in the sense that they easily enter into a trance state. They are called Adja, the title of the initiate who has reached the highest level.

intention of taking her the Good News, asking her to choose Jesus as her personal saviour, and having her put a stop to her services to Ginen."

"What did Zanna answer?"

"Zanna is wise. She simply thanked him and invited him to come back to see her."

"I would have put him in his place."

"He is there already, *pitit an mwen*, owing to his ignorance. He proved that he misunderstood the pwen of Jesus, by condemning someone who had known how to win that same power."

"Then why did Zanna want him to come back to visit?"

"I am sure that Zanna is going to teach him something. This pastor was very lucky. It is the Spirit that sent him to Zanna. This story should be closely followed."

"Have you spoken to Zanna?"

"Of course."

"How does she see the incident?"

"Like me, she thinks that it portends Ginen."

"This will be a difficult struggle, in my opinion."

"You are right, Zanna will have a hard job. It is not easy to convince a Christian. He has a tendency to reject any method that demands a different kind of discipline from his own. Christians '*soufri maladi-lapèrèz*' (suffer from paranoia). If a faithful Christian, Catholic or Protestant, comes upon someone walking on water or passing through a concrete wall, or floating in the air, he will stone him as a demon, in the name of Jesus. Yet Jesus taught his disciples how to master these elements."

"You are criticizing the Church severely, which is hypocritical, since you go there every day."

"I criticize it because it doesn't teach any practical method that might help its faithful to develop their personal power. On the contrary, it does nothing but depress their spirit in a sort of inertia. I go to church every day because it is a place where power resides."

"Are the faithful aware of all that?"

"They don't have full consciousness of it. Ninety-five percent of Christian faithful are Bible illiterates. According to them, there is no place where power resides except Rome and Judea. They believe without exception that Jesus is the only personage possessing power. What a lack of maturity! It is sad to acknowledge it."

"Should they receive a different kind of instruction?"

"Only the elect have this opportunity, but they are not numerous. They are the *fran-Ginen*★ (intiated into true Ginen) of the new order."

"Do you believe that a Catholic or a Protestant can be sufficiently open to grasp the teaching of Ginen and become fran-Ginen?"

"Yes. If the Spirit has reclaimed him, anything is possible."

"Even a Protestant can be reclaimed?"

"The Spirit chooses whomever it wants."

"How can that be done? The Protestant is indoctrinated in such a way that it doesn't seem easy for him to elevate his consciousness to another level. What is the process that brings about this transmutation?"

"It is true that the Protestant faithful are self-important and their egos are enormous. This stems from training that inculcates the idea that to know Scripture is to possess True Knowledge, which leads to their use of the intellect to learn Biblical verses by heart only to prove their superiority. Nonetheless, when the Spirit seizes its prey, it does not let go until it is transformed, fragmented, and its very origin has disappeared. The nannan-rèv plays an important role in this change. Since it is a primary mediator between the known world and the Unknown, it covers the elect just as a hen covers her chicks, waiting for the transformation. Meanwhile, an increase of strength delivers the elect from the thick shell of his *kantamwa*★ (his ego). The indoctrination that has caused indifference to the double must be effaced so that it may be filled with light."

"Is that true for everyone, Aunt?"

"It is not so only for Protestants. In general, human nature is the same. We all have a tendency to make our reason and our will the slaves of our kantamwa. That impoverishes our source of energy."

It was a pleasure to hear Aunt Tansia speak. I felt freed of a kind of tension. Her message was so strong that it passed through my whole being and brought about the uprooting of certain thoughts that made me a prisoner of the world of reason.

"If I were able to fly, I would go far away above this earth," I sighed.

"You cannot flee your obligations. Even if you knew how to fly, you would still have many things to learn. While you are waiting, learn to know your nannan in order to bring your dream to maturity."

"What is it like, this nannan?"

"It is the replica of your physical body. The only difference is that it is not as solid."

"Why did Beke's appear as a black mass?"

"Wait! You perceived it first as a black mass, but then as two luminous shafts of light, isn't that so? That means that Beke was not alone. Two shafts of light represent two bodies."

Suddenly, I recalled that the bird's cries alternated and did not have the same pitch. At times they were low-pitched, at other times they were very high-pitched. I commented on this to Aunt Tansia.

"I believe that Beke's cry is high-pitched. I know it. As for the other, perhaps it is a new apprentice," she said.

It was four o'clock when Lòlò and I got home. We had spent more than ten hours talking with Aunt Tansia. The subject was intriguing. There were so many mysteries to uncover. I spent the rest of the afternoon meditating on the things she had revealed to us.

That night in a dream I saw myself flying. I did not see the sky, only the ground, which was the color of terra-cotta. I flew toward its center and I recognized that I was in Haiti. I passed through a world with two suns. There was no vegetation. I was feeling the desire to approach one of these suns when I was brusquely awakened by the voice of a *pratik*★ (merchant)—a vegetable vendor who passed by each Saturday at dawn to offer fresh produce. I was furious at being disturbed. My dream had been interrupted precisely at the moment when I was going to make an important decision. I screamed at the vendor: "You savage! *Lanmèd!* (Fuck off!)" Lòlò, who was also awakened, reproached me, "Don't talk like that!" I stopped, but in my mind I continued bombarding the vendor with all kinds of names, even calling him a lougarou. I didn't get over my anger until late in the afternoon.

As usual, I went to visit my parents that day. My mother and I were seated on a slope eating some *batiste* mangoes—a kind of mango highly prized for its flavor. I was cutting the fleshy parts of my mangoes with a knife and putting them aside in a saucer to eat. With my tongue I removed the rest of the pulp from the pits. I was doing this when a duck of a luminous whiteness appeared and took the two slices that were left in the saucer. I was immediately inflamed with anger and I threw the knife at the duck, which fled like a flash and disappeared. I had missed. I wanted to get up to chase it and give it the punishment it deserved. But my body was heavy and I couldn't move. I tried again, but I lacked the strength. I couldn't feel my body; it was as if I was numb. Then I gave it up and recognized that I was still dreaming. I tried to speak but no sound came out. I said sadly to myself, "Am I about to die?" I began to imagine my burial. I was sad. I cried for myself. I opened my eyes wide to look around me, perhaps for the last time, and I saw my mother. She saw me turn. She came to me and touched my forehead. I heard her voice saying, "You look strange. What's wrong?"

She shook my legs. Her gesture woke me up.

"The duck stole my mango," I told her, not quite awake.

"What duck? What are you talking about? You are eating your mango right now."

"No, it stole the last two slices I had on my saucer."

"They are in your hand, wake up!"

In fact, I did awaken fully to see that that I was gripping the mango slices tightly in the palm of my hand.

Confusion. Silence spread through my being. Then I realized that I was praying. I mumbled a few words. I asked myself a thousand and one questions at the same time: "O, *Bondje-man-man-mwen!* What is this ? Am I going mad?"

I went to look for Aunt Tansia, hoping for answers. I explained my problem to her. What puzzled me was the fact that I was certain I had seen the white duck with my own eyes, even if my mother assured me no duck had been in the vicinity. On one hand, I felt very disturbed about not having been able to act rationally; on the other hand, I was convinced that I had reached a state in which the image I had of myself had to change, because of my inner duality.

I began to feel less self-assured And then I felt something like a pain in the pit of my stomach. I couldn't breathe. Aunt Tansia made a poultice of *lanmidon* (manioc flour) moistened with fresh water, which she placed on my left breast. She had me drink sugar water. The pain stopped immediately.

Aunt Tansia did not comment on my new experience that day. When I reviewed it, I concluded that I had acted in a gross and violent manner.

Two days later, I confessed my thoughts to Aunt Tansia.

"The fact that you have seen it yourself is already better than nothing. You are violent. In effect, you wanted to mistreat the duck because you felt wounded in your self-esteem by the fact that you let yourself be wronged by an animal that you consider an inferior being. Yet this white duck was nothing but the reflection of your own hand. Luckily, you were agile enough to change the direction of your gesture, otherwise you would have hurt yourself badly with the knife."

"Why did I see a duck in place of my own hand? How can a duck be the reflection of a hand?" I asked.

"I don't know," Aunt Tansia said. "Now you must provide me with me some explanations. Gather together everything you saw."

She exhorted me to recall what I had done since the morning. I recounted my dream and my contentment at traveling through the air, my annoyance and behavior with the vegetable vendor, my pleasure in eating the batiste mangoes, my anger at the duck. I noticed as I was speaking that my day consisted in thwarted pleasures followed by outbursts of anger. Aunt Tansia took some time to respond. She closed her eyes and began with a severe tone of voice: "The cause of your violence lies in the importance you give to your personality. It is urgent that you recover control of your being."

"How can I do that?" I asked.

"By losing your personality."

"I find this approach contradictory. On the one hand, I must lose my personality, while on the other hand I am expected to recover mastery of my being. If I must lose my personality, how can I regain what I have undertaken to lose voluntarily? It's crazy!"

"You don't understand, your personality is not your being. You must understand that."

"What is the difference, Aunt?" I asked, completely confused.

"Your personality has been constructed by this world for the functioning of this world. You have been given a name, a class and an education. You have been taught about *tout sa ki te fèt ak sa ou pa dwe fè* (everything that has been made and everything that no one has the right to make—what could translate as "norms and prohibitions"). Thus you have acquired an image of yourself, by concentrating your perception on one aspect of the being you are. On the other hand, deep inside this image there is a being that no one knows, who is a mystery. This being constitutes an essence that forms part of the Essence of everything that lives."

The impact of this teaching was extraordinary. It convinced me that human beings are mysterious and that I must make a definitive effort to pierce the mystery of who I am. In order to achieve that, I realized, I must exchange my way of living for another more powerful way. Therefore I must adjust to the principles and rules of this new world. My first move was to submit to Aunt Tansia's regulations. So, little by little, I became the "prey" and readied myself to blend into the Spirit that rules this world of *power*. Aunt Tansia ordered me never again to yield to violence.

"Violent people are hedonists," she said. "*Y ap boule touttan* (they are always burning) their energy and perturbing their vision. They deform everything they see. A dreamer does not have the right to be violent. Quite the contrary, he must cultivate patience, kindness, cunning, suppleness and firmness."

"It isn't easy to be all those things, all the time and on all occasions."

"Everything can be learned. Besides, you shouldn't speak of time. You are not in time anymore. . . ."

As she spoke, she took my hands and made me turn around seven times. I experienced vertigo and a kind of pressure in my solar plexus. I wanted to vomit. She pressed my temples. Everything turned to black, but at the same time I attained another level of awareness. An awareness that does not know time, one in which only the present moment counts.

"I no longer have the desire to live!" I cried in a voice that my own ears did not recognize.

"Move, move quickly, as if you had to die this very instant. Make every one of your gestures unique." She lowered her voice to a whisper. "Dance a final dance for the earth, for me, for this world." Then, her voice boomed. "Dance!" she cried.

I opened my arms in a gesture of abandon but with the decisiveness of someone who was going to leave for another place, never to return. I felt no regret. I was ready. Then I began to dance. My body was light. I was not thinking of anything. I entered a state where everything remained the same. I was free!

I don't know how long that state lasted. Perhaps for several weeks. Unfortunately, I ended up finding myself in my previous state. I didn't know how or why I came back down again. I was calm and dreamy, but I was not happy. I wanted to reclaim my liberty, since my equilibrium completely depended on it. I had fallen back into the eternal chains of my self-importance, into the doubts and cares of this world. I was sad because I knew that my efforts to leave it again must be redoubled. My despair was palpable.

Aunt Tansia did not fail to come see me. She perceived my dilemma and avowed that it was not in her power to get me out of the state into which I had fallen.

"You alone have the key."

"Aunt," I said to her in a supplicating tone of voice, "How can I do it? Help me, I beg you! Tell me how to protect myself from falling back into the snares of this world."

"Fight against your violence," she urged. "Hound yourself constantly and think of your violence as only a mask. Tell yourself that you can take off this mask at will and put it back on if necessary."

I listened carefully. I was thirsty for her advice. She knew it and she generously explained many things to me that I had already known but had forgotten. She reminded me that violence often takes the nannan hostage and prevents the dreamer from remaining in equilibrium (freedom) between the two worlds (the Known and the Unknown). She confessed to me that she herself had been very violent. Her violence had manifested itself in the form of a fatal love affair. She had been capable of destroying the happiness of others and breaking up households. Her beauty was her No. 1 trump card. She had used her violence, driven by mad passion, because she did not know the path of Perfection, of the Spirit, of Ginen, of Liberty.

## CHAPTER 5

# The Purification

## *Kanzo*

We were sitting on the ground, half-naked. The ceremony took place in silence, but even still I did not feel well. The intense heat of the fire burning on the thunderstones, the smoke, the odor of the leaves were all suffocating me. I said to myself: "My God! I am burning up.... I can't breathe anymore.... I see nothing but fire everywhere, it is too painful.... I don't think that I will get out alive from this experience.... So much the worse.... I'll die in the midst of doing research: That is better than dying pitifully in a bed, fighting an illness." I was almost certain that I had only a few hours left to live.

Suddenly a sound was heard in the darkness.

"He is coming...," said the officiating houngan. As I looked straight ahead, I saw something that shone in the blackness. I adjusted my vision and saw two pairs of luminous points. They were watching me. I guessed that they were the eyes of G.B.I. and R.B., eyes like those of a bird of prey. They projected shafts of light that traced a direct line between them and me. I was trembling, afraid.

R.B. asked me about my fear and my sense of malaise. He had guessed that my real problem was that I had too many prejudices. He suggested that I leave the tent. "Go outside and get a hold of yourself with *lachòy* (sage). ...Then come back to the tent." I didn't want to leave the tent for fear of meeting G.B.I., but I left. The darkness was so dense I couldn't see. Suddenly, the cry of a bird rent the silence. I pissed where I was standing. I wanted to cry, to run for shelter inside the tent, but the entrance was guarded by R.B. and the houngan. I thought I would go mad with fear. I closed my eyes and let myself fall to the ground. I stretched out on my back, opening my arms to form a cross. . . . I was ready for anything, even death. I stayed there, waiting. I prayed: "*Bondje-manman-mwen, ede m non, souple. Ede m sipòte eprèv sa a. Pa lage m non!* (My God, my mother, help me, I beg you. Help me to undergo this trial. Don't abandon me!)" I automatically recited the "Hail Mary" and sang "Tantum Ergo" at least six times.

Suddenly I felt a kind of internal peace come over me, and I began to laugh at myself. Comical scenes from my childhood popped up in my memory. I used to wet my bed every night. One such night, when I was nine, I was awakened in the night (for the third time) by the need to urinate. I was about to get up but stopped because I heard a song and footsteps coming toward the house. "It's a *galipòt*★ (member of a secret society)," I said to myself. The voice was grave and beautiful. It couldn't be anyone, I imagined—shaking from head to foot—other than Master Midnight passing by. My only hope, I told myself, was to hide under the bed, since the legs of that giant were so long that he wouldn't be able to bend down and see me. I got up from the *nestri*—a kind of mat that my mother had had made by an artisan from Mont-Organisè, near Ouanaminthe—which had served as a bed because my continuous bed-wetting rotted the cotton mattress. I headed for the bed of my big sister, with whom I shared the bedroom, in order to hide under it. I knocked over the enameled cast iron chamber pot, making an infernal racket and spilling its contents on the tiled floor. "Who is there?" a voice called out—it was my father, whose voice I didn't recognize right away. I didn't answer. My father got up and also bumped into the chamber pot, which made a loud noise. He slipped on the urine spreading across the floor, staggered and fell down noisily. "Manman!" I yelled. "What's the matter"? she cried. "I'm afraid!" I responded, my voice trembling. "Emilie, light the small lamp. Get some light quickly and then you'll see," my father said. As soon as there was light I began to talk, but with difficulty, for my jaws were clacking together against my will as when I had a fever. "I heard the voice of a lougarou outside." My mother said, "What is this talk about a lougarou?"

Meanwhile, the voice that had been singing had gone silent. But suddenly it began again and stopped in front of the house. "What is the name of the child who keeps pissing in her bed? I have stopped by tonight to eat her up." "Who are you?" my mother asked in a strong, aggressive voice. Then she went to open the door of the living room and I overheard a discussion between her and the supposed galipòt/Master Midnight/lougarou.

"It's me, Kasou, Madame Ovide. I passed by at the request of your servant, Charité, to scare the child so that she'll stop peeing in her bed."

"What right does Charité have to ask you to do that?" my mother said, and made a loud *kwipe* (sound made with the lips to express annoyance or disappointment). She slammed the door hard behind her. Before she went back to bed, she took care to comfort me: "Momose, go back to bed. The Good God did not create lougarou."

I learned later that Charité was Kasou's mistress. This was information I gleaned the next day from snatches of conversation I overheard between my mother and my godmother, Lise Jean Antoine, when she recounted the events of the night before. Kasou was an odd, scatterbrained tafyatè.

I had laughed heartily, above all at my father, who had to wash up because his pajamas were soaked with pee. He complained because the water was too cold, and because he had to open the back door to go outside to get it from the big tub. He didn't stop repeating, "*Kalao! Ki tentennad sa!* (Damn it! What a mess!)."

After that, I established a deep bond with the dark. In the evenings when my mother sent me to buy bread at Brenard Joachim's—the only baker at the time—I used to sing all along the way. I was happy, I loved the dark. I always walked with my eyes closed. It was a way of blocking fear by concentrating hard. This game with darkness helped me to develop a kind of intuition. I was able to sense and recognize from far off someone who was coming along the road. I knew the smell and the sound of the footsteps of my neighbors, my friends, and the friends of my parents. I was even able to avoid stepping on the *kaka-chen*—the dog turds—that I had spotted in the course of the day.

As I evoked these memories while lying on the ground outside of the tent I was able to sense in the depths of my being a sacred and consecrated space: the site of my inner temple. A phrase of Aunt Tansia's came to mind: "The body has its own understanding and its own memory." I heard a small voice inside that was singing an old song. It was the voice of my childhood: "*Kamèl! Kamèl, O! Vin pran yon boul sik mant. . . .* (Carmel! Carmel, oh! Come take a mint bonbon. . . .")"

After a good half hour, I returned to take my place among the others inside the tent. Everyone was waiting for me. Someone took my hand in the dark. It was a woman who was suffering from a cancer of the head. I sat down quietly by her side. She held out a packet of sage. I thanked her. I had the feeling of being an intruder, as if I was disturbing the atmosphere in some way by delaying the normal development of the ceremony. I excused myself. No one responded, and I understood that it was not necessary to make the gesture.

In truth the purification was hard. The heat was frightful, but I persisted in following the session. I farted and pissed several times right where I was. I sweated copiously, I was wet from head to foot. I lost all the water in my body. At a certain point I was feeling sorry for myself and I began to cry. My tears burned my face and my neck. R.B. held out a packet of leaves. I took it from his hands, in the dark and swabbed my nostrils and my ears with the leaves. I breathed deeply the scent of the leaves, and then I put the rest on my shoulders. Quietly, I placed my hands, the right one on my left shoulder and the left one on the right. I made myself very small and, as if by a miracle, I relaxed. I felt the process of my physical diminishing start to happen. I was leaving gradually, and this time I was fully aware of it: I was able to take the measure of my size. One more moment and I was reduced to the very smallest bit, or at least to a vanishing point, as we usually say in ordinary speech. A moment more and I was no longer anything. Nonetheless, I was able to integrate myself into everything: the fire, the large rocks, the earth, the air, the wind and the plants, and the ant and the bird. For an instant, I was the bird in perfect harmony with its environment, and with the air that all of a sudden had no secrets for me. It gave me its code and I was flying. I went everywhere, free as the wind, freed from all my prejudices, and I went about without a precise destination. Free! Free at last!

Suddenly I noticed that I could no longer see my companions. I left that state as soon as I asked myself: "Where have the others gone?" Scarcely did I have that thought when I saw that we numbered about twelve, seated side by side, in a circle inside the tent, a kind of teepee whose conical canvas form granted total obscurity symbolizing the darkness of the womb.

An inner voice asked me, "Who are you, Mimerose?" I understood that Mimerose was *anyen* in the *Anyen*★ (a void in the Void).[55]

The answer came from Anyen: "I am—I am not: I. . . ."

It was five in the morning when R.B. had me pour a large quantity of cold water over my head. Then he sprinkled my whole body. I didn't speak a word during the entire day that followed. But I understood that I was no longer the same.

I do not know how much longer my pilgrimage will take. But I do know that:

> *Ala pase m'pase!*
> *Rele Lwa yo pou mwen!*
> *Danbala Wèdo![56] Ago e!*
> *Mwen sèvi. . . .*

> Let me pass—I am passing.
> Call the lwa for me
> Damballah Wedo! Attention!
> I'm serving. . . .[57]

---

55 Anyen is the concept that defines the central void. The name "Mimerose" has no mystical significance. It is not a power name. It is nothing.

56 Danbala and Ayida Wèdo: mystery of creation, symbolized by two snakes that represent duality, harmony, understanding; the egg placed between the snakes symbolizes the Word.

57 In this context to *serve* means to be devoted to this or that spirit, or all the spirits. In Vodou the idea of *service* tends to replace the idea of *belief.*

## CHAPTER 6

# Manipulating the Double

*Vire tounen nan nannan-rèv-ou jan ou pito*

Once again I asked Aunt Tansia to explain to me what the Ti Bonnanj was. With a great deal of patience, she remarked: "It is not a state that can be defined."

"And the double, what is it exactly?"

"It is another name for the nannan. It is the other body. It is the nannan which nourishes the Gwo Bonnanj. The nannan participates in all the acts of the kadav kò. Without it, the body would be an inert mass, she reminded me."

"Tell me, where do I find the double?"

"It constitutes part of our being. It is our mystery side. '*Se nan leten, li pran nesans. Li fèt ak leten menm.*' ('It is born in the ether. It is made of ether.') This fifth element contributes to the totality of our being. The double is the body that is conscious of the two states—the state of being awake, and the dreaming state. However, in Nan Dòmi, it is enveloped in light and becomes light: the nannan-rèv. It is the double that goes to and fro between the Gwo Bonnanj and the Ti Bonnanj."

I knew all that already. Nothing in all that she explained to me was strange or new to me, but I didn't feel that I was understanding it well. "Is the double visible?"

"Yes," she answered, "but it is fluid."

"I can't imagine it."

"It is not a question of imagination, either you know it or you don't know it."

"I find all this so complicated."

"In effect, the world of the Unknown is just as complex as the known world. Our inability to remain in permanent contact with the Ti Bonnanj comes from the fact that we have favored the development of our right side to the detriment of the left."

"What do you mean by that, Aunt?"

"I am going to explain the event to you that has marked all civilizations since the Middle Ages."

"An event that happened in the Middle Ages? How did you come to know about it?"

She said, cutting me off, "I should really call it a misfortune. It was Abodourine who told me about it.

"The mystics in old times, wanting to experiment magically with only one side of the human being, wished to place all their disciplines according to a protocol that they would establish. They decided on the right side. They then promulgated a decree, law or prohibition with a subsequent program of education. In order to convince any recalcitrants, they invented the thesis according to which the left side must be protected because it contains the heart. It was necessary to pay attention only to the right side and leave the left in repose in order not to tire the heart and provoke a premature death. So it is that by following this orientation humanity lost its sense of many things and the human being lost his equilibrium."

"What can we do to recover our sense of equilibrium?" I asked, eager for an explanation.

"Thank you for asking. There is only one way: to forget everything that we have learned and start again at zero."

"Meaning?"

"To be reborn."

"Are you talking about reincarnation?"

"Where did you learn that big word? Don't repeat what you don't know. Haitian intellectuals have this unfortunate tendency. It is demagoguery. Pay close attention."

"Why only Haitian intellectuals?"

"I don't know any others."

"As far as I am concerned, I simply want to make the connection between the language and the word."

"It is an unfortunate mania. Sometimes words do not translate what has been comprehended."

I knew that Aunt Tansia was right, but my pride had taken a blow. I tried to defend myself.

"Stop playing this game. What you are setting out to do is very dangerous. You don't have the right to lie to yourself. That amounts to causing pain to the Holy Spirit," she admonished me.

I bowed my head, ashamed. I recognized that I did indeed have the habit of using words whose meaning I only knew through the *Petit Larousse* dictionary. I realized that that would not be enough to come to a profound understanding. I discovered at the same time that my state of confusion resulted from the way I thought. I depended too much on definitions from the *Petit Larousse*, and, when I was not satisfied with an explanation, my imagination took over and ended up furnishing words and concepts. I also had an annoying tendency to find ways to disapprove of all discourse that did not conform to a learned way of speaking, even if it made good sense and had an educational goal. Learned speech for me meant the use of grand phrases (*gwo franse*[58]). I tolerated discourse empty of meaning as long as the orator rolled his r's well and didn't commit any grammatical mistakes.

Aunt Tansia knew about this tendency in me. When she reproached me, she tried to draw my attention to my other side.

"Don't play the role of the intellectual. It amounts to *move mès* (bad manners) that you picked up at school. Get rid of this defect immediately. It may serve you as a mask, but don't let it stick to you. It makes you look ugly and it is the cause of your weakness."

"I don't know how to get rid of it."

"Act as if you had never learned anything. Be like a child, it's easy."

Tears flowed from my eyes. I wasn't sure why. She wiped my eyes with the edge of her skirt and asked me to blow my nose into it. I hesitated. She insisted and I obeyed. I kept on crying. I could not stop. In my inner being I felt a kind of lack of strength

---

58 For certain people, "speaking good French" is equivalent to using rarely used words, unfamiliar to ordinary people.

to change myself completely. Too many things had contributed to cast me in a mold.

"Why are you crying?"

"Because I am discouraged."

"Why are you discouraged?"

"Because I am incapable of carrying on a fight to change myself. I cannot learn what my intellect doesn't grasp. I don't know how to act differently."

"Begin by manipulating your nannan. The advantage you have is that Ginen-an has called you. You cannot reject the experiences that it has had you undergo."

"What do you mean when you ask me to manipulate my double?"

"That means that even when you act externally, that is to say with your physical body, you must retire into the inner part of yourself. Even when, in the eyes of others, you are taking care of worldly affairs, you are no longer of this world. It is extremely urgent that you begin to practice this way of being. Like an actor, play your role in the theater of this world, knowing all the while that the stage is only a place you are passing through and that you must leave when the curtain falls."

"In other words, you are asking me to lose consciousness of my surroundings. . . ."

"To manipulate your nannan is not to lose consciousness of your surroundings, of your physical being, of objects or your intellect. Rather it is to detach yourself from them."

"Thank you, Aunt, I am going to apply myself so as to live like that. Now I have another problem: *Ki bò sa ap mennen-m?* (Where will this lead me?)"

"Into the Ginen mold."

## CHAPTER 7

# Walking in the Swarm of Stars

## *Palmannaze nan Lapousiyè*

One morning Aunt Tansia visited us. She was in a hurry: "I must go to five a.m. Mass. I have passed by to ask you not to leave and to wait for me. I want to discuss something important with you."

She returned at midday. She announced that she had begun to make preparations for our journey *pou nou monte Anwo*★ (toward ecstasy) and the *Lapousiyè* (the Milky Way). I made a movement of surprise because I did not feel ready for such an adventure. But she insisted: "You must undertake this voyage. It represents one of the most important obligations of the initiate." Before leaving she invited us to go to her house. Lòlò went first, and I joined them at six o'clock. They told me they had been waiting for me. Aunt Tansia opened out a mat that was near the door and I sat down. Zann, the servant, brought me a big cup of hot verbena tea. I thanked her and drank it all. Then Aunt Tansia indicated that Zann should leave us alone. She put on her straw hat and left in the direction of the public square.

"Do you think that I am ready to undertake this journey? I'm not sure of myself," I began.

"If you let yourself be guided by faith alone, you can do anything you want."

"How many times have I thought I could succeed in a project of this kind only to find to my great disappointment that I have reaped the opposite?"

"You didn't believe, my child. You merely thought. And thought is not always true. Faith itself is capricious. It is like a virgin who awaits her fiancé: patient, beautiful, ingenuous, attractive, innocent."

"I would like to know how to strengthen my faith."

"In order to undertake such an initiative, the initiate must conform to certain practices; for example, avoiding toxic substances. That is to rid both Ti Bonnanj and Gwo Bonnanj of their imaginary side."

A long silence ensued. Then I questioned her about the pleasure that I would experience. At least, I wanted to know what it would be. She responded that the goal of this voyage was not my amusement but rather the accomplishment of a specific mission. "Furthermore," she explained, "it is not a simple *voye je gade* (voyage of exploration). Your sole task is to penetrate, see and return. You will leave from Anyen and you will transcend the physical universe."

I did not answer right away. I was curious and skeptical at the same time.

Aunt Tansia left and came back with a tchatcha which she shook gently three times. The sound was agreeable and did me good. Then she said: "*Ann ay monte Anwo. N apray palmannaze nan Lapousiyè*. . . . (Let's ascend toward ecstasy. We are going to walk in the Milky Way.)" Then, to arouse my curiosity, she told me stories about the *pronmnade*—the promenade—of the dreamer. She again shook the tchatcha; I counted nine times. I asked myself how I could go so far away without being transported by some kind of engine. What was the science that authorized me to undertake such an exploit? Aunt Tansia understood my thought and answered: "*Fòk ou kapab mete ou toutouni*. (You must get completely naked.)"

"I must strip? I don't understand."

Aunt Tansia doubled up laughing. I looked at her in astonishment.

"*Se lougarou sèlman ki konn fè jan de bagay sa yo*. (Only lougarou do that.) You must get rid of all thought processes."

"I can't concentrate with the noise."

"The sound of the tchatcha and the darkness will help you. Lift your head toward the sky and look to the East."

I lifted my head and saw a group of stars, like a swarm of

*koukouy* (fireflies) sparkling in the sky. I pointed them out with my finger, but Aunt Tansia corrected my gesture by closing my index finger and straightening the little finger.

"Never show the index finger."

"Why not?

"*Pou rezon* (just because)," she answered quite simply.

I continued to admire the beautiful, luminous carpet of stars overhead. I was calm and happy. Suddenly, I felt the need to speak: "I see many stars. It seems that there are more tonight than on other nights." The sky was truly beautiful, splendid, majestic and sparkling with stars.

"Do you see *Wa Jipitèr* (King Jupiter)?"

"Do you mean the planet? I can't distinguish it from the others. . . ."

"I'm talking about the divinity. He rules the world of atmospheric phenomena," she responded.

Then she began to sing in a voice I didn't recognize at first. It was so different from the one I was used to hearing, strong and soft at the same time. She sang making her tongue vibrate and with an accent that was rather guttural and nasal. She shook the tchatcha to a rhythm that recalled the *Nago*★[59]:

> *Ife Ile*
> *Ife kèlè kèlè*
> *Omi Nannan!*
> *Ile lakoun O!*
> *Ife Ile, kèlè kèlè!*[60]

> Center of the earth
> *Ife kèlè kèlè*
> Sacred mother water!
> Grand house, O!
> Center of the earth, *kèlè kèlè!*

I sang with her. This song's melody reminded me of a lullaby.

---

59 A rhythm accentuated by three weak beats and one strong.
60 Untranslatable, a rhythmic sound.

We were seated face to face in the half-light. I closed my eyes and let myself drift into somnolence. I could not say how long it took us to enter into a state of concentration. But at a certain moment, I was conscious of walking in a place where everything was colored mauve. "My God, it's extraordinary!" I heard myself say. I found myself facing a stretch of deeper blue, like the ink that Aunt Tansia called "the black sea." At intervals, an abyss opened and then fell away. A prolonged movement like the swell of big waves broke into foam the color of yellow saffron. The scenes before me came and went, fast and fascinating. I plunged into them as one plunges into the sea. The waves rocked me, and suddenly I saw myself as a baby. I watched my own birth. As soon as I left the womb for good, I folded back on myself. I looked for something to reattach myself to. I searched in vain for the sounds and regular beats I was used to hearing. Instead, I heard a faint sound that I tried to identify. I cried out, then saw a little light. It was love gazing at me—my mother's eyes. In a moment's time, the color disappeared and I lost the recovered memory.

## CHAPTER 8

# Knowledgeable in Mystical Consciousness

## *Kore*

From a linguistic point of view, *kore*,⋆ a word derived from the word *kòr*, should mean: to make one with the body. Nevertheless, from the time she began teaching me, Aunt Tansia taught me that the word was of African origin. In effect, among the Bambara (Mande speakers) kore means "the highest degree of consciousness." In the Haitian vocabulary, based on the French lexicon, when this word is attributed to a human being, "*Mche kore. . . ,*" you understand right away that it refers to someone who is respected by others, because of either his intellectual knowledge or his magical power. The meaning of kore changes according to the context in which it's used. For example, you also say to someone who has gorged on food, "*Vant ou kore.* (Your stomach is well filled.)"

Aunt Tansia's teaching on the word kore encompassed all of these dimensions. In material terms, it is illustrated by a necklace made of grains filled with magic power. Spiritually, the initiate who wears this necklace is one who, in the view of the master, is deemed capable of assuming this responsibility. Right at the beginning of her teaching on the kore, I waited for Aunt Tansia to prepare solutions of poison antidotes so that I would be *djògwe* (protected) against the *kout poud* (powder attacks, bursts of powder caused by a chemical reaction perpetrated by evildoers. By *poud* (powder) I understood the substance to be composed of toxic plants, which certain individuals use against their enemies, even innocents—whether to avenge themselves or cause harm. I was truly excited at the prospect of an antidote, for who in Haiti doesn't fear that kind of violence? Though poud in the time of slavery may have been a justified form of fighting back on the part of runaway slaves, in our day this practice still exists, causing everyone great fear. Prevention is better than a cure, I said to myself. When I showed my joy at the idea of being kore, hence protected from *kout poud*, Aunt Tansia looked at me as if to say: "Do you think that I am going to lower myself to counter such a practice?" I was puzzled and annoyed.

"Aunt, do you know that children and adults die after being exposed to poud?

"And?"

"I would like to be protected against it."

"Protect yourself."

"How?"

"With your Je!" she said in a biting tone of voice.

"I hadn't thought of that."

"You refuse to live with complete spontaneity. Your head is harder than a rock. How many times have I told you that if you don't have Je, you will be blocked inside only one world?"

"Tell me five hundred thirty-nine times!" That was my way of telling her not to become discouraged. We had a good laugh together, and me above all at my mania for drawing everything into the realm of thought! I considered myself stupid and ridiculous. Finally, I was able to laugh at myself. At least it was proof that I had learned something.

Once, Aunt Tansia and I were seated on the ground, under the kénépier where we customarily went to talk or listen to the tree sing. This tree—it's still there—forms part of the landscape of the courtyard of our house in Ouanaminthe. Very big, it is over one hundred years old. Its numerous branches, leafy, and green, provide generous and agreeable shade.

"This tree has witnessed many things, I love it very much. The tree and I have a lot in common. We grew up together. We know each other well," Aunt Tansia said.

I admired this kind of emotion in Aunt Tansia. She always bore witness to her love of the least of things.

"Don't forget that I am the daughter of Erzulie Pierre," she added, proudly. She had served this spirit ever since the shock she experienced at the time of the deaths of her husband and son. Every time she evoked this lwa, a light passed through her eyes. Suddenly she asked me, "Didn't you hear something?"

"No, there is total silence."

"You didn't see anything either?"

No, I answered, absolutely nothing.

"She killed herself to make us hear."

"Who? Who are you talking about?"

"Nature!"

"No more joking, why now? Why would Nature be dead?"

"Go cover yourself, quickly," Aunt Tansia said in response.

The tone of her voice had changed. This answer made me anxious. Because in magical parlance covering oneself conveys the sense of protecting oneself.

"From what? From what?" I continued to ask her, warned of danger by the tone of her voice.

"Go quickly to fetch me your *kwiy* (half-calabash). And bring the water from your pitcher. We'll need it."

Suddenly she took me by the hand as if to help me get up. She held out her cane with the other hand. I took it and kneeled in preparation for getting up completely. Instinctively, I raised my eyes toward the tree and I saw a gray snake coiled around a branch.

For a moment our gazes met. I wanted to flee, but my legs refused to obey. I remained nailed to the spot, watching the snake come down at an angle toward me. Aunt Tansia rapped me smartly on the inside of my knee and I fell to the ground. The sound of my body striking the ground was so strong that I felt the ground give way under the shock. I heard the earth complain, but at the same time I never took my eyes off the snake coming down toward me. It moved over my stomach. For a moment I thought it was going to encircle my waist. I felt cut in two. For half an hour I lay on the ground. I was astonished at my passive behavior. "Why haven't I reacted?" I asked myself.

Aunt Tansia leaned toward me and said to me very softly as if in a single breath: "I told you to cover yourself."

"I am not whole, the snake took away my soul."

"*Ou nan dlo.* (You are in the water.)"

These words made me fearful because in ordinary speech, they point to a bad omen. I felt weak and defenseless.

Aunt Tansia encouraged me, "Get up. Don't let yourself be carried off by this current. Get hold of yourself."

"What can I do? I'm lost."

"Go get me your calabash filled with water from your pitcher. I'm going to show you a place in the water where you can find an exit point. You know, only the water can erase the mark left by the snake. Look. . . ."

As she spoke, she kneaded my waist and recited a kind of prayer.

"I'm afraid, Aunt. What do you think of this incident?"

"She is reclaiming you."

"I don't want it. It is not up to her to choose me. I hate her!" I cried.

"Nevertheless, there was no hatred in your gaze just now. You were hypnotized by her."

"That does not prevent me from hating her."

"Why do you hate her?"

"I don't know. She contains too many mysteries."

"She wants to make you understand them. All you have to do is open yourself to her, be her friend."

"How am I going to communicate with a snake? I could never do that."

"It is not a snake. It is your allié. Be careful! You have perceived her as a snake because you have not changed position, that is: you have remained a prisoner of your fear."

"I do not want this animal to symbolize my allié. I would have preferred to see a fish, a dog or even a lion, but never, a big never, could I get used to a snake."

"The allié may take the form of whatever animal it wishes, or even appear in the form of light. That depends on your gaze. What is essential is that you be able to go beyond the form in order to become one with your allié."

"Can that happen once and for all?"

"Don't you know that form is nothing but appearance? Change your perception and the forms will change at the same time."

"I know all these things, but I don't know how to be without a form and no longer see a snake."

"Make the sacrifice."

"I am afraid of suffering."

"You are honest. However, if you don't make the necessary sacrifice, you will remain a prisoner of time and tradition."

"Tradition, that is to say, culture. Is there something wrong in remaining attached to it?"

"You are right. Tradition and culture are one and the same. Nonetheless, culture is one thing and initiation is another. The goal of initiation is to reach the kore. Now, you well know that tradition recommends repeated sacrifices, while initiation only asks for one. It is precisely this difference that one must pay attention to."

"Speak to me about this sacrifice, Aunt, if you would."

"It is in the *bay tèt a ou kivledi: kite Ginen an kor w. Kite Ginen an sele w, non, pitit an mwen* (giving of oneself, which means: surrender your body to Ginen-an. Let yourself be possessed by the Spirit, my child)!"

Her answer reminded me of the lessons of catechism, and that made me feel ill at ease.

"Be a little clearer, Aunt."

"Well now, enough said. Go get me your kwiy."

I went looking for my kwiy and took advantage of the search to look at myself in the mirror. There were traces of swelling all around my waist.

"Did you look at yourself?" Aunt Tansia asked me when I came back.

From her *djakout★* (straw bag) she took out a *sakit★* (a small sack) and emptied its contents onto her skirt. Some seeds fell out. She sorted out twenty seeds of *madlèn* (red and yellow fruits), which she put in the kwiy. Then she chose twenty seeds of *legliz* (fruit of a kind of acacia) twenty white peas, twenty red and twenty black peas. When she finished, she emptied the water from the pitcher into the kwiy, which she had taken care in advance to place on the roof of the kitchen—a small building constructed at the foot of the courtyard to the west of the house and the kénépier.

"I hope that with this you will obtain grace and compassion. In a word, redemption."

"What is going to happen to me? What have I done wrong?"

"I don't know. But remain alert. *M kwè ou pare pou ou kore.* (I believe that you are ready for the kore.)"

"Meaning?"

"The snake passing over you is an omen. It takes seventy-two hours to ascend to the *kalis* (chalice, suffering recalling that of Christ)."

Then she began to sing:

> *Kore, kore, nou kore nan Gore*
> *Si Gore pa t kore*
> *Yo ta dechouke Gore*
> *Kore, nou kore nan Gore*

> Supported in mystical consciousness
> Are we after Gorée
> If Gorée were not a place of power
> One would have already uprooted it
> Supported in mystical consciousness
> Are we after Gorée

We both sang. This song put me into a kind of trance. Perhaps because of its meaning. It was an invitation to the initiate not to allow himself to give up, and to persevere in the search for consciousness. By making kore and *Gore* rhyme, this song gave the word its most profound meaning. In effect, the word *Gore* refers to an herb that is not easy to uproot; once cut, it comes up again the following morning. But it is also the name of the port—in Senegal—from which the slaves embarked for America. It symbolizes the determination to live.

Aunt Tansia left without saying goodbye, leaving me in my state of beatitude. I forgot to ask her the date of our next meeting. I spent two days and two nights in a feverish state, without closing my eyes so as to count the hours. My body was shaken with trembling. I thought about death. Lòlò was uneasy.

"Maybe fear is the cause of all this. How do you feel?"

"Neither good nor bad. I know that I am feverish, but my body isn't suffering."

My teeth clacked together when I opened my mouth. He brought me lemon juice and aspirin. I drank the juice and put aside the pills.

"I'm going to look for your mother."

"No, go get Aunt Tansia instead."

He returned accompanied by Aunt Tansia and Aya, a relative of my grandmother. She was like a nanny to my mother's children.

"Èske ou pare (Are you ready)?" Aya asked me.

At Aunt Tansia's request, she went into the courtyard to get the kwiy, and she took from her basket a packet of herbs that I recognized: zèb gore★ (a very hardy dwarf herb). She asked me to hold the zèb gore in my hands, joined together in a gesture that strangely resembled the gesture of praying. She made five small packets, drew out the discolored seeds from the water and blew on them. She lit five candles and put the seeds next to each packet. She then threaded three threads, black, red and green, through a big needle. One by one and following a predetermined order she threaded the seeds, all the while reciting a prayer that I didn't understand very well. When that was done, she added twenty-one pieces of maldyòk★ (pieces of porcelain) which were red, white, royal blue and yellow. Then she knotted the ends of the three threads and asked me to untie them myself, without breaking them. My hands trembled with fever and emotion. It was difficult. I was sweating from head to foot.

I succeeded in untying them after an hour of work. Suddenly, the fever broke.

"Come here so that I can cover you, my child," Aunt Tansia said to me affectionately.

I got up from the bed and approached her. She asked me to lift my blouse and repeat after her this solemn oath: "Pa pouvwa papa Loko, mwen resevwa grenn maldyòk. Mwen pran an temwen St

*Iv Bakonwa ak St Jwachen, Sen Nicola,* (Sen may refer to a Vodou lwa and a Catholic saint), *Sen Pyè, mwen jire pou mwen pa janm touye moun.*" It meant: "I receive the twenty-one pieces of mal-dyòk in the name of papa Loko and, taking as witnesses St. Yves Bakonwa and St. Joachim, St. Nicolas, St. Peter, I swear that I will never kill a human being." She ceremoniously placed the beautiful belt around my waist, a symbol of kore. Next she asked me to Jete, which I always did with joy. Once she had assembled the herbs, she asked me to scrub them in the water in the kwiy. She rubbed my fourteen active and seven passive Ginen pòtay-mistè with *Koko Ginen* oil, then poured the water from the kwiy over my head and told me to drink it as it trickled down my face.

"Now I am going to show you the opening, the passage in the water. Fill your pitcher with water."

"And then, Aunt?"

"*Poze san ou non pitti an mwen* (Calm down, my child)," Aya said to me.

"We will wait for the full moon. Your pitcher needs the moon's energy for the next operation," Aunt Tansia said.

Then they both left, leaving me alone with a mystery to discover: living in kore.

## CHAPTER 9

# The Eye of the Water

*Ja dlo a ou dlo gen "Je"*

I began the *limen*\* (candle lighting ritual) from the beginning of the Angelus, a ritual I always followed at the full moon. Early in the morning, I plunged my *cruche* (pitcher) into the water of the *ganmèl* (wooden pan), meticulously cleaned the house and the courtyard, and placed bouquets of roses in every corner. As Aunt Tansia had instructed me, I poured the water from my cruche into my kwiy, which I put on the roof of the kitchen, climbing up on a chair to reach it. At the moment I came down, I heard a bird singing overhead. To my great surprise there was a column of tako flying above the house. You would think that they were choreographed. It was truly impressive to see. For about fifteen minutes, those birds offered me a sight so marvelous I shall never forget it.

The next morning, I went to five o'clock Mass. Aunt Tansia and Ton De were in the church, seated side by side. I found a seat in the front row. During the Mass I remained seated, my eyes closed. I opened them at the moment of the offertory, and to my great astonishment saw Aunt Tansia and Ton De soliciting offerings. When she passed in front of me, Aunt Tansia held out the collection basket and shook it before my eyes. I gently pushed it away and Aunt Tansia said, "*Bay tèt a ou.* (Make a gift of yourself.)"

Then she held out a candle to me and said very quickly: "*Priye anwo y, apre sa, w a depoze y nan panyen kèt la.* (Pray over your offering, then put it in the basket.)"

Three or four minutes later, she passed in front of me with the basket, and I put in the candle laden with prayers.

When we left the church, she asked me to accompany her to the market. She bought snuff, cassava—a kind of biscuit made from manioc flour—a packet of watercress, and two gallons of mabi. She offered me one of the gallons. I accepted gladly.

On the way back Aunt Tansia asked me to stop by her house to deposit her provisions before going home. She told me how, on the days of full moon, Abodourine only ate one meal, consisting of a cassava, watercress and avocado sandwich. She knew how much I loved Abodourine. "Each full moon is a unique occasion, not to be wasted, to formulate one's vows. Abodourine taught me this practice."

"Every full moon," she confided to me, "*Nannan Bou-louklou*[61] inspects the lakou-Bitasyon (or demanbre) to make *Omi Nannan* descend. It is she who chooses all the sèvitè and inspires them in the building of the kay mistè. In the initiation pact, the sèvitè takes charge of building the *houmfò*★ (temple)— or the kay mistè, *badji ou sobadji*★ (private temple of the Vodou priest)—which is the sacred place on a pwen that Nannan herself has given him. It is in the houmfò that the new initiates will be *kouche* (literally, "seated," which means initiated) on the pwen of the kay, obviously. On the demanbre, which represents the ancestral inheritance, on the first day of the month of May of the year following his entry into service, the initiate must plant: *yon mapou, yon monben, yon bwacyhènè, yon bwadòm, yon palmis, yon pye siwèl, yon pye flanboyan osinon yon pye seriz, yon pye kalbas, yon pye metsiyen, yon pye sitwon, yon pye mango, yon pye bwapen, yon pye gonmye, yon pye kenèp, de pye koton—yon blan ake yon wouj* (a mapou—a big tree—a yellow mombin, an oak, an elm, a cabbage palm, a Spanish plum, a flame tree or a cherry tree, a calabash, a pinon, a lemon tree, a mango tree, a pine tree, a gum tree, a kénépier, and two cotton plants—one red and one white). The mapou will be the largest initiated tree of all the *pyebwa sèvi*★ (initiated big trees serving as altars). It will

61 Nannan Boulouklou or Naa Bukuu, a divinity who represents the first female principle.

serve as a resting place for *Mawou Lisa*,[62] the elm for *Mètrès Dantò*[63] and her cohort, the cabbage palm for *Kebyesou*,[64] the calabash for Ogou Feray, the flame or cherry tree for *Kouzen Zaka*,[65] the Spanish plum for *Erzulie Freda Daronmen*,[66] the gum tree for Loko, the pinon for A-Legba, the lemon tree for the Gedes, the kénépier for *Agaou*,[67] the cotton for Danbala and Ayida Wèdo."

"I have never unveiled this secret to you, my child: At the time of the full moon the center of the earth opens up to allow the beings who live there to come out. The earth is hollow and it is inhabited, *anba tankou anwo* (below as well as above the surface). *Tout sous dlo gen pasaj ki memmen anba tè a, nan gwòt yo gen pasaj pou ale anba dlo, nan nannan laté.* (All springs are places of passage to go beneath the surface of the earth; in the grottoes there are passages to go into the depths of the water, to the center of the earth.)" Then she began to sing and dance the *zèpòl*—the shoulder dance. People stopped on their way to look at us and applaud the spectacle before them, this old woman so full of life and gaiety:

> *Ile Ife, Ile lakou, Manbo Ile. . . .*
> *Nannan Boulouklou O!*
> *Masa-Wè vodoule! Ile lakou O!*

> Center of the earth, Great House, Great Priestess
> Nannan Boulouklou Oh!
> The child of Vodou moves from one mystery to the other
> He encounters the terrestrial Master of water!
> Great House Oh!

---

62 Mawou Lisa, the Unsurpassable, was engendered by O'Batala who himself was engendered by Nannan Boulouklou.
63 Purifying and exorcising god.
64 Lwa of lightning.
65 Zaka or Azaka Mede: guardian spirit of Haitian culture. His other names are: Minister Azaka, Kouzen.
66 A female lwa.
67 A male healer lwa.

"But why don't you have a lakou, Aunt," I interrupted her.

"It isn't given to everyone to do the same thing. I have been chosen to accomplish another task."

"Aunt, can you tell me in what era the lakou was established and the reason for its existence?"

"Abodourine taught me that the lakou has always existed. Its primary role is to spread the cult of Nannan Boulouklou. . . ."

In retrospect, this conversation turned out to be hugely important to my understanding, but at the time I doubted everything Aunt Tansia said. It would not be until about thirteen years later that I was able to confirm the precious teachings of Aunt Tansia: that the lakou, contrary to other definitions, comes from the word *Ile-Lakoun* (or *Ile Lakun*) which means "grand house" or "center of the diffusion of the cult of *Naa Bukuu*."

Our musical group, Boukman Eksperyans, had been invited to the West African nation of Benin for the festival Ouidah 92 organized by the Benin government. A party was organized in our honor on the evening before our return to Haiti. Among the African guests I noticed a young man who had been staring at Lòlò and me all evening. Before leaving, he came up to us and addressed us politely. "My name is Otè Atnanase Badjaou, I have an important commission for you." Then, without giving us time to respond, he handed us his essay on the cultural foundations of the unity of the pre-Odudua Yoruba—it was his thesis for a Master of Sociology and Anthropology—a small paper bag filled with multicolored kernels of corn, and another plastic bag filled with soil. "All this comes from Ile Lakoun," he said, "I would like to offer it to you."

"Did you say the *lakou*?" I asked him, surprised at having heard him pronounce this word.

He opened his eyes very wide and said, "Yes, madame, I have no other home. I am the slave and serviteur of the house of Naa Bukuu. . . . This soil and these kernels come directly from the granary of Ile Lakoun. . . ."

That was what we heard from the young man.

Lòlò was waiting for us at the entrance door.

"Go take a look at the east side of the gallery," he said, uneasily.

I went and saw some food placed here and there: *diri kole ak pwa*★ (rice and beans, the Haitian national dish), *anmizman* (grilled peanut) candy and cakes, *mayi griy* grilled corn) and more.

"Aunt Tansia," I called out, "Come look!"

She approached slowly, registered the display of food and told me not to be afraid. "It's just an offering. Your house is situated on a strong point, *nan kalfou* (at a crossroads). It is like an altar. It is perfectly normal that people should use it to deposit their offerings."

"I don't like this, Aunt. It's going to take me forever to clean up. And it's disgusting to see so much food on the ground when people are hungry. It's wasteful!"

"You resemble those moralists who want to appear sensible and concerned but who are not generous enough to share their time with a child. You call an offering wasteful? Come, my child, don't waste your words. Simply clean the gallery or let the dogs enjoy themselves; they will be happy, and that's all. Why lose your time criticizing what you don't understand?"

This remark went straight to my heart. We had reached the courtyard. Aunt Tansia told me to get the kwiy and put it on a chair that I should place in the center of the courtyard.

"I'll be back. I'm going to prepare the meal for my children." She always referred to prisoners and the poor as her children.

Aunt Tansia came back at midday. The sun was hot but not burning. The weather was lovely.

"At the time of the full moon the sun is a gentle lover," Aunt Tansia joked.

We both laughed. The witticism sounded false.

"What a paradox, Aunt."

"It is the special touch of Tansia," she responded. "Sometimes I say things that may seem funny but have a hidden meaning. You mustn't forget that I am an artist."

"I didn't know that. What art do you pursue?"

"I live."

"That is not enough to be an artist."

"You are wrong, my child. Living is an art."

"Do you mean, knowing how to live?"

"I said living is an art, don't confuse things. Living is to be conscious of one's luck, of one's personal power, it is to feel everything in the moment; it is to be at the heart of everything, in a single *bat Je* (blink of an eye). The charm of life is woven with mysteries. Consciousness is the key."

I had not noticed that she and I were kneeling next to the chair on which I had placed the kwiy. I listened religiously. I loved the sound of her voice so much that I could have spent my life listening to her speak.

"Look at the water in your kwiy," she said.

It was boiling. Bubbles formed at the bottom of the water. Aunt Tansia covered my head with a white headscarf and told me to be attentive. I remained in front of the kwiy, my head down. Suddenly, the form at the bottom of the kwiy was not a bubble but an eye—and it was looking at me intensely. It emerged from the water and entered my left eye. I felt coolness and registered that that my eye saw more clearly than before. I continued contemplating the water and, one by one, the bubbles rose up and bathed my face. At the bottom of the kwiy, in the place of the bubbles, an opening had formed—or rather, an empty space.

"Ah! I see! I see! I see! I see it!" I cried, "I see the opening!"

As in a dream I heard Aunt Tansia's voice saying: "*Omi-Nannan! Adja-hou!* (The water of Nannan! God be praised!)" I repeated it after her without understanding anything. Suddenly she placed her hands with all her strength on my shoulders, which made me fall down on my back. I lay on the ground, eyes open, filled with my beautiful vision.

"*Fikse solèy-la, pito.* (Look at the sun.)"

I obeyed her, not without regret, but I felt right away such a sensation of well-being that I wanted to laugh and cry at the same time. I felt that I was at the heart of life, inundated with light. I was light! I had before my eyes the bubbles of water, in my pores, on my skin, on my eyelids. They emerged everywhere on my face. I saw them rising, heading for the sun. They became drops of light. Was it an illusion? It didn't matter. It was marvelous.

"You have just seen the mysteries of water. The droplets are the vapors. They rise up to the sun to return charged with new energy. They will come back at nightfall."

"Aunt, I am amazed!"

"Rather, be mindful of the lesson. What you have just seen is the manifestation of a *makonnay an twa* (triune formula, three-in-one, as in the Christian trinity)—the water, the sun and the wind together bring about the whole mystery of renewal: '*Ma a/Nannan/vodou-Ile.*' It is a code: Ma a (the pond) represents the field of magical forces. Nannan represents the primary feminine principle. Vodou Ile represents the Great Spirit—the Holy Spirit." Then she cried loudly while she beat her breast, "*Adja vodoule! Adja-houn! Adja-nou! Adja-houn!* (Child of Vodou, dance Vodou until you enter into trance! God be praised! God be praised! God be praised!)"

Many years later, one night in September 1992 when I was lying on my back, I saw an unusual brightness through the window of my room. Contrary to my custom, I had forgotten to consult the calendar concerning the ceremony of the candles on the day of the full moon. I got up to go dip my pitcher and my kwiy, write a prayer and place it on the altar, prepare the wicks with holy oil, light them, and proceed to the ritual of the full moon. I placed the lit candles at the foot of each tree altar in the courtyard of the house. I thought intensely about Aunt Tansia, and about my father, who had died four years earlier. I prayed for them. I put sprigs of basil in each water pot, by the side of the candles. It was midnight when the ceremony was done. My children—there are three—and my little niece Lovelie were lined up in my bed. There was no more room for me, so I stretched out on the parquet. All of a sudden, without knowing why, I began to cry. The tears soothed me and I went to sleep. Suddenly I heard the voice of my daughter, Laura: "Look, Manmie, there is a fire in the courtyard!"

Lòlò and I ran to the window to see a flame rising up to a considerable height. It was under a passion fruit tree where I had lit a candle before going to bed. The flame almost had the look of a human form. We stood there a moment to look at it.

It didn't have an evil or destructive air. It was a kind of half-white, half-red light. To me, it was a vision. It stayed in the same place for five minutes, then slowly disappeared. At the moment when we returned to lie down on our improvised bed, the flame reappeared, this time in our room. From the place where I had lit the wicks, it took shape and rose up to the ceiling. Lòlò, our daughter and I were stilled in awe before such a phenomenon. I didn't try to understand its meaning. I was happy merely to be a witness to such a marvelous sight. The flame disappeared just as it had come, and all three of us intertwined went to sleep on the parquet.

The next morning, I went to the altar and I found two drawings traced over the leaves of paper on which I had written my thanksgiving prayer: one representing a face and the other the form of a fetus. I carefully saved these drawings. Man Choune, whom I told about this, explained to me that it was a coded message: "*Ou konnen, monfi, tout desen se ekriti.* (You know, my child, that every design is a form of writing.)"

Of course, I knew it and that was why I was curious about the meaning of the message. I went to a cousin of my grandmother who had also passed through Aunt Tansia's school: Aya, who served *Ti Jean Dantò*, a male Lwa who uses suggestive remarks exclusively to convey his messages. Aya gave me the following explanation: "*Genlè se pwòp fòm a ou Ginen-an a montre-w.* (It seems that it is your own likeness that Ginen-an is showing you.)" I found this explanation bizarre.

From another friend—Marie Hélène Beauséjour Nau—to whom I had shown the drawings, I obtained this response: "The face reminds me of the face on the Shroud of Turin." I was not satisfied. I would have liked an explanation that was fuller, more logical. Up to this very day, I am still searching for the meaning of these drawings.

On the night of December 10, 1993—fifteen months after this experience—I was awakened by an unusual noise. I got up and checked the bolts on all the doors and windows to make sure that they were shut tight. We had just moved into our new house, and I didn't know the habits of the people living in the area. I always took a thousand precautions, though at Lakou Jean-Gilles everything seemed calm. Then I sat myself in the rocking chair. I couldn't sleep. I looked at the time: it was four a.m. I went back to bed in the hope of having a little *kabicha*★ (nap) before getting up for good to undertake my daily round of tasks: prepare the breakfast, clean the house, etc. In my head I planned the small budget corresponding to the day's program. In the absence of a much-wished-for nap, I tried to fill up my time. I lit a candle, which I placed at the foot of the poto mitan. I saluted the four cardinal points while omitting the gestures of the Jete. Then I began to recite a prayer to Nannan Boulouklou, a Yoruba divinity adopted by several lakou in Haiti. She represents the first feminine principle. I had been reciting this prayer since my return from Benin where I had met Otè Badjaou, who was also an adept of Naa. It was he who had given me the codes of Naa.

I was about to begin the first words—*Nannan Boulouklou, Oke tililewu, ognigni-gnigni. Ale koto ahure kprakprawo! Ten'te Ure* . . . (Nannan Boulouklou, you who are infinite Grandeur, the prime force of all time! You, the able Artisan . . .), when I sensed a presence in the room, as if someone were moving forward majestically and standing in front of my altar. Since my eyes were closed, I hesitated between the desire to open them and that of staying in the same position. I did not at all want to disturb the silence by a maladroit gesture. So I chose to keep my eyes shut and to wait, calm and attentive. I then began to feel a sweet sleepiness coming over me. I blinked several times in the hope of glimpsing the visitor before letting myself glide into this new state. But instead of a face, I saw nothing but the color red, then white. At that, I understood that I was already in Nan Dòmi. A voice gave me a message: "Sacrifice." The voice was strong and gentle at the same time.

"What sacrifice, Bondje-manman-mwen?" I repeated my question two more times.

I felt as though I were drowning. A moment came when I wasn't breathing anymore. I was waiting for orders.

"The sacrifice of the form," the voice answered, very close to me now. "I saw you in the water. You saw me too without recognizing me. You have been anba dlo for too long, I'm going to help you rise up to the surface."

I opened my arms to be helped, even raised up if it were necessary. Instead, I received in my right hand an object in the form of a locked chain. In the left hand, I received a key. The objects were enormous.

"Open . . . open it," the voice said. "Create the passage yourself. . . . What you have before you is your deliverance."

I wanted to obey immediately, but I was not sufficiently dexterous. I tried many times to lift the object so as to put the key in the opening, but the weight of the chain was greater than the strength of my wrist. I persisted in my need, as if it were a puzzle to be solved. I put down the object and kneeled before it. I enclosed it in my arms and kissed it. Then I sat on the chain. I caressed it with my free hand. I looked down the better to see it, and discovered that its opening was on the left side. With considerable pain and effort I managed to open it. At that very moment, I found myself in a strange world in which beings moved about like mollusks in the water. I was awakened brusquely by the voices of children entering the room noisily.

After this experience, I again took up Auut Tansia's lessons on the subject of Je in order to find the passage to prepare for "my Janbe." This teaching was very difficult for me. I didn't stop asking myself: "What is the transition like?" I looked for possible references in the hope of understanding it a little better. She had taken pains to explain that this power would not be accorded me until I consented to be *toutouni*★ (naked, without form). She had tried to define toutouni as a move toward definitive rejection of the intellectual mode (denying forevermore knowledge gained through the intellect). That seemed truly difficult to me. I imagined not being able to know any longer what a glass was, or a napkin, a house, a dog—everything that I had carefully stored in my memory—so as to protect my reason from general confusion. However, she always avoided choosing words that were not able to contain the essence of her message. She always went on coolly with what she was saying. She gave me the explanation. I was satisfied with it, for I had, at last, understood everything. Nevertheless, I must confess that I had a hard head.

She waited a month to let me absorb the content of the message before launching into a more complicated discourse. I understood at last that water was a symbol, that it is the only element with which you can make clean what is soiled. I told myself that to fill my memory with useless recollections is like soiling my mental state, as well as my dream body—of which my memory is a part. One word always came to mind: the trace. I had never meditated on this word before. Since it was impossible for me to find an explanation, I had asked Aunt Tansia to speak on the subject of the trace. Her response plunged me into reflection that was still more profound, so profound that it only came to the surface thirteen years later. When I asked her to tell me about the trace, she responded: "The trace is the emanation of the spirit."

"What is the form?"

"The form is the expression of the trace *nan yon dire ki vid: longè, lajè, otè ak pezantè* (length, breadth, height and weight)." I interpreted this as space-time.

"Can you tell me what problem form represents?"

"The only problem is that of letting oneself be trapped *nan yon dire ki vid* (an expression that one can translate as space-time) and never leaving it except by death."

"But how can one liberate oneself?"

"Through sacrifice. To leave one's form is to liberate oneself from death."

"Tell me, what must I do to leave my form?"

Aunt Tansia took a deep breath before she answered me: "*Aprann vire rad a ou lanvè.* (Learn how to turn your clothes inside out.) Learn to change your mentality/perception. You must make this change clear."

By *vire rad lanvè*★ she was indicating the passage from one state to another. And *Lanvè* is also another name for Ti Bonnanj. Thus I finally understood that once and for all I ought to let the spiritual side of my being reach fulfillment in order to live my life as an initiate. Aunt Tansia encouraged me to do so. She used solid arguments to convince me that without my passage under water, I would remain *mofreze*★ (infirm) in the unknown world. I imagined all kinds of stories on the subject of water. It is true that popular legend was full of stories of children and adults who, bathing in a river basin, didn't reemerge until several years later with stones of power. These people didn't remember their past and didn't speak further about their life anba dlo. But as for me, I was scared stiff of water. At the time, I simply suppressed the desire to bathe in the river. However, in spite of everything, I had not abandoned the ritual of jete dlo. I knew that I couldn't get lost or drown in a kwiy of water, or in a pot, or in a pitcher.

## CHAPTER 10

# Establishing a Means of Communication

*Pase pa filyè oubyen trase yon filyè*

Aunt Tansia often repeated to me that my shell—my logical mind—was cracked but not entirely broken. That is what kept me prisoner of this world. I was trapped by a barrage of passions and desires. In order to avoid bothersome missteps, she told me, I should work patiently but firmly to develop Attention to my left side. I should also establish a communication link with the Unknown and strengthen this link by concentrating my attention. To do this I had to cleanse my nannan-rèv. She took time to explain this to me in down-to-earth language: "It's like an injured fingernail that must fall off to let another grow in its place. The injured nail, while it is cracked is still attached to the flesh."

The image was clear, and I said sadly, "I understand."

Following Aunt Tansia's advice, I began to take care of myself. That allowed me to acquire a broader vision of my responsibilities. For an entire year I had to take, three times a day, in order, tea from *mouton zenzen*,★ from *ti bonm* (a plant whose leaves are good for special baths and whose perfumed infusion is highly valued), from flowers of *toli*★ (a shrub), verbena and basil. The dose was very specific, and I had to follow the prescription to the letter for the effects to be noticeable.

Aunt Tansia told me that one of the most important objectives in reaching Ginen was to find the key to one's personal power, which can be attained by developing one's gifts, ensuring thereby the rigorous treatment and removal of all kinds of internal blockages. She claimed that not being conscious of one's personal power was equivalent to a kind of infirmity. I was fascinated by her words.

"My child," Aunt Tansia said, "there is no magic unless there is communication between the Ti Bonnanj (Selidò) and the Gwo Bonnanj (Sèmèdò). Magic = personal power = energy = luck."

"What I fear is the immensity of it all. In the face of it I feel so alone."

She took my hand. "It is a difficult experience but you cannot retreat from where you are now. *Djètò-a ak Djehoun a ake.* (The *Djètò* as well as the *Djehoun* are with you.) Ask your allié to help you."

Then she began to clap her hands while singing a song:

> *Pwen sa a se pwen manman an mwen*
> *M di sa yo ka fè wen*
> *Pwen sa a se pwen papa an mwen*
> *M ape mande sa yo ka fè wen*
> *M apwèy nan Gran Bwa*
> *M apwèy chache fèy o*
> *Si m pa ka pote*
> *M a woule.*

> This pwen is the pwen of my mother
> I say, what can they do (to me)
> This pwen is the pwen of my father
> I wonder, what can they do (to me)
> I'm going into the Great Forest
> I'm going to look for leaves
> If I can't carry (the weight)
> I'll roll it.[68]

This song did me good. Like a balm, it calmed my anguish. The melody was there for a reason. I learned it.

---

68 *Pwen* is a magical power which is often but not always bound into a physical object, such as the leaves to be searched for. Gran Bwa has a double meaning here, not only the material forest where medicinal herbs can be found, but also the lwa named Gran Bwa, associated with initiation, herbal healing and the untamed wilderness. The weight which may be hard to carry here is the burden of inherited spirits.

"Aunt," I asked her, "does one really have need of magic if detachment removes all striving for ambition? What is it good for? You have told me that according to the way of Ginen, one needs nothing."

She opened her eyes wide. "All living creatures need magic. The lion's strength is its magic, the cunning of the cat is its magic, the deification of man is his magic. I could cite thousands of examples for you in the animal as well as in the mineral and vegetable kingdoms. In following the Ginen way you consent to lose everything in order to win the only thing one really has need of: one's personal power."

"I was not conscious of that. You say that even the vegetables and the minerals possess magic of their own. It's incredible."

"But true, my child. Now I am going to explain it to you. Pay close attention."

She wiped her mouth and face with the pink handkerchief that she always had in her djakout. "The natives of this land—that is, the Taino—discovered the magic of the *woukou*[69] as well as that of the *wòch dife*★ (stones that make fire when they are rubbed together)."

"How were they able to do that? What led them to it?"

"The need to communicate."

"I haven't really grasped the importance of their approach."

*"Pitit an mwen, sa w pa konnen pi gran pase w.* (My child, what you don't know is bigger than you are.) Listen to me, I'm going to show you something."

She left and returned with two stones, presenting them to me. I put out my hand to take them, but she stopped me. I didn't understand.

"You do not have the right to touch them without my permission."

"Why not?" I retorted, incredulously.

"You could do yourself harm."

"Let's see, " I said playfully, "I want to find out."

"If you wish, but it's your responsibility."

---

69 A plant whose fruit serves as a coloring agent. Native people of the island of Hispaniola used it as a cosmetic. Modern Haitians use it as a food coloring in sauces.

"What are they good for?"

"For displacing passive energies, those of a body too weakened by some kind of leak. They can heal as well."

"How can they do that?"

"By their magic."

"I want to see in order to believe."

"Happy are those who believe without seeing. Obviously, you have the right to not believe."

I sensed impatience on her part. She told me to stretch out my hands. I obeyed her. She put one of the stones in the palm of my right hand. When the stone hit my hand, I felt vertigo. Colored points appeared before my eyes. I couldn't see Aunt Tansia anymore. I was seized with panic.

"Aunt, where are you?" I cried out in desperation.

"I am here," her voice replied.

"I don't see you!" I cried louder.

"I am here, by your side. Don't you believe it? Be calm."

"Yes, I believe you, I hear you, but I don't see you," I said in a calmer voice.

"I am here though. Don't you feel it?"

I didn't answer. She asked, "What is wrong with you?"

"My head is spinning, I have vertigo, I need to vomit. I am blind!"

"You have only changed worlds. Don't be afraid. Look for a point of color and fix your attention on it."

I saw points of white, red, saffron yellow and indigo blue pass by, but couldn't focus on any of them.

"Don't be afraid," Aunt Tansia reassured me. "Cling to your allié. It is your faithful guide."

"I see many colors. I can't fix on one."

"Choose one. Choose the color of your allié."

I had a hard time choosing. The colors passed by too quickly and my nausea grew worse. Aunt Tansia pressed my temples. I fixed on the indigo blue, and I felt better right away. Suddenly, I saw Aunt Tansia in the form of light on my left. I also saw another form of light, which held out its right hand to me. I recognized it as the stone. It greeted me, I responded to its greeting with a smile of satisfaction."

"Welcome!" it said.

"Thank you," I answered.

"What do you want?"

"Nothing. I only wanted to see. . . ."

"The world to which I belong?"

"Yes, if you like."

"Come," the luminous body said to me, "I'll take you with me."

I went through a world that I wouldn't know how to describe. It was beauty and magnificence and made of many colors, unknown to me until then. Nevertheless, I was not completely at ease.

"Here, this is our world. Each one of us has power. Humans have misinterpreted our role alongside them. Each human being has his correspondent in our world," the luminous body told me.

"Is this true for me, too?"

"Of course."

This explanation plunged me into profound reflection, and I lost my vision. But I was not returned to myself again, that is to say, to my normal state. I continued to pose questions. I heard answers coming from very far away; then I lost contact with my interlocutor. I heard nothing more. I turned to see whether Aunt Tansia was with me, but to my great surprise I was alone in my parents' room.

*It's not possible*, I thought to myself. *How did I land here?*

I looked at myself in a mirror. My eyelids were swollen like those of someone who had slept too long. I looked around to see whether I was being watched. I went through all the rooms; there was no one there. My parents were gone. The servants too. I hastened to get back to Aunt Tansia's house. I ran all the way. I found her at the exact place where we had been talking a moment before.

"What happened to me?" I asked her.

"You ran too fast."

"How could I end up in my parents' house?"

"You left me. Where did you go?"

I told her about my trip. As I spoke, I held her hand. I was overwhelmed by my experience. I needed human warmth to help me bear the weight of this enigma. Like a child reciting her lessons, I kept repeating, "Every human being has a stone as correspondent."

"Yes, that is true. And sometimes, many correspondents."

"Do I also have a correspondent?"

"Yes, you too."

"What is it called?"

"A stone of power."

"Why is it called a stone of power?"

"Because it is a stone of power."

"But what is its real name?"

"You must find it first, then give it the name you like."

"How did you find yours?"

"They came to me. I didn't look for them. I didn't buy them."

"Can we buy them?"

"Whoever gets a stone buys it at the same time. He doesn't pay money, but there is still a price to pay. Many buy them just as one buys a pair of shoes. As for me, I'd advise you not to do it that way. *Gen anpil moun ki konn ranmase pongongon mete nan kòr a yo.* (There are many people who are trapped by getting things that will cause them problems later.) Be careful not to envy someone else's stone, to borrow one, or to touch one without the permission of its owner."

"Why not?"

"Because of what happened to you when you touched my stone, that's why. If your allié had not taken you to your parents' house, you would be lost."

"Ah, good. I understand now."

"Finally!" Aunt Tansia said, in a relieved tone.

"Aunt, do you know other people who have stones?"

"Yes, I do. Vivil has five of them. He even worked with Anacaona's stone for a certain amount of time in order to make several voyages through the island. He was the courier of the Cacos."

"Anacaona, the Taino queen?"[70]

---

70 Anacaona (1474–1503) was a Taino chief, married to Caonabo, a chief in the territory of Maguama. Anacaona initially negotiated with Columbus's invaders but was later accused of conspiracy and hanged by the Spanish Governor.

"Yes."

"Explain it to me."

"Anacaona and Caonabo each had a stone. Theirs was a mystical marriage. Anacaona was Taino. She was beautiful and flirtatious, but her beauty stemmed from more than physical appearance. Rather, it consisted of grace and love that emanated from her being. She was called 'Sun Queen.' Everyone loved her. The few who thought they hated her admired her in the depths of their beings. Their hatred was more the result of a kind of jealousy or misplaced envy. She was a great poet and loved dance. In one of her poems she said:

> Taïno,
> We need dance,
> Poetry, sound,
> Music and dreams
> To nourish our bond of
> Communication
> With the Unknown.

"She was a dreamer and used her stone as a means to travel through the unknown world. This magnificent stone was recovered. So it is that Vivil—Rosainvil Pierre, who was an obstetrician/midwife—had the honor of benefiting from the powers of this stone."

"And Caonabo. What was he like?"

"He was the most beautiful man in the land of Ayiti. He was a colossus. He symbolized strength and determination. He was a Carib[71]. He had a violent temperament, but he only used his strength against whatever blind force might try to disturb the peace in Ayiti. He had prophesied: 'Ayiti is going to experience two hundred years of tribulations. However, she will not perish. If I must return so that she can recover her pride and her peace, I, Caonabo, *Ayabombe! Ayabombe!* (Victory! Victory!) I shall return.'"

---

71 Caonabo (?–1496) was one of the principal Taino chiefs (*caciques*) of Hispaniola at the time of Columbus's arrival in 1493. Thought by Hernando Colón to have been a Carib, he was married to Anacaona. His attacks against the Spaniards brought about his arrest. He drowned in a shipwreck as he was being taken to Spain.

"How can he return?"

"Through the person to whom he gives the stone."

"I don't understand."

"Certain Ginen meet other Ginen in the dream state who counsel them and perhaps offer them gifts, stones of power, for example."

"But how could Caonabo, an Indian, be a Ginen?"

"In the unknown world, the notion of race does not exist. It is not exclusive only to Africans or their descendants to become Ginen. Anyone can become Ginen under the guidance of the Spirit. I repeat to you once again: He who has discovered the totality of his being is Ginen."

"I didn't know that the African and the Indian could meet anywhere."

"In Ginen everything is possible. The principle of Ginen is a universal principle. There are degrees and an Order, the Order of the star, which is the crossing of five roads guarded by *Brav/Kalfou senk*."[72]

She struck her chest and said, "*So djèmè twa fwa,★ nan Ginen tande★!* (Three times in truth, I take Ginen as witness!)"—the solemn oath of Vodou initiates. "The Order of the star is the pwen of the first inhabitants of Ayiti. When the African disembarked on the island, his Ti Bonnanj was already on guard. Without the Ti Bonnanj, there would not have been a single survivor during the crossing, I swear it to you.

"Nonetheless, the African, who had lost a part of himself because of the shock caused by his humiliation, sought a way to restore his wholeness, however much it might cost. If not, he would have gone mad. For him the land of Ayiti had to provide the remedy for his disintegration. He encountered the Native and made a pact with him. He found that the Native had preserved his magic, intact. The African profited from that, learning the secrets of the island's plants, grottos, and waters. That is why the Haitian—the descendant of the African—when he leaves the *Djèvo★* (Vodou convent) at the time of his initiation, is obliged to

---

72 Brav is also called the Brave Being, the Good Being, who is Christ. Associated with "the five crossroads"—"Kalfou senk"—the place of all the intentions and decisions taken by initiates, Kalfou is also Legba, who is the Master of Intention.

salute first of all the spirit *Aryètò* and also to bear the mark of the star with five points. *So djèmè twa fwa, nan Ginen tande!*"

I listened attentively to Aunt Tansia. She had the enthusiasm of a real history professor. From time to time she paused to take a little tobacco from her small jar. I didn't ask her any questions. For once, I understood perfectly well everything she was saying to me. She blew her nose and resumed the conversation.

"The *Ayitien*★ (ancient inhabitants of Haiti) had the same problems as the African, but he chose Janbe. He let himself be torn to pieces, worked to death, scattered in space in order to go in search of the unknown world after having severed all his attachments. Certainly he chose not to fight physically with his enemy. Because for him, bloody physical combat would have led him to another point of the known world and attached him to this world. He preferred Janbe. Anacaona had foreseen all that from afar and had incited Caonabo to form an army arranged along transversal lines of the Order five so as to protect the Djèto belonging to the surviving Ayitiens."

"Where are they? Where do these supposed survivors live?"

"They are the *zing dlo*.[73]"

"That I don't understand very well, Aunt. What do you mean when you talk about an army? You have just told me that there was no response to the colonialists' aggression."

"It was then that the gad were formed: the gad *Malawe* and the gad *Makaya*. The latter are the most ferocious," she continued, without responding directly to my question.

"What did they do? What was their role?"

"It is an army of iron that protects the Djèto of the Ayitien."

"You speak of this army in the present tense."

"Of course. It still exists. However, only the Haitian can locate it."

"Were there no Haitians from the time of Caonabo? I am completely confused, I've noticed that you do not speak of Indians."

"Pardon me, you are right. In fact, the Ayitiens were the first inhabitants of the island, those we call Indians. Then came

---

73 A savage, a hermit whose hair never felt a razor.

the Haitians, the inheritors of the island who created the new nation. The truth is that the Haitians took up the challenge of hatred, racism and exploitation. Because the island was the place where the fusion of Indian, African and European cultures occurred, they are the legitimate trustees and direct heirs of these three cultures. They constitute the point of reconciliation between Africa, Europe and America. Europe is at the junction of Africa and America."

"I understand," I said, quite satisfied, "But one thing intrigues me. Why are there five roads instead of six, twenty, one hundred, or one alone?"

"There are a thousand and one roads. The Ayitien, for his part, has always chosen the star with five points. It was his mystery, his pwen. He truly searched for total liberty, illumination."

We both became silent. For a long, long time we gazed at each other. I wanted to ask her another question. My lips opened, but no sound came out. I wanted to ask her how she was able to retain all these stories. She understood my thought and smiled. She explained that since our culture is oral, every Ginen receives the teaching and the history of the Danti who have preceded him. She emphasized that every element of our culture constitutes an important aspect of our entire being. Thus we have the obligation to gather together all the elements that have served to form our deepest being. However, she taught me that we must guard against an obsessive interest. She considered herself affected by such an obsession, as well as all the Ginen without exception.

"Each person must construct his own line of communication. So long as one has not attained the integration of his being, he remains on the level of passions and desires," she said.

I talked about this subject for a long time. The image I had of myself was that of a black woman, an inheritor of African culture, only. For Aunt Tansia, having black skin had nothing to do with my being. I did not understand what she wanted to prove with that assertion. She calmly persevered without concerning herself with my confusion.

"You could just as well be a *quadroon*[74] or a *bata* (a blend of Indian and black)—both amounting to the same thing. *Pa fikse Je a ou anwo pròp tèt a ou, anwo kadav kò-a ou.* (Don't fix your Eyes on yourself, on your physical body.) If you make the effort to recall who you are, you will see that you are 'consciousness.' In this space where you are materialized in order to construct your own experience, there already exists Ayitien, African and European culture. Now, your consciousness, having assembled these three cultures, has stitched them together and made for itself a garment that is the Gwo Bonnanj. But remove the garment and you remain as consciousness. That is what you are. Don't ever forget it."

"*Bondye!* (My God!)" I exclaimed. "What you say to me here is very hard to understand."

"On the day when you are able to master the dream state, your consciousness will at the same time reach other levels of Attention. There are three levels of consciousness that each human being must experience to be able to Janbe. The first is called *Je klè*. The second, Nan Dòmi. And the third, which is the most important, is called *Pinga-pye*★. Keep this well in mind. Attention equals Consciousness."

At the time, I didn't understand where Aunt Tansia wanted to go with this. I thought that she was trying to take away my pride at being black as well as my sense of racial belonging. Now I know that she wanted to protect my nannan. She told me: "Obsession blocks the will. Now, with the will we can transform the nannan-rèv into whatever we want. Don't cling to anything, my girl, be free! You are a dreamer. You have the opportunity to find everything you need to create your line of communication. Don't waste your chance!"

Convinced by her words, I embarked on this adventure like a child plunged into the universe of play. Thus, little by little, I have learned to play with my myths and my poetry, which for me have become at times an independent reality, at other times elements of my own culture, and often both at once. In this way,

---

74 Child of a mulatto and a white, or a mulatto and a mulatto, with very light skin easily mistaken for white.

I have learned to become the referee of my own play with the help of my gift: dreaming.

Such is the paradox I have drawn from Aunt Tansia's Ginen teaching. From now on, it is my way of living *Jodia*★ (living in the moment). I have ended by at last accepting the Ginen principle. I have received the Order, but I still have many things to learn and, above all, to experience.

## CHAPTER 11

# Manipulating One's Gift

### *Sèvi ak fòs ou*

My entry into the dream state has undergone small changes, beginning in 1990. But I must confess that many years earlier I was completely blocked. Since it was evident that I was not progressing, I tried to recall certain lessons from Aunt Tansia in order to preserve the habit of heeding her influence, so as not to reside in the world of one single perception. The very fact of wanting to remember led me to induce silence within myself. And that brought about the birth of the desire to know and explore myself.

Painful evidence led me to realize that my inertia was caused by my stupidity—I remained dependent on concrete structures. I was living without hope because I had not given myself an abstract objective. I was incapable of developing my spontaneity, which would have made me more supple and much more attentive to the signs of Ginen-an.

I had searched for and wanted to know the secrets of the lakou and of Vodou, but I had never realized how complex this culture was, nor that the Spirit of this culture could in itself determine my consciousness. Thus, I spent long moments in proving myself. I ended by saying to myself, "When one is blocked at an impasse, the only solution is to fly over it."

On many occasions, I tried to fly above the barriers I had created for myself because of my need for the concrete. But the departure of Aunt Tansia had created real turbulence around me, which caused a forced landing every time I tried. The worst of it is that I was aware of the fact that there was only one issue: My obligation was to transcend my history, to efface the continuity of my existence to be able to live my other life—the one that offered me Liberty. But I lacked the courage to do what I had to do.

It took me a long time to recover what I wanted: the sensation I had experienced the first time I saw the small spark of light. I was convinced that this very sensation was connected to a change of perception. Recovering it would help me to *see*. I also knew that if I came to perfect this consciousness on my own, doing so would indicate a change in my level of consciousness. I concentrated on the points of color that I was already used to seeing. I sought a point of reference. I tried out and succeeded in re-creating—all alone—a rhythm in my surroundings, a generator of other underlying rhythms.

Everything came together to contribute to the success of my attempts: rivers, trees, music, wind, sea, rain, birds, stones, dance, sounds, children. I finally succeeded in holding my attention on everything that existed within my ken. This exercise helped me to review the Ginen order. This period of time fortified me morally. I felt regenerated from one day to the next.

One night at around three o'clock I was awakened by a sound like that of a ship entering port. While I was concentrating on the sound, I heard the sound of gurgling water filling my stomach, I suddenly felt a blow on my neck; a memory was spontaneously activated that involved my entire body, which quivered with joy: I saw again the indigo blue light.

I dreamed again that night, after ten years of constant struggle. I awakened Lòlò then to tell him my dream. He asked me, "What time is it?" It was 3:10 a.m. Looking at the alarm clock, he yawned and sat on the edge of the bed.

I told him what I had just seen. The scenes unrolled as in a film—that is, in three dimensions.

The story amazed Lòlò.

"You must write it all down quickly. When did you have this dream?"

"Just now, at about three a.m."

"That's not possible. When you woke me up it was 3:10. How could you have seen so much in so little time?"

"I don't know," I said. "I really can't explain it."

*Dream, story, history, myth, legend?*

In the course of my dream, next to the indigo blue light, I saw another light. Through the light a form slowly took shape, permitting a woman of an indescribable grandeur to appear. Next to her, I was like a particle of dust. She was taller than the roofs of houses, but there was nothing outlandish about her appearance; on the contrary, she was majestic. She was like a Haitian peasant woman, her hair bound with a sky-blue headscarf. She was barefoot and carried a naked baby on her left arm. She wore a blouse of blinding white, a grass-green skirt, and a red belt cinched tightly around her waist.

She called me by my name. I approached her. I raised my head to look at her and she said to me:

*"Chak Pèp gen pwòp lejann pa l. Tout lejann yo sèvi pou fè fomasyon ak edikasyon. Yon lejann, se tankou yon jaden ki gen anpil bèt vivan k ap ladan li. Se yon bagay ki toutafè natirèl. Epi nan mitan tout bèt sa yo, gen yon ti bèt tou pitipiti yo rele mit. Ago! Gen de kalite de mit. Gen yon seri de mit ki koze nizans, yo manje twèl ak plantation kilte jaden. Men nan menm tan sa tou, gen yon lòt seri de mit ki konn bay tradisyon yon pèp fòs ak andirans, ki kapab kenbe lèspri yon pèp fèm menm devan lanmò. Yo rele mit sa yo: Mit-a-lojik, Mit-a-lojik, Mit pou lojik.*

(Every people has its own legends. All these legends are used for training and education. A legend is like a garden with a lot of little creatures living inside it. That's a completely natural thing. And then, in the midst of all these critters, there's one tiny beast that they call *mit*. Pay attention! There are two different kind of *mit*. One's a kind of bug that causes trouble; they eat cloth, or whatever you plant in your garden. But at the same time there is also another kind of *mit* which can give the tradition of a people power and endurance, which can hold the spirit of a people firm, even in the face of death. *Mit* like that are called Mythology—Myths with their own logic.)

"All the personages who form the base of a culture, its

foundation, are mythological. All the entities that lend it dynamism, enrich it and embellish it so that it may live are mythological. Each culture has its myths, inevitably. In Haitian culture we find key personages. Today I have come to speak to you of the person who is the guardian of this culture. I want to speak about Minister *Azaka Médée*, who sends this message to more than one listener: 'Men and women of the whole world, you do not know true social justice. This is because you neglect the integral development of the human being. If you do not come together to protect the foundation of your culture and your genetic patrimony, you will not see the evolution you dream of.'"

Then, in a strong and melodious voice, she sang:

*Jacques Roumain ki Gadò yon leta*
*Li di: O! mezanmi! gade yon leta!*
*Ala de wont! Nou desann ba!*
*Pa gen jistis O! O!*

Jacques Roumain, who is Guardian of the state[75]
He says: O! my friends! look at a state like that!
For shame! We have fallen low!
There is no justice, O! O!

*Minis Azaka*
*Ki chita l ap gade yo*
*"Peyi yo pou yo*
*Y a fè sa yo vle"*

Minister Azaka[76]
who sits down to watch what they do
[Says] "It's their country,
Let them do whatever they want."

---

75 Jacques Roumain (1907–1944), writer, politician and founder in 1934 of the Haitian Communist Party. Author of the important novel *Masters of the Dew* (1944).
76 A lwa called Minister because he is thought of as the Minister of Haitian agriculture.

"This song," the majestic woman said, "is an antidote against the poison of injustice. You sing it, too."

When I opened my eyes, she had disappeared. But I heard her voice from far away telling me, "I will return to tell you other stories."

CHAPTER 12

# The Importance of *Je*

I spent the rest of the night thinking about my vision. This experience exceeded my expectations. It must be said that all that was the result of my perseverance in practicing the ritual of jete dlo, in accordance with Aunt Tansia's teachings. The jete dlo can open up innumerable doors. The mystery of water, she told me, plays a powerful role in the creation of the world. It is salutary for every living being to know the signs of water. Plants and animals, she explained, know by instinct certain possibilities that water offers. Human beings know it too, but for about a quarter of a century we have ceased to experience the mystical aspect of water. The ancient Ginen were baptized anba dlo (under water). The life of men today is organized so as to prevent them from knowing the truth about water.

"Aunt," I asked her, "How can we discover a truth by means of the jete dlo, when there are so many situations in which we do not see clearly. Is there a direct and general formula?"

"Can you tell me what your life today consists of?" she asked in response.

"It consists of my dream and my creations."

"I agree. But can you give up your dream and your creations?"

"No, not easily."

"If you have the power of Je, you can do it. You can do it by looking squarely at your dream and your creations and asking yourself, 'What is it that I have to give up?' You will then feel the solitude of the Sabbath and the detachment of the sage, and you will be able to say to yourself: '*TRUTH IS. I DO NOT NEED TO SEARCH FOR IT OR PUT IT TO A PROOF.*'"

Aunt Tansia had a hard time convincing me that the strength of my desires would create serious conflicts between the idea of truth and that of detachment. My desire to create and to produce was an internal necessity that I steadfastly wanted to fulfill. Life would become dull if I no longer harbored desire.

At the time, I was listening to Bob Marley, whose music was a kind of revelation to me. It reawakened my musical-artistic vocation. I wanted Haitian music to spread as widely and as powefully as his. I concentrated my energy on realizing this dream.

Aunt Tansia said: "In order for your dream to become possible, if you are truly filled with the desire to make Haitian music known, you must take into account all the circumstances and demands that seek to become reality in this conflicted world. Do you have enough courage to convince yourself that this desire can enter into conflict with other desires that also seek to come to fruition? Do you know the principles or the rules that lead to glory?"

"I do not think that I should have to fight for a place that belongs to me. I believe I am right in telling myself that Haitian music ought to be known by all other people. It is good music; all cultures ought to recognize it and profit from its 'therapeutic' effects."

"If only you had as much interest in Ginen!"

"It is in the interest of Ginen that I want to do my work!"

"No, it is your own interest you are defending. You are working for yourself: Your pride, your vanity, your nationalism, your Haitianism."

Aunt Tansia was too hard on me. I did not want to listen to her or even try to understand her point of view. My dream and I were one.

"Listen!" she said. "Just as your Gwo Bonnanj can block you because of your attachments, your nannan-rèv can give you a hard time. You will never be able to master it if you allow your intention to imprison you in one single perception."

"Why bring my nannan-rèv into all this? I don't see the

harm my nannan-rèv can cause me by my desiring something good."

"It is the wise man who said, 'What you have bound on high will be bound below. What you have unbound on high will be unbound below.'"

"I know that saying, but what do you mean to tell me?"

"When you make a vow, it is a contract made with the Invisible. If the response is positive, it will also be positive in what is visible. Consequently, everything which is involved with the nannan-rèv is registered by it."

"Tell me, Aunt, is there a method for avoiding problems?"

"Problems vary according to our perceptions. Each world has its problems. You can evade them by changing perception any time you feel caught in the trap of your desires. In the face of fear or joy, dissatisfaction or glory, make a sideways movement of your eyes in order to escape the two complicit lines: the vertical and the horizontal, which are the chains of the dimension Earth/Sky."

"Is it so important to make that gesture?" I asked, thinking she literally meant executing this movement with my eyes.

"Yes, you really ought to do it," she said, without further explanation. Then she began to sing:

*Agaou, pito m vole*
*pase dyab la manje m*

Agaou, I would rather fly through the air
Than be eaten by the devil

One can imagine, however, another less literal translation: Prevention is better than a cure.

Filled with Aunt Tansia's lessons, I became a scrupulous practitioner. I wanted to grasp the relation that exists between water and the invisible world. I needed above all to understand the effect of water on my nannan-rèv. I applied myself to act in accord with Aunt Tansia's advice in order to free myself each time I felt trapped.

On the night when I saw the majestic woman, I saw the

danger of the attachment I could feel for visions. I experienced an intense pleasure in recounting the story to myself. "That is where the trap lies," I told myself. "How could I ever manage to change my mode of perception if I take on the role of storyteller?" I remembered Aunt Tansia's severity when she spoke to me of energy. "*I am not jesting. Changing the mode of perception is the only engine capable of activating energy and fortifying the power of the nannan-rèv*," she had warned.

"I would like very much to change my perception, but I do not know how to do it. I am weak when it comes to my desires and needs," I replied quietly.

"Your problem stems from the fact that you become immobilized as a result of observing yourself only in Nan Dòmi. That is depressing, because for the duration of nannan-rèv the kantamwa expands and becomes a deforming mirror for contemplation, and that hinders energy's dynamic."

"I am not conscious of that."

"Do you usually know when you are tired?"

"Yes, indeed. I always feel my eyelids grow heavy, and a lack of interest in the outside world overtakes me. But I always fall asleep without being aware of doing so."

"That lack of interest comes from the fact that your consciousness has tired of remaining on only one level: the level of the material world. It invites you to change the level, whether you want to or not. Nonetheless, it will proceed to this change while preserving your dreams and phantasms, which are projections of the Gwo Bonnanj."

"How is that possible?"

"Because consciousness is a magnetic band that registers everything you are and everything you represent, whether in the physical world or in the immaterial world. Consciousness is attention. This is why you must work seriously to liberate yourself from the kantamwa, which is the creation of the Gwo Bonnanj, its own cherished child."

"How can I do that?"

"By practicing Nan Dòmi consciously. That is to say, with a special kind of attention."

"Do you mean a conscious sleep?"

"Nan Dòmi is not sleep. It is simply a state that resembles sleep. It is the state that precedes deep sleep. It is the place of revelation. Artists, above all painters and storytellers, enter easily into this state. They have the power to do so at birth." She was silent for a moment. "I must warn you of this: On the day that you become conscious of this state, do not attach yourself to it above all else!"

"Why not?"

"You risk losing communication with your Gwo Bonnanj. Remember that each state has its own snares. What is essential is always to remain attentive to what is happening. For attention alone can help you free yourself from your hindrances."

"What is this 'attention' you are talking about?"

"I want to speak to you about the movement that makes us ready for the kounye a-la-a, the present moment. That is what inevitably develops the Je."

"How do you explain the Je?"

"It is a gift."

"How does one acquire this gift? Or at the very at least, how does one come to deserve it?"

"*Merite pa mande*," she replied. It means: Deserving is not asking. She meant to say that every effort deserves reward, or that everything comes to fruition for the one who knows how to wait. "The Je cannot be acquired. It is developed in Nan Dòmi. However, when one has achieved mastery in the Je, one must consolidate one's power in the Je klè in order to reassure the Gwo Bonnanj regarding its role as interpreter. The Gwo Bonnanj is the only part of our being that has the capacity of explaining and giving form to the vision."

"What does it mean exactly to have Je?"

"*Je se wè.* (Je is seeing.) To have Je means to be the active and conscious witness of a scene that becomes reality. It is to live in two parallel worlds. It is to be in the position of evolving in these two worlds at the same time. It is to be in the present."

"Is it true that one can lose one's Je? I have heard stories about such things."

"Of course. It is true of neurotics who are inattentive dreamers, and who have let themselves be blinded by their phantasms because of lack of energy. They are caught in the snare of their illusions. The images they evoke are the projection of their kantamwa, which becomes their sole source of information and inspiration. Now there are all kinds of inspirations: good, bad, informative, malignant."

On the cassette where I recorded this teaching, I noticed that the timbre of Aunt Tansia's voice had changed. It became grave and nasal. I explained this change in her tone of voice by telling myself that perhaps a lwa possessed her that day. But a little further on, I found the correct explanation when I said to her: "I do not understand your gaze, Aunt. It is vague and lifeless."

"I am in Nan Dòmi, now. It is the voice of my nannan-rèv speaking to you. The pitch of my voice astonishes you, isn't that so?" (Laughter) "It doesn't belong to the world where you are now. Do you want to join me?" (Laughter)

"I would like to very much."

"Come," the voice invited me.

I cannot explain what happened next. I still do not have enough energy to lend form to what I lived at that time. I did not feel my body any longer. But at the same time everything became clearer and more brilliant in my eyes.

"You are in the process of receiving your baptism of fire and of the spirit," Aunt Tansia explained. "You are now in the *M la-M pa la*★ (I'm there—I'm not there; a concept that defines the state of internal silence). It's up to you to see."

I had barely heard this word when a change suddenly took place in me. I saw a tall tree whose leaves and branches were made of drops of water as brilliant as crystal. What I saw impressed me greatly: A young man came toward me with flames of fire shooting out from his eyes. He greeted me and said, "On this tree there is a djakout for you. It has been there for a long time. I have been waiting to give it to you." He held the basket out to me. I opened it and saw two lamps *tèt gridap*. I closed it and lost my vision. Aunt Tansia and I resumed our conversation. She asked me, "Did you recognize this man?"

"No," I said.

"You will meet him again in the flesh in fifteen years. On that day you will understand the whole vision."

I heard a voice resembling Aunt Tansia's saying, "Have you finished seeing?"

I heard myself ask her, "What happened? Am I still in Nan Dòmi?" I wanted to assure myself that I really understood that state.

"Now you have a lot of energy. You have just made a double intervention. One, on your Gwo Bonnanj, the other on your nannan-rèv. The state that you have experienced just now is marvelous," Aunt Tansia explained. "Did you understand that? Did you notice that there is no *Lòt bò ake Isit* (the near and the far), but only the *Isit la*★ (the here), for everything happens in the *kounye a-la-a* (now) and not in the *Isit epi La* (here and there). This is the secret of Je."

When I asked her what she thought of fortune tellers, she replied: "Pursue your research."

This evasive response, which I would understand better after numerous interventions that I had to carry out in many lakou, tormented me for a long time. It pushed me to have many conversations on the subject of Je with houngans and mambos in order to comply with Aunt Tansia's instructions. By chance, I also ran into a fortune teller. That day Lòlò and I had gone to the Dominican Embassy to get a visa. A woman came in and sat next to me. She opened her purse and took out a deck of cards. A card representing the Queen of Clubs fell down at my feet. As she picked up the card, she said to me, "The black queen is traveling with you. There is a woman in your group who is your cruel enemy. She is going to exert all her power in order to make your life difficult, but you will conquer her because the black queen, the mother of earth, will protect you. You are very lucky. That is what makes you the object of so much jealousy."

I didn't answer her. She tried to convince me of her Je by recounting things about my past. Perhaps she wanted to extract a little money from me. I pretended not to understand.

"Come to my house, I live in Nazon," she told me. "I have some things to reveal to you about your life: many things that will help you later on."

I did not answer this woman. At bottom, I knew that I didn't want to see her again. It did not interest me at all to hear someone speak to me about the past or the future. That was not the object of my research. I only wanted to gather information about Je. But I have discovered, not without regret, that people have a greater tendency to make a display of their knowledge than to put the investigator in the presence of mystery.

Aunt Tansia had warned me on many occasions that charlatans swarmed around Vodou venues, and that it was important for me to learn how to detect them.

"How can I do that?" I had asked.

"By developing your Je."

"How can I achieve that?"

"The Je develops in two ways. First, thanks to well-absorbed dosages of certain roots of plants, *plant ki chaje, wi* (power plants). Second, by a gesture."

At that time, I was convinced that the gesture must be a physical movement such as batting one's eyes. Aunt Tansia burst out laughing when I confessed it to her.

"*Non, pitit an mwen.* (No, my child.) It is not a matter of batting one's eyes. One only makes eyes for declarations of love." She laughed. "The gesture of Je is simple."

"What is it?"

"It is nothing," she answered.

"I don't understand, Aunt."

"The Je is a spiritual attitude. It is *pa gade anyen* (not looking at anything). It is the immobilization of the gaze. It is quite a difficult discipline because we have a marked tendency to let our gaze—even in closing our eyes—pass over images. A wandering gaze endangers thought, which strives to go back and forth between the Bon-konprann and the Ti Bonnanj."

"Can I immobilize my gaze on an object?"

"No, that would still be to agitate it. Immobilize your gaze on nothing."

"On the void. But that is impossible! I don't think that I will be able to do it. And worse yet, I'm afraid of the void."

"Are you afraid of the Spirit, of the Abstract, of Ginen? You are so busy *doing* that you forget how to *do nothing*. You are caught in the snares of time."

She had scarcely finished speaking when she got up from

her seat and came up to me. She put her forehead against mine, looking me straight in the eyes. And I saw the void. Then she lifted her left hand and firmly pressed her thumb and her index finger on my temples. It hurt for a moment, but little by little the pain went away and the light became darkness. She loosened her fingers on my temples and then repeated her gesture three times. On the third I began to see balls of light. I couldn't think. I struggled a bit, but I felt her fingers, like pincers, restrain me. I had the sensation of being suspended in the void, held by a thread. Then, right there, I suddenly understood what she wanted to teach me: how to enter the kounye a-la-a, which is also the void, which we labor to fill with our projects. She breathed on my eyes, which I again closed instinctively For a second I was conscious of knowing something: I had the key to a door, the door of *isit-la*. I could open this door and see, but I hesitated for no reason.

"What are you feeling?" Aunt Tansia asked.

"I am waiting," I heard myself answer.

"Very good, stay in that state. Now you are capable of seeing without my intervention—you understand, don't you? You are sure of the place of Je, *ti manzè* (little lady). Do you finally want to make an inventory of your powers?"

I promised I would.

Then she blew once again on my eyes. Her breath was sweet and beneficial.

In fact, it had taken me a long time to be able to appreciate the importance of Je. It was necessary for me to live through a painful experience before I could accept putting the formula of Je into practice. For inexplicable reasons, I always presented the profile of a lazy initiate.


I will not enter here into theories that could support this study; rather I will try to limit their importance in regard to Haitian Vodou. The subject is immense, but I am going to propose to the reader the witness borne by a sèvitè of a lakou. My visits in these lakou have been fruitful. I have learned that the initiation into the mystery of Vodou consists primarily in the development of Je. Each master has his own techniques and his tactics. However,

I am convinced that the disciplines of traditional Vodou are not solely abstract. Once they are internalized, the initiate is obliged to put his faith into practice and demonstrate its works. The goal of the initiation is :

1. Sèvi;
2. *Rive* (becoming) fran-Ginen;
3. Having the power of Janbe nan Ginen.

Now, without Je or *zye* (eyes), one remains blocked in only one dimension. One cannot Janbe without Je. Janbe and having Je are two necessities, for they are two prerequisites for being able to journey through other dimensions.

Aunt Tansia insisted on the mystic drama of man. She justified her point of view by explaining, "The human being must be transmuted in order to change his *kadav kò* into lwa. Whether this be through the Je klè or in the Nan Dòmi, the initiate must have the capacity to see *liy-nan* (the passage, line or divide) that separates the worlds. This line is the image of water. It is why water is indispensable for the initiate and for every living being."

For Aunt Tansia the mystic drama of the human being is equivalent to his or her *Pozisyon granmoun* (faultlessness), to her *Lwafication* (deification). The profound meaning of the ritual of water is clear: to reintegrate the state of germination. "*Nou se dlo, n ap tounen nan dlo.* (We are water, and to water we return.)" She took as an example the sperm and the ovum, two waters that give life. To possess Je, for Aunt Tansia, is, in other words, to enter into the water to find one's true nature. It is *konnen Mistè*, that is, to experience consciousness of several things in silence. It is to be fluid like water, capable of assuming any form.

## CHAPTER 13

# I Remember

This chapter is a report on my inquiries into Je, undertaken during a distressing time in my life. I had lost a child and I was having a hard time recovering. I dragged along my unhappiness like a shadow covering my spirit. I had no strength, no will to efface the frightening and macabre picture: the lifeless body of my child, who until then had been in apparent good health.

I blamed myself for not having reacted promptly, since I had been forewarned on the very morning of the drama. In Nan Dòmi I had glimpsed something like a misfortune. But I lacked decisiveness, and I was not sufficiently experienced to interpret and reconstitute my vision. In Nan Dòmi, I had seen myself at the Plaza of Arms in Ouanaminthe, walking during a torrential downpour, splashing through muddy water with my child in my arms. I came upon an infirm woman who, after greeting me, said: "Madame, it is not prudent to walk in this sea of mud with your child. You risk falling and losing him!" Her warning had suddenly taken me into Je klè. My heart beat wildly. I was afraid. I awakened Lòlò to tell him my vision. He proposed that I pray and remain in Pinga-pye. But I didn't have enough energy to forestall misfortune. I prayed, but there was no coherence in my message to Ginen-an. I had prayed without faith. In short, this experience cost me dearly. I poured torrents of tears into it. I recognized my weakness and my negligence. Afterwards, I learned that the decision taken by an initiate must be irrevocable and instantaneous.

Later I went to Ouanaminthe to recharge myself with new energy. The calm of the village and its people have always helped me to get back on my feet. Charité, a resident of Ouanaminthe, was always one of the most helpful. He followed us everywhere—Lòlò and the children had accompanied me to Ouanaminthe. One night, when we were coming back from Capotille, a suburb, a lwa Gede "rode" him (possessed him) along the way. This lwa held me back by the hands, for I wanted to flee—a reaction I still can't explain. As the lwa Gede spoke, it looked me straight in the eyes:

"*Madame, pitit a w la te mouri mò natirèl, tande?* (Madame, your child died of natural causes, you understand?) You must not harbor bad thoughts. People often blame the lougarou for the death of their children. *Men sa m ap di ou la se laverite: pitit a w la te malad nan kè.* (But I am telling you the truth: your child had a heart condition.)" I was startled when I heard this, because the autopsy had indicated the same thing the day after my child's death.

"How do you know that?"

"*Je-an mwen pèmèt mwen wè y.* (My Je allows me to see it.)"

I let out a deep sigh. The lwa Gede approached me and rubbed its forehead against mine, and after that it struck my solar plexus and shoulders with a hard, dry blow, like two hands clapping for a bravura performance. At the same time, I felt a pocket of gas rise up from my stomach to my breastbone. I was in anguish, fearing that I would die from it. The lwa understood and asked me to cry out. I obeyed. When it struck the same blow the air came out and emerged with a thunderous sound. At the same time a strange phenomenon took hold of me: I was no longer sad; suddenly I was relieved.

I was free of the shadow that had been following me. Miracle or magic, I don't know. What matters is that I was cured of a malady and the healing formula did not come from any medication. The lwa explained many things that night: That the new moon would be an unfavorable time to become pregnant because the child would be born ugly. It told me it was inadvisable for pregnant women to bathe in the river during the new moon because the eyes of the water could cause the fetus to be malformed. Many children are born with a heart condition because of negligence in this regard, he said. I did not place blind faith in his statements; it was impossible to verify them. But this was not the first time I had heard such things. Popular lore is full of such stories. Yet, the lwa had convinced me of one thing: The efficacy of its methods for curing me of my malady.

The importance of Je was confirmed to me subsequently through the testimony of various houngan and mambo attached to different disciplines. My goal in the course of this research on Je was to clarify certain points in regard to Vodou. It was my intention to establish the existence of a basic principle that is one of the pillars in the foundation of Vodou: Je. After assiduous attendance at many lakou, I ended up with a genuine document woven from things seen and heard.

Aunt Tansia often asked what was most important to me. My answers always varied. Sometimes I said finding God; at others, understanding the truth of Haitian Vodou. She burst out laughing every time, as if she didn't take me seriously.

Once, I was so upset I got the hiccups. She patted me on the back to calm me down. Her gesture only increased my nervousness. My hands began to tremble. Between hiccups, I managed to ask, "What are you laughing at?"

"You!"

"Me? Why do I make you laugh?"

"Because you are laughable, that's all."

These words reawakened my sadness. I felt consigned to the lowest level. I had always thought of myself as a confident woman. Now, as the result of her laughter I lost all my self-assurance and began to doubt myself. The hiccups shaking my body only made me look more ridiculous.

"Do I seem mad in your eyes because I am searching for truth?" I asked her in a tone of reproach.

She did not stop laughing. I was on the point of shedding tears, but I closed my eyes so as to hold them back. I made a last effort to appear indifferent, but my hands betrayed me. They were trembling. She shook me forcefully and said, "You are laughable not because you are searching for truth, but because you have such fixed ideas on the subject of truth."

Her words comforted me. My hiccups disappeared. "How can you say that I have ideas that are completely fixed? That is a 'prejudice,' Aunt."

"Which truth are you seeking? Can you at least state what truth is?

"I mean supreme logic," I answered. I would never have given this response if I had known that my own thought had in fact trapped me.

"You contradict yourself. On the one hand, if you know the definition of truth, what do your steps to seek it represent? On the other hand, if it is supreme logic, how can your limited intellect find it in order to put it to the proof and explain it? For it contains in itself its own proof. As for me, I'm telling you the truth: that there are things that cannot be proven."

"For example?" I asked, excited by the idea of "catching her up," just to satisfy my need for revenge for having been subjected to her derision.

"The Spirit. If you are a researcher you must know that the truth is unfathomable, even if sometimes it is not absolute. There will always be some points left in question as if they could not be completely understood. Nevertheless, the proverb that says, 'He who proceeds slowly will surely arrive' can be applied during the entire course of time one dedicates to a work of research. It is a correct attitude for one who seeks the Truth."

"I disagree."

"Why?"

"Because it is not completely true that by going slowly one will surely arrive, because one risks wasting one's time and perhaps even dying on the way before having attained the desired goal."

"What logic! You are as right as I am. However, through experience, I know that going slowly at least allows us to be attentive to small details. For it is small details one has forgotten that often hinder the success of our efforts. Through these small details one discerns reality, and in reality there is truth."

"I want to know quickly, above all when the facts are there before me."

"Why such relentless drive?"

"So that nothing that concerns me can escape me! I love clear and precise answers for the things that interest me!"

"Answers about God and truth, isn't that so?"

"About God and Vodou," I replied forcefully. "It is my right to know the truth about Haitian Vodou. It is my culture. It is fair that I should at least possess this consciousness."

"Consciousness is only acquired through experience."

"How do you want me to be able to experience things without being able to formulate them?"

"Ask and you shall receive."

"I have been asking now for two years, but I've received nothing."

"You do not receive because you don't know how to ask."

"Do you dare to make me responsible for the fact that my questions have not been approved? Am I responsible for not knowing how to ask? I have followed your teachings to the letter. I have applied them as much as possible. Am I responsible for not knowing things that have not been revealed to me?"

"You are completely responsible. I am sorry for you."

"What else must I do, tell me! Lord, should I look for another master?" I cried out in desperation. "Who will teach me what to do?"

"No one. However, if you accept deep down the education that Ginen offers you, you will know how to act," Aunt Tansia answered me gently.

"That is blackmail!" I exclaimed.

"In effect, yes. However, it is also the path that will help you find the codes that will open up the door of Consciousness."

"Let's suppose that I accept everything, who will guarantee that I shall find the key to this door?"

"I will," Aunt Tansia answered in a dry, firm tone of voice. The sound of her voice touched the depths of my being. I looked at her. Our eyes met for a moment and I knew that she was telling me the truth. I stopped defending myself. I took her hand in a gesture of consent.

Four years later I had a similar conversation with father Bien-Aimé. He was more reserved but he evinced the same firmness. He was about eighty years old when I knew him. His physical appearance impressed me greatly. Slight of build, he was scarcely five feet four inches tall. He had a long face, slanting eyes and thin lips that inspired respect and evoked a kind of wisdom.

In his demeanor was firmness mixed with gentleness. I loved him from the moment I saw him. The timbre of his voice and the harmonious gestures of his hands when he spoke transported me to a place of trust and peace. I loved to talk with him. For the most part, I asked him questions about the structure of the lakou. What interested me was to learn from him the history of famous lakou such as Nan Kanpèch and Lakou Souvnans, to understand the inhabitants' way of life and also to understand the common bond uniting the members of the lakou.

"Ninety-nine-point-nine percent of the people in the lakou practice Vodou," he told me. "The vodouisant defines himself within his social group. Normally, he has been educated according to the principles of his group. His upbringing is such that his reactions are normally geared toward the cohesion of his group. And that is true from every point of view."

"I know that the lakou has its own principles. But who oversees them and on what foundation were they formed?"

"By Ginen-an. The foundation rests on a certain logic: The earth is indivisible."

"What are the reasons for such a rule?"

"It is because the price of land is also the price of life. The cost of living rises with the cost of land. When a population begins to multiply, the space becomes crowded and the price of land rises. When the price of land rises, everything becomes more expensive. That is why Ginen-an has ordered the protection of a portion of land that must remain indivisible: It is the demanbre, which we nevertheless continue to exploit for the profit of the whole group. The demanbre constitutes the savings bank in our economy."

Father Bien-Aimé was one of the people who most encouraged me in my research. He was not very talkative, but his answers always opened other doors for me. He reminded me all the time that he wasn't good at math; he didn't have a head for maps or numbers, he said. He was always so humble and frank that I was always very much at ease following our meetings.

"Father," I once asked him, "are there different kinds of lakou? Can you tell me that?"

"Yes, each lakou has its own character," he said quietly.

"How does one define the character of a lakou?"

"By its rituals and the Legba. One must always pay attention to that."

"What do you mean, 'pay attention?'"

"Ask the Spirit and it will tell you."

All three of us became quiet—Lòlò was there too. Then, after a rather long time, I dreamily repeated, thinking about Aunt Tansia, "Ask the Spirit?"

"Yes, but you must know how to do it. If you don't, you will not get an answer."

"Who can teach me the best way to ask a question so as to receive an answer?"

"Ginen-an. It is only then that you will know how to open doors."

"What sign will indicate to me that I have acquired this power?"

"The lwa will descend when you call and they will let you in on their secret."

"Where is the guarantee of truth in this practice? Who can attest to the authenticity of the scene of the descent of the lwa?"

"I can," he cut me off firmly.

Then he changed the conversation and said to me, "*Isit, nou sèvi lwa Ginen, lwa dawonmen.* (Here we serve the lwa Ginen, the lwa of Dahomey.)"

"In that case, is the character of the lakou Fon or Gede?" I included the Gedes because the Dahomey site belonged to them before the Fons. According to my reasoning, I told myself that the Gedes took their natural place in Rada rituals and in all the lakou of a Dahomey character. I situated the Gedes in the same pantheon.

"I don't know what you are talking about when you refer to 'Fon.' But as far as the Gede is concerned, this lakou does not have this character. Our lwa are instead *'dawonmen' fran-Ginen* (they originated in a "pure" vodou rite from Dahomey)."

In my innermost being I did not believe this last declaration because once I encountered a lwa Gede in the lakou. I was pregnant at the time. When the lwa saw me, it approached and lifted me up, despite my weight. When it put me back on the ground it gave me a loud kiss on the lips. With an authoritative gesture it lifted my dress almost over my head and moistened my stomach with its drink—a concoction much appreciated by the Gedes: a mixture of clairin and peppers. Then, with a complicit glance it said to me, "*Pa kite tèt zozo kale a konnen sa mwen sòt fè la pou ou-a.*" (It isn't necessary to tell the bald head [slang for a circumcised penis] what I just did for you.)" Traditionally, the Gedes are great hosts who create diversions around them and use bawdy language. I knew that he was talking about father Bien-Aimé.

As I recalled the scene I asked father Bien-Aimé, "Do I have the right to know the reasons for this limitation?"

"We respect the Gedes and we never fail to salute them in our ceremonies, but we have received a formal order not to let them dance freely in the lakou."

"Why not?"

"It is the principle ruling this lakou. Such is the order left us by Nèg Ginen. That's the way it is. We don't receive other lwa, above all, those who are not Ginen."

"I thought that all the lwa were Ginen because, by definition, a lwa is an enlightened being."

"My child, all lights do not have the same intensity. And it is so that all colors do not have the same hue. Apart from primary colors, there are others that are nuanced and modulated. Therefore, there are lwa Ginen and there are also those who are *vapé* (emanations) from a lwa Ginen."

"Well, what is a lwa Ginen?"

Father Bien-Aimé did not answer my question right away. He got up from his chair and stood before me face to face. His gesture reminded me of my mother, who waited that way for me—when I was a child—to take me somewhere. He looked me straight in the eyes, and I tried in vain to evade his glance. Because, like a lover, his eyes attracted me and held me. He smiled, and his face was open and illuminated by a light that came from inside. He was beautiful. His left eye sparkled.

I didn't understand right away what he expected of me. Then I, in turn, got up from my seat and joined him. We were face to face contemplating each other. My heart was beating wildly. Still, I was not afraid. I scarcely felt so much as apprehension. He took both my hands and breathed on my palms. He closed my hands in a gesture of prayer.

I didn't entirely understand his gesture. He came very close to me and rubbed his forehead against mine. I felt a kind of warmth, a bit above my eyelids, between my eyebrows. Suddenly I became conscious of a quivering at the level of my neck and a sort of tingling on my scalp. I wanted to scratch it, but he stopped me and said, "Don't touch anything, let it come."

I didn't move, but, in an instant, I lost all sense of continuity. I was both conscious and unconscious at the same time. I moved between two states, completely whole at one and the same time in these two parallel worlds. I saw myself standing up in the place where I was before, and at the same time I saw myself perched on the poto mitan. I don't know how long it lasted. But finally, I saw father Bien-Aimé, who offered me a jug of water. I drank from it, then he sprinkled my face and my head with it. I was filled with new energy. I had no doubt about the animating force behind it. But I had no desire to talk about it. I had understood something for which I had no explanation that could be put into words. "Aunt Tansia was right," I confessed to myself, "when she told me that the truth is not always verifiable."

After that, I visited many lakou. I came to know at least one hundred. From north to south, passing through the Artibonite and the west, Lòlò and I visited lakou whose character was Kongo, Rada, Petwo, Mandingo, Bizango, and so on. Lòlò always went first, and then he took me there when I notified him that I was ready. I pursued my investigations of the idea of Je.

The heads of these lakou always made us welcome. They had a highly developed sense of hospitality. To begin with, we always waited before the entrance of Legba, for the *adjenikon*[77] or someone to come escort us into the sites and present us to the different personalities of the society. We were always served a cup of coffee as a gesture of welcome.

According to Aunt Tansia, all these good manners were

---

77 A sacristan, of sorts, who knows all the secrets of the kay mistè, often responsible for the lakou chorale.

taught to us by our African and native ancestors. We must follow the rules of hospitality; all visitors have a right to respect. The person who enters your house does you the honor of his presence and must be made to feel appreciated.

"Is this rule generally observed?" I asked her once. "I don't know how I could show sympathy to an enemy who might enter my house. Frankly, my heart would not be open to receive him. I would not even dare to open the door to him."

"First of all, you shouldn't have enemies," she advised me.

"Impossible, Aunt, impossible!" I cried. "Are you asking me to love the person who has done me wrong?"

"Listen carefully. I'm not asking you either to love or hate. But rather to remain equal to yourself."

"Indifferent?"

"No, being equal to yourself means being above events and situations, it is to be in a watchful state of Pinga-pye, it is to remain in kounye a-la-a."

"It is truly difficult to achieve self-mastery."

"It must be won. It is not only a question of knowing what the other represents for you, but also of taking what he brings to you and transforming or manipulating it. That is the secret leading to mastery of our personal power."

"But if someone comes to my house with the intention of killing me, would I have enough power to manipulate or transform his intention?"

"I don't know whether you have cultivated your power so as to be able to do that. Because that takes a lot of energy, but normally every responsible person ought to have enough magic to be able to manipulate no matter what kind of force. If not, the lakou would not have enjoyed this stability."

"That is true, you are right. I have noticed that in all the lakou I have visited, the people are extremely amiable. They welcome anyone without the least formality. I used to say to myself that these people were too naïve and that misfortune could strike them."

"Don't fool yourself. They aren't naïve. On the contrary, it is the stranger who ought to watch out after his visits. If not, he risks emptying himself of energy."

"How? I don't know what you mean."

"Do you think that all lakou have the same orientation? The stranger will always be welcome, of course, but that isn't the end of it."

"Then, their hospitality is feigned?"

"It is a mask and at the same time a sign of being well brought-up. It does not follow that to be well received in a lakou means that one is accepted by the lwa of that lakou."

"Aunt, when one is accepted, will one have access at the same time to certain secrets?"

"There is still another step to be taken in order to achieve that. Even a lakou head doesn't know all the secrets of the lakou for which he is responsible."

"What must be done to gain the intimacy of the lwa?"

"Nothing special. Ginen-an confides what he wishes to whom he wishes."

"Does this hold true for even superficial things?"

"Everything is implanted in the *nan rasin nan* (in the root). The lakou space is organized according to principles that are universal and rigorous."

"But why doesn't it evolve? Why is there so much misery? Where there is so much discipline shouldn't there be a kind of evolution at the same time?"

"There is no misery in the lakou," Aunt Tansia corrected me. "There is poverty and modesty. They must not be confused."

"Can you explain to me the reason for this poverty?"

"First, I want to say one thing: The lakou is always on the defensive. The lakou heads do not have sufficient courage to take the offensive against other systems that tend to invade us. The effects of slavery have left us with a fear of expressing ourselves completely. Our expressions are always *mawonnen* (coded)."

"Do you think that this can explain the economic poverty of the lakou?"

"I have told you that there is no economic poverty."

"But do you agree that a static economy is necessarily in crisis?"

"Tell me about the economy of the lakou, you who know about it."

"In the lakou, people do not own any material goods. They are all penniless, like outcasts."

"You lie when you say that they do not possess any goods. You do not know the economy of the lakou. Go do your research on the demanbre, then you can tell me what the economy of the lakou is like. Whoever wants to talk about the economy must necessarily speak also of the common holdings. Do you know that the demanbre represents the holdings of the lakou?"

Then, in a rather long discourse, she continued to instruct me on the structure of the lakou, which she explained as follows:

1. The demanbre or Bitasyon represents the familial patrimony. It is the place reserved for divinities, where one finds the altar trees, the *pyebwa sèvi*. "The powers are transmitted from one generation to the next."

2. The sacred place called the *houmfò*, *badji*, *sobadji* or *kay mistè* is where the Pe are erected and also serves as a convent where the *kouche* (procedures, initiation rituals) are carried out for the new initiates.

3. The *peristil* or *lasal* is the place favored by the initiates and the profane when they join together to dance and celebrate with the lwa.

"The structure of the lakou," she told me, "is designed in accord with the state of consciousness of the founder; that is, it is based on a direct rapport with the unknown world, which can only be reached through trance. There are different degrees of trance. There are trances so deep that the *chwal* (individual possed by a lwa) can spend a month or more outside himself. There is the inspirational trance that writers, musicians, poets and artists in general are familiar with. There is the trance in which one sees and hears the spirits, the one that dreamers know. The trance of ecstasy in which one travels through distant regions in full consciousness. The ecstatic trance that the *dòktè fèy* (leaf doctor, or healer) knows, in which the initiate acts lucidly while his spirit communicates at the same time with other spirits."

This conversation helped me greatly. It also changed my

points of view on the lakou. Thus, in my conversations with father Bien-Aimé, I presented my arguments on the lakou and, awkwardly, asked him to help me in my research. Since I am reserved I do not generally like to ask anyone about anything. Father Bien-Aimé knew that about me, and, discreet as he was, he pretended not to have sensed anything so as not to embarrass me. He promised his good services and all possible information. I was honored by such a mark of collaboration and sympathy, proud of it.

Right at the outset of our meetings, I explained to him that I was not an imposter, but I needed to be certain on the subject of things about which I was doubtful. It was not my plan to play the role of the intellectual, for I was sincerely seeking knowledge. Since the lakou had attracted me, I searched for the codes of its existence, if only to satisfy my need for consciousness and to reassure myself about my theses. Father Bien-Aimé had pressed my hands as if to tell me that he believed in my sincerity. After that, a certain bond was forged between us.

"Whoever says 'codes' means numbers or letters," he told me. "I know neither. I am illiterate. I cannot help you in this area. However, I am ready to teach you things in other areas."

That day he spoke to us a lot about Jacques Stephen Alexis,[78] whom he appreciated greatly, and of Madame Odette Mennesson Rigaud,[79] whom he cherished. We spoke so much about these two that I felt very close to them, without having met them or even having read their works.

"These are the two most sincere intellectuals I have ever known. They poured their souls into their research," father Bien-Aimé said. "Jacques was brilliant. Ginen would have revealed everything to him, but he was in too much of a hurry. His visage shone with light, but he was not patient. He would have been one of the greatest Haitian heads of state if he had waited for the order of Ginen-an."

---

78 Jacques Stephen Alexis (1927–1961), a medical doctor, was a member of the Haitian Communist Party with international contacts. He was also a successful novelist.
79 Madame Rigaud (1936– ) is an ethnographer, photographer and student of Vodou who worked alongside her husband Milo Rigaud.

According to father Bien-Aimé, Madame Odette was an attentive and patient woman. She was remarkable and discreet at the same time. All her gestures were marked by simplicity and purity. "When she visited the lakou, before addressing whomever it might be, she unfolded her large white sheet right on the ground. She placed a white faience plate on it along with a candle and a jug of water; then she sat down and waited with open hands."

"What did these gestures mean?"

"She was a respectful woman. Her gestures translated for one thing into an offering, for another a prayer, an offering to Ginen-an in which the plate symbolized an invisible meal. A prayer to the guardian spirit of the lakou asking it to open the passage for her was symbolized by the candle. Madame Odette was truly filled with consciousness. She was also a humble woman. That is why Ginen-an gave her the gift of Je."

"Where is she? Does she come often to Souvnans?"

"I don't know where she is. But she always comes to Souvnans, though not in her physical form."

"Have you never thought to ask her what she was doing?"

"No, I didn't find that necessary. Since I know that she is called 'Ordre,' I am not going to bother her with such a fatuous and indiscreet question. Because she is optimistic and insistent, I know that she works to find complete enlightenment in her whole being. In a word, I know what she is doing."

Odette seemed like an extraordinary woman. This thought made me wish to meet her in the flesh in order to talk to her about my projects and ask her advice. I had a strong notion that she would be the only person capable of helping me. If I could have done so, when I took leave of father Bien-Aimé I would have turned back and returned to Port-au-Prince in order to satisfy my desire. But I hesitated to alter our itinerary.

Lòlò and I had been planning for three months to do research on Vodou in the border towns, researching the correlation between the Dominican *fandango* rhythm and the *salie* rhythm. Certain songs interpreted in Ouanaminthe to open the *sèvis*★ (rituals) fascinated us with their poetry, their melodies and the dances that accompanied their rhythms. The latter rhythm resembles a kind of Rada but has an added measure. Lòlò was interested in this rhythm and I was too; both of us had the intention of introducing it in new compositions for Boukman Eksperyans. But I also wanted to get away from Port-au-Prince, where prickly political problems disrupted social life. Nightlife, so to speak, had disappeared. I preferred to go *andèyo* (into the countryside, or the country beyond, as Gérard Barthélémy[80] has so well put it) rather than live in that chaos. Above all, I had a wild desire to see the town of my birth and my old friends.

So, after we left father Bien-Aimé, we went directly to Ouanaminthe; then to Cana, on the outskirts of Ouanaminthe. Both towns lie on Haiti's border with the Dominican Republic. In Cana we met a young boy who guided us to the very beautiful Jean-de-Nantes River that waters the eastern side of Haiti. On the road, we tried to strike up a conversation by asking about how people in the area lived. He told us that all the land to our left was a demanbre. The work there was done in *konbit*★ (collectively).

"Is it a lakou?" I asked him.

"Cana is a big lakou."

"Is everyone Vodouisant in Cana?"

"*Vodou! Adje! M pa konnen, non* (Vodou! For pity's sake! I don't know what that is)," he responded innocently. As he spoke, he smiled and rubbed his hands in a strange way. His gesture caught my attention, and I noted with surprise that his hands were very big. The size of his fist was not that of a child but that of an adult. The skin was wrinkled like an old man's. That intrigued me. I asked him if he worked with a hoe, thinking that perhaps working with that tool would have built up his muscles and prematurely aged his skin. He told me that he had never touched a hoe. "Is it because of my hands that you ask me that?" he asked.

"Yes," I confessed. "Your hands are too big for your age."

"Ah, well! Do you know how old I am?"

---

80 Gérard Barthélémy (1934–2007). French anthropologist and writer whose works on rural Haiti include *Haiti, la perle nue* (1999) and *Le pays en dehors* (1989).

"Not exactly. But since I have children I can say that according to your appearance you are eight or nine years old at most."

He burst out laughing. His laughter was contagious. We all laughed together and he took advantage of that moment of distraction to ask us to look at a cashew tree on our right, "I am as old as that tree," he said to us.

"Hmm," I murmured.

I went back to look at the tree, which was heavy with fruit. It dominated the space around it. Placed on a green hillock, the tree lent a special touch to the landscape. The three p.m. sun was shooting its rays through the branches. When I turned to speak to the boy, he was no longer there. Since we were walking along a path in the middle of fields of Congo peas, sugar cane and corn, I thought he must be hidden in the fields.

Then we came upon an old woman carrying a calabash on her head. After we greeted her, we asked whether she had seen a boy on the path.

"What does he look like?" she asked.

I thought for a moment. I realized that I had not noticed anything but the boy's hands and could remember nothing else about his appearance. We tried to describe him.

"It is Ti Dye, my grandson!" she exclaimed. "I left him at the river. He is getting ready to bathe. But how did you meet him? Who are you?"

Lòlò answered her. "We met him under the mango tree as you enter Cana. He offered us his services to guide us to the river. We are strangers and didn't know the way."

"Good luck, *mesye-dam pran bon ti beny!* (Monsieur, madame, have a good bath!)," she replied.

We walked more than fifteen minutes from that place without encountering a living soul. The area seemed sinister to me. We bathed for about two hours. At the very moment when we decided to leave we saw Ti Dye on the bank on the other side of the river, while his supposed grandmother was on our side. They faced each other and were tugging at a vine, like two children playing with a cord. They were having fun, laughing hard and ignoring us completely. For a moment I had the strong conviction that they were not human beings. I confided my feeling to Lòlò who said, "I also strongly doubt that they are human. Let's go."

We left hastily. There was no living soul on the return path. I was shaking. As I walked, I heard bursts of laughter coming from all sides. When we got to the place where we had parked our car, we had a surprise: Ti Dye and his grandmother were there, waiting for us. The two were still laughing. We got in the car without saying a word and drove off like a shot, not daring to look back. An hour later we were in Ouanaminthe. We went to my family's house, where they were glad to see us again. That night in Ouanaminthe, I couldn't close my eyes. I was in a hurry to find father Bien-Aimé to tell him about the scene in Cana.

At dawn we decided to leave, cost what it may, despite my parents' urging us to stay longer. Before coming, I had told them that we would spend at least two weeks, and they were vexed to see us go away so soon. But I didn't want to explain my sudden need to go.

As we passed through Gonaïves en route to Port-au-Prince, we stopped to see father Bien-Aimé and told him what had happened in Cana. We were very shaken by the story. "Don't be afraid of anything," he reassured us. "You encountered the guardian spirit of the Cana lakou."

"But they were living humans. An old woman and a child."

"The spirit is alive."

"They were flesh and blood, two distinct people."

"They merely appeared so."

"How can that be?"

Father Bien-Aimé smiled. "You remind me of Odette, when she saw Brav for the first time in the kay mistè, eating food that had been prepared for the lwa Marasa.[81] She could not believe her eyes. She spent a whole day asking questions on the subject of the Spirit. She has good Je, but sometimes has doubts about it."

"I would give anything to meet Odette."

---

81 Literally "twins," or doubles, representing the vertical and horizontal line, symbolizing innocence and humility; the active and passive force.

"What prevents you from meeting her?"

"No one can prevent me from seeing her. I am almost certain that I have some connection with this woman," I answered forcefully.

We left father Bien-Aimé very late in the afternoon to return, not without regrets, to Port-au-Prince.

Starting the next day, I began to discreetly question several people on the subject of Odette. I wanted to know if she was still alive. One person confirmed for me that she was living in Pétion-Ville. But in spite of the directions I received, I was never able to find her house. I ardently wished to see her, but this desire was never satisfied. Sensing my frustration, Lòlò asked, "Why do you want to see her?"

"I am sure that if I see her, something will become clear at the same time that will permit me to *see*. I have something to ask her."

"If this enters into the plan of the Spirit, you will meet her in any case. Whatever it may be, father Bien-Aimé on his own is a very good source of information. He can help you with your thesis."

"I know, but I have a great desire to see Odette physically and speak to her."

From that moment on, everyone I met and asked for information about Odette's residence kept telling me that she had left the country. That did not weaken my will to pursue my research on the lakou. On the contrary, the more advanced my research became, the more convinced I was of not being far from Odette, spiritually speaking.

In all the other lakou I visited after that, I always tried to direct the conversation to the characteristics belonging to the different models of lakou.

"Every lakou has its own character," each lakou head always assured us, as if it was an established fact and there was nothing more to discuss. But because each one instructed us according to how his own lakou was set up, I noted a difference between the *lakou-andèyo*★ (lakou in the countryside) and the *lakou-lavil* (urban lakou). I was able to see changes in the organization of the lakou-lavil. So it was that I never saw a demanbre, but I saw misery in all its filthy manifestations.

"You must pay close attention," man Choune warned us.

"Why?" I asked her.

"Because you could be duped by charlatans. Things have changed in the town."

"In what sense?"

"In the sense that certain lakou say they are Ginen but in fact they aren't. You must always ask the name of the lwa who dance in the lakou that you visit so that you will be aware in advance and won't stupidly make useless and regrettable promises. Above all, be careful about giving certain gifts—animals, for example."

The head of Lakou Déréal gave us a similar warning, with certain precise insinuations concerning certain families of lwa. He also assured me that Déréal was a lakou Ginen and only served lwa Ginen.

"What are the characteristics of a lakou Ginen?" I asked him.

"*Gen degre. Rada pa vle di Ginen, Kongo pa vle di Ginen, Petwo pa vle di Ginen. Lwa Ginen se Limyè-fran.* (There are degrees. Rada is not Ginen. Kongo is not Ginen. Petwo is not Ginen. The lwa Ginen is loyalty itself.)

Man Choune, sèvitè of the Lakou Nan Jisou—whom we had known for a number of years and in whom we had great confidence—gave us some other, similar definitions of Ginen. She taught us that there are nuances among the lwa, and that only someone possessing Je could see the difference. She also told us that the lwa Ginen didn't make the same demands as a lwa Kongo, a lwa Rada or a lwa Petwo, etc.

"Do you want to talk about rituals?" I asked her.

"The Ginen service is simple, and the magic is instantaneous. Even marriage (the contract) with a lwa Ginen is arranged differently."

"Man Choune, a marriage is always giving, giving, isn't it? Therefore, as I see it, the formulas must be the same?" I replied.

"You are partly right. However, there is a difference: The lwa Ginen never takes what has not been given to it, and with it the transaction is always very clear."

"Meaning?"

"It will never ask you for a chicken or a *kabrit* (goat). . . . only to take the life of your child, without your knowing."

"That would be an act of malice. How can one avoid being trapped?" I asked, sickened by this revelation.

"The lwa who say: Give me this or that and I will do this in return do not act in accord with true clarity. *Lwa Ginen se Limyè fran. Lwa Ginen pa mande bwè san moun.* (The lwa Ginen is an honest light [speaks with genuine clarity]. It never drinks human blood.) One must always be very aware of that."

We had spent more than half of that day conversing with man Choune about the lwa. At about six in the evening when we were hurrying to leave Nan Jisou to go back to Cap-Haïtien, Mike Tarr, a friend who was accompanying Lòlò to help with a ceremony, came to tell man Choune and me that he had heard something that sounded like drums.

"*Blan an gen bon zòrèy, wi!* (The foreigner has a good ear!)," man Choune exclaimed.

"*Se pètèt yon seremoni vodou k ap fèt. Annou pwofite ale ladan non?* (Perhaps it's a Vodou ceremony? Why don't we take advantage of this opportunity and attend it?)," Mike proposed.

"No," man Choune said, "I advise you not to go. I know the sèvitè of this lakou, *li mele, li sèvi ak de men, se yon ipokrit, se yon malfetè* (he is mixed up, he plays a double game, he serves with both hands, he is a hypocrite, an evildoer). His name is 'G.' He does not perform a Ginen ceremony. He plays at Rada, but the rhythm of the *ountongi* (the second drum) is not stable, which indicates his intention to do harm. Listen carefully to the rhythm."

A silence ensued after man Choune's remarks.

"I want to attend this ceremony. We won't stay long, nothing more than a quick look," Mike insisted.

"Go if you wish, but I'm warning you to be vigilant."

Lòlò and Mike left at about eight p,m., accompanied by César, one of man Choune's adopted sons. Three hours later, they knocked at the entry door of man Chouane's house. Blood was running down Mike's head, staining his T-shirt and slacks.

"Mike is wounded . . . ," Lòlò started to say, but man Choune interrupted him. "How did this happen?" she asked.

"I was looking at the drummers," Mike explained, "when I was suddenly hit in the head by a stone. I can't explain where the stone that hit me came from, since the door was shut tight and there were many people in the room where the ceremony was taking place. . . ."

"I told you not to go there, because this G is an evil man. This is not his first attempt. He has a nasty habit of doing things like this. The lwa he serves love human blood."

"I am afraid, man Choune," Mike said to her.

"Don't be afraid of anything. Let me dress the wound. It is not necessary to set off on a road to who knows where, and it doesn't matter how it happened. If you possessed Je, you would be able to see who struck you."

"I don't understand, man Choune," Mike said. "There were a lot of people in the room, why did he choose me?"

"That's what happens when one doesn't pay attention."

A long silence ensued following her reflection. Then we all began to laugh, with a laughter that was contagious. Mike laughed even more than the others. But I was trying to understand something. I was distressed.

"Man Choune, tell me, how were the elders able to learn to distinguish one lwa from another? How were they able then to pass on this teaching?" I asked.

"It was an immense labor, *monfi* (my child). For a long time there have been two kinds of sèvitè. First, those who are chosen by the Spirit in their mother's womb. They received all their instructions in Nan Dòmi. From all the information they received they devised a set of rules and began a line that has never been broken. This is what causes their teaching to remain authentic while at the same time it is always changing. All that is a mystery."

"How is the message transmitted?"

"Ginen an chooses the sèvitè and makes the connection between the liberated spiritual head (who has died) and his successor. One always has confidence in the one chosen by Ginenan. He always has Je. He is an Adja. '*Yon moun ki sèvi toujou Rete sou gad.* (An initiate always remains in a state of transcendent consciousness.)' "

Nevertheless, there is also the *Asogwe*.*[82] The latter is chosen either by the lwa or by men who force him to assume certain responsibilities. In that case, the Asogwe may be seconded by the Lanperè. This is because the Asogwe doesn't always possess Je."

"Is there a big difference between the Adja and the Asogwe?"

"The difference is that one uses his hands to make the lwa descend, the other uses his *Ason** (a sacred/ceremonial rattle, an attribute of magical power)."

I tried on many occasions to take up this subject again with man Choune. But she proved to be reticent. Once, when she was resting during the siesta, I took advantage of the moment to explain to her that I was not completely satisfied with her explanations on the subject of Adja and Asogwe. I wanted to know which of these servants had more power.

"The Adja is supposed to have more magical power. But if, after he has been chosen, he does not exercise his gifts, he is worth nothing."

"Does all that enter into consideration in defining the particular character of a lakou?"

"Yes, the Adja only becomes fran-Ginen when he fulfills the totality of his being. His lakou will be Ginen when all the lwa whom he has chosen to work in his lakou are Ginen. *Ginen pa pran kaka Je pou bè.* ('Ginen does not mistake shit for butter,' meaning the Spirit is not a dupe.) One must possess Je to know that not all the lwa are necessarily good. There are some who are very bad."

Her acknowledgement pushed me to reexamine my points of view on the subject of the lwa. Formerly, I thought that all the healing, helpful and jovial lwa were good lwa and therefore lwa Ginen. I never would have thought that a healing lwa could kill at the same time.

"A lwa is a being in search of energy," Aunt Tansia told me. "This is why he always has need of a human being to help him maintain his reserve of energy so he can remain alive. Nonetheless, not all the lwa have the same technique."

---

82 Initiate, *kouche*, that is to say someone who has followed the teaching of a line of priests in Djèvo.

In a rather long discourse, she explained to me again the behavior of certain lwa, "Some among them, looking after their earthly needs, demand that their chwal and their protégés provide for all these needs at a given date. They are to deposit their offerings on the Pe or under the altar tree consecrated for that purpose. They will receive favors in return: pwen, wealth, fecundity, health, protection against *wanga* (magic), *movezè* (the evil fortunes cast by magicians) and accidents of all kinds. Certain lwa take human lives in exchange for a magical power or a service rendered."

After a service over which she presided in Madjoro (a neighborhood not far from Pétion-Ville), I met madan Jacques, the sèvitè of that lakou. It was a friend who introduced us. He was so enthusiastic that we responded with a strong desire to meet her, and one night he took us to her house.

She was waiting for us on the verandah. She welcomed us with a jug filled with fresh water and a lit candle. She performed the Jete before the door then asked us to do likewise. I found her calm demeanor agreeable. She began the conversation with these words, "*Ginen pa Bizango.* (Ginen is not Bizango.) Whoever searches for Ginen must make his approach with pure hands."

We talked at length about Ginen and Bizango. She revealed many things on the subject that comforted me greatly. When I confided to her the false idea I had that all lwa were good since they were capable of doing good, she explained to me that a good lwa normally does good, but that there are lwa Bizango who also do good, although that does not make them Ginen.

"*Ginen pa Bizango.* That is a mystery," Madame Jacques affirmed.

"There is something I do not see clearly. I have always wanted to know the whole truth concerning the basic relationship between the lakou and Vodou. Certain revelations disconcert me. I don't know where to begin. Every time I have thought that I understood something I have always had to begin again."

"You must create a certain distance between you and your project. That is the only advice I can give you. Let yourself be guided by Ginen-an and you will find the right inspiration. Everything will be clarified for you."

"But I do not place any conditions on Ginen. Quite the contrary, I am always ready to sacrifice my life to my research. What leads me to despair is that I am not making any progress. The lakou interests me. I sense that there is something strong in this way of life but no one wants to reveal its secret to me. I feel abandoned by everyone."

"The secret is in the konbit, my child. Communitarian life is guaranteed by sharing, solidarity and mutual aid. That defines the economic dynamic."

"Have all these behaviors been imposed from without?" I asked.

"Everything has been studied and planned by the lwa."

"How is it that these rules are observed without any apparent pressure?"

"There are codes that are written in a certain way, somewhere, with their prohibitions."

"Where and when were they written?"—I was thinking of the ceremony at Bois Caïman.

"In the memory of every Haitian," Madame Jacques responded.

"I thought for a moment that during the ceremony at Bois Caïman the ancients had taken the occasion to write down these codes. Bois Caïman is a corruption of *bwa Kay Iman* (the woods of the house of the Iman)."

"Vodou is a very ancient religion. There was Vodou before the ceremony at Bois Caïman. Vodou is the Spirit, the Mystery, the Invisible. The Unknowable. It is a complete philosophy of life. One need only live it to comprehend it. Everything has been elaborated over the centuries with a great deal of care. Among other things, are you aware of *sèp*?[83]"

"Yes, I saw it at Lakou Souvnans. What do you make of this phenomenon? Explain it to me, if you please."

---

83 Immobilization of the legs; a kind of punishment inflicted on slaves whose legs—one folded over the other—were enclosed in a sort of wooden box. In certain lakou, the adepts who strayed beyond Vodou morality—that is to say its prohibitions—punished themselves with this sèp by the order of the lwa.

"The sèp," she responded, with a certain pride, "is the test that is very closely monitored by the lwa, for correction is the result of this form of pressure."

*A society built on such structures would be ideal,* I said to myself. *People would be more responsible. Perhaps it is the best way to change mentalities.*

"Do you know why Haiti is in this state right now?" Madame Jacques went on. "It's because people have ceased to fear Ginen-an. This generation has many prejudices that are unfavorable to *rasin nan* (culture). Young people let themselves be influenced instead by other currents that carry them far from their roots. This is unfortunate for Haiti."

This conversation plunged me into a more profound meditation.

"The lakou," Aunt Tansia told me, "is a well-defined geographical space. Yet, civil authorities have no power over this space. And in 1915 even the American military was only able to touch the foundations of the lakou in a superficial way. The lakou has undergone many humiliations. That is why it seems moribund and no one bothers about its fate. A campaign of disinformation has made Vodou responsible for the country's poverty with the goal of leading Haitians to choose a different way of life. The inaction of the lakou heads makes them complicit. Are you aware that all of that contributes to the degradation of the country? *Se konmsi pa gen granmoun nan lakou a.* (It's as if there were no adults exercising good judgment in the lakou.) Do you know what has caused all this misery in Haiti? It is because people have profaned it by violating the sex of its plants. Haiti weeps at having been separated from its trees, its dearest friends. It is filled with sorrow at the disappearance of its birds and animals. When I was young there were forests everywhere. Giant, majestic mapous, *anakayit,* coconuts and palm trees embellished every public plaza and elegantly covered all the hills with splendor. The life of the people and the animals was less threatened. There were few illnesses. The trees protected us. We nourished ourselves with their fruits. In those days the air was pure and filled with bird song. Domestic animals roamed happily through the streets. They did not fear for their lives; little meat was eaten, not to say never. One gave only a *tisisin*★ (a small quantity of it) to children. People were healthy. Only with the arrival of the Americans did the eating habits of Haitians change."

"How did they bring about that change?"

"By introducing *manje nan bwèt* (canned food). *Gen yon seri de maladi ki tou debake an Ayiti an menm tan tou.* (From then on certain maladies also appeared in Haiti.) Eating too much red meat is also a cause of illness. Nowadays, even a doctor advises eating meat though he knows that certain kinds of meat cause *abse nan kannkès* (an abcess in the colon). Thus he becomes an accomplice in the destruction of the country. And this is so although the role of a doctor should be identical to that of a lakou head or a priest. But that is not the case, unfortunately."

"Is that all that illness consists of, Aunt?"

"*Kadav-ko a fenyan anpil. Depi li pa jwenn bonne nouriturre, l ap tonbe an fèblès epi l ap rive tonbe anba nenpòt lòt bagay ki pi fò pase li.* (The human body is so fragile! If it isn't well nourished it can easily fall into a dependent state at its first contact with another body stronger than itself.) Do you know that certain sentiments such as hate and rancor, for example, can provoke illness? Displacing a stone, killing a plant or any animal whatever can also be the cause of illness. The body's resistance keeps pace with the spirit that leads it. A sound mind lodged in a sound body. Illness is the effect of the mental state on the physical body. I tell you, it starts there. There is one rule and it applies to everyone. Do you know that the act of killing provokes illness?"

"In that case, Aunt, there is no escape, since man does nothing but kill to assure his survival."

"Rather, it should be said, to assure his supremacy. Man surrounds himself with cadavers and eats them to the point of satiety up to the moment when his own progressive degradation converts him in turn into a cadaver. The worst of it is that he has become the No. 1 enemy of plants and animals, and does not care. Man is constantly pursued by the conscience of these beings. Trees are the most rancorous."

"Is one pursued even when one kills in order to make sacrifices to God?"

"God does not ask for this kind of sacrifice."

"Nevertheless, in Vodou, one does not forbid offering animals whose throats have been cut to the lwa. Judaism has also done this in the past."

"There is a mystery in this practice. Certain lwa demand the blood of their protégés. Sacrifices stem from this belief. The sacrificed animal consents to give his life, he accepts his dying as a sacrifice. What is more, the officiating priest assumes responsibility for the involvement of the faithful who are present. Religions have invented the rite of purification so as to exempt the priests from all the consequences of the blood they have shed."

"I would like to act differently toward plants and animals, but how can one manage to live without them? There is no other choice."

"You are quite right. We cannot live without them. We are made to cohabit. It follows that we must help each other. Like all living things, they have a right to respect. Even when one cuts a leaf on a branch it is always necessary to ask permission from the plant and make sure to cut the branch at the knot and never in the middle. Then it is necessary to dress the wound by putting a bit of mud on it. Above all, it is necessary to talk to it during the whole time of the operation."

"Telling it what?" I asked her, in disbelief.

"Asking for its cooperation, to give a little of its energy through its leaf or its bark, to grant pardon for having hurt it, for wounding a part of it and for having made its blood run." She was referring to its sap.

I burst out laughing. I found that childish, and I told her so. "All that for a plant?" I exclaimed. "It's too naïve."

"It's necessary to be polite to all living things without exception as much as to human beings. Listen, would you like for someone to lift up your dress and *rache pwèl anwo do bouboun a ou* (pluck out hairs from your pubis)?"

I burst out laughing and she seized the opportunity to tickle me under the armpits. I laughed harder still. I never imagined that Aunt Tansia would speak to me of sex at that moment. She also laughed heartily.

"It's not the same thing, Aunt."

"When you touch the leaves or the flowers of a plant you are touching its sex. The structure of a plant is inverted. Its head is in the ground—its roots. Its torso is its trunk, and its sex are its branches and its leaves."

Then she made me understand a lot of things on the subject of plants: for example, that certain plants are allied, that birds and even some insects can become allies, and also the role played by birds and bees during the time of flowering, which is the time when plants are pollinated.

What she told me concurred with what I had learned of plant physiology. She convinced me that plants were living beings that could suffer, love and hate. That is to say, they can experience feelings just as human beings do.

There was regret and anger in her voice all at the same time. I listened religiously. She bent down and wrote on the ground with her finger. I didn't understand the markings. They resembled Indian (Taino) writing. She stood up and struck her chest three times, crying out in a strong voice, "*So djèmè twa fwa! Nan Ginen tande!* (In truth three times! I take Guinea as witness!)" Then she said, "Listen, I am going to tell you a story. Be sure not to forget it."

"No, I'm not going to forget it."

"But if that happens, don't hesitate to tell me so."

"I won't."

"You must tell it to the children some day." She asked me for a chair, and I brought it to her.

Aunt Tansia sat down, took out some tobacco from her little jar, stuffed it in her nose, and then began to sing:

*Fèy o! sove lavi mwen.*
*Nan mizè mwen ye, O*
*Pitit mwen malad*
*Mwen kouri kay Gangan (Ougan) Similò*
*Si li bon Gangan (Ougan)*
*Wa sove lavi mwen*
*Nan mizè mwen ye O!*

Leaves! Oh! Save his life for me

194

I am miserable, oh
My child is sick
I'm going to visit Ougan Similò
If he is a good Ougan
He will save his life for me
I am in misery, oh!

When she finished singing, she said:

"There was a country, a very small country, the most beautiful in the whole world. There was not a single flower one could not find there. This country exuded a soft and sensual perfume. The sky and the clouds were enamoured of it. They looked lovingly at it, sprinkling its land with rain all day long, by way of a caress. The land smelled of life. This land was blessed, and its bosom was fecund. It was verdant. There was no lack of food. Everywhere one could see waterways crisscrossing the mountains, cooling the temperature of the plains, which the sun's amorous ardor burned with its fire. There was not a living soul who, after discovering this country did not love it to the point of obsession. Even strangers who set foot on its soil didn't want to return to their own country.

"Among the clouds there was an enormous and frivolous one in particular that nourished a kind of crazy passion for this country. For centuries it looked for ways to seduce this small country in order to have the exclusive right to water its land. Jealous and possessive, it wanted the country for itself. It would have made war on the other clouds if it hadn't been chained—the consequence of an amorous overture that it had previously undertaken with a continent. Compelled by its devouring love, it had descended on it with all its strength during their amorous effusions, which caused the continent to be swallowed up tragically. The Spirit put the lover in chains for a period of about one thousand years, while periodically granting it a day of freedom every twenty-five years.

"However, despite all these precautions, this cloud caused nothing but irreparable material and spiritual harm throughout the land on each day of its freedom. Whence its surname, *Mèt*

*Dega*★ (destroyer of celebrations). For five hundred years men of all countries worked on plans and projects making use of nature to strengthen their constructions in order to defend against the misfortunes caused by the frightful cloud. But during the passage of Mèt Dega a mere second sufficed to wreak total destruction on an entire town.

"Mèt Dega enchained was frustrated and hateful when it saw the incessant flirting of the little country with the other clouds, this country it so desired to caress in its turn. Filled with bitterness while it waited for the day of its liberation, it increased its moisture until it turned an opaque gray.

"In addition, a woman whom no one ever called by her name also lived in this country. Everyone called her *man*. She was a woman of exceptional beauty. She didn't wear jewels and always dressed in cloth made of raw cotton. According to public opinion, she was fulfilling a vow, perhaps in order to have a child. She was, however, over sixty, but who knows whether she was waiting for a miracle—like Elizabeth, the mother of John the Baptist. Nevertheless, her house was full of children of all ages, whom she called *pitit an mwen-yo* (my children). There were some *vye granmoun* (old men) as well, who also called her *man*. This woman always got up at the first cock crow, four a.m. sharp. Her first act was to open the back door of her house. Provided with a white jug filled with water in her right hand, every morning she always went to the same spot, her left hand placed on her stomach and the other holding the jug over her head. Then she turned to the east, patiently waiting for sunrise. From the moment she saw its first rays pierce the sky she began to mumble things no one could understand. She spoke *langaj* (coded, onomatopoeic words), the old people said. Then, with a supple movement, she poured out the water from her white jug, bowing to the four cardinal points.

"When she finished, she stood under a large mapou tree in the courtyard of her house to make the coffee. During the day, the branches of the tree served as an arbor where she could rest and work. She used to sit either on one of the many above-ground roots of the tree or on a small chair. And, with her hands, she carefully sifted through a big pile of ashes left by years of cooking fires. What intrigued some people and confounded others was that this woman had neither a piece of pinewood nor a match to light the fire. With her hands, she tirelessly sifted the cinders, her head raised, until she sensed the heat of a spark. Then she smiled and bent her head to look more closely. She scattered the cinders, just as a chicken does with dirt, and when she spotted the spark, began to blow on it until it turned into a big fire. Then she placed *twa wòch dife* around it as a support for the pot in which she prepared the *manje pou ti moun yo* (the children's food). Next she poured out the coffee, filling up her white jug with it and sprinkling it on all the roots of the mapou tree. Then she called all the children and gave it to them with bread for breakfast.

"All day long she fed her fire with the dry wood of the *bayawonn* (mesquite). She fanned it with a big *layo* that also served to winnow the foodstuffs with which she prepared her recipes.

"One day, while this woman was facing the sun and performing her habitual rites, behold, suddenly a shadow covered the whole land. Passing her left hand over her eyes and thinking that she had lost her Je, she cried, 'Have I lost my sight?' She knelt and said a prayer, '*Bondje pran swen ti moun yo, souple*. (My Lord, I pray that you will take care of my children.)'

"During this time, laborers in the fields found themselves nailed to the spot, while the animals let out cries of distress and a chorus of dogs began to *wouke* (howl). People heading for their offices bumped into each other in the streets. The darkness was so dense that no one could see anyone else.

"Groping their way through the dark, women searched out matches for a little light in their houses. Some found them. But others searched in vain. In these houses, despair took hold; children cried, overcome with fright.

"During all this time, the woman dressed in syam cloth was on her knees until an inner voice finally revealed to her that that day marked the day of freedom for Mèt Dega. She struck her chest three times as if she were taking an oath. Then, following this gesture, the memory of her commitment came to mind, the vow of chastity that she had taken in exchange for grace and the safety of this little country from the evil designs of Mèt Dega. Her prayers and her dress of raw cotton were proof of it. Feeling betrayed, she got up and stepping firmly she strode into the darkness as if it were broad daylight. She walked without hesitation toward the east. She walked with the stride of a warrior.

"She was going to fight to demand justice. She went forward, decidedly, toward the place where the sun rises. When she got there, she raised her left hand and began to sift through the clouds just as she was used to doing with the cinders. But this time her head was lowered, concentrated on what she was doing. As soon as she felt warmth on her fingertips, she raised her head and saw a small spark of light. Then she began to expel her breath with all her strength. She blew hard to dislodge them and the clouds opened up in a space as big as a fist. She inserted her whole right hand, with her white jug filled with water, using all her strength in order not to *bite* (stumble). The sun recognized the white jug and the hand of the woman who waited every morning at dawn to greet him. He asked her, 'Woman, what are you bringing me?' 'A jug filled with tears.' 'Why are you crying, woman?' 'I am crying for my country. Behold that today Mèt Dega is free. He is standing in front of your door and hides your face from us. He is going to profit by taking over all the terrain of my country, at the price of our lives.' 'What do you want me to do, woman?' 'Remove him from in front of your face and before all the land. You alone have the energy necessary to make the darkness disappear, I ask for your help.' 'You shall have it, woman,' the sun reassured her.

Then the woman began to sing:

*Mwen vini kote a w. O! Mouche sole*
*M vin mande w limyè*
*Pou pitit a ou ki nan twou fè nwa.*

I've come to your side. O! My dear Sun
I've come to ask for light
For your children who're in the hole where it's dark.

"The sun didn't stop smiling warmly while she sang,

charmed by her sweet voice. As the sun smiled, the cloud dissipated. It contained water, a lot of water, *Lavalas*★ . . . *dlo desann!* (A massive torrent of water came down!). Houses collapsed. Furniture, animals, people, armoires, jewel boxes, and tools were carried off by the flood. 'What misfortune!' the survivors cried out, 'What have we done to deserve this?' The wild and pitiless water also carried along poisons that infected children whose small bodies jerked with *malkadi*★ (epilepsy). A strange and contagious tic attacked adults—their mouths gaped open as if they were starving. This absurd gesture filled their heads with a torrent of air that muddled their reason. It was impossible under the circumstances to imagine how to meet Mèt Dega's challenge. They began to groan like weaklings and blame each other for the collapse of the country.

"Then the women decided to ask for help from strangers who had loved the country. The woman dressed in syam cloth returned and as she viewed this sight sang still more strongly for the sun:

*Mwen vini kote a w. O! Mouche sole*
*M vin mande w limyè*
*Pou pitit a ou ki nan twou fènwa*
*M vin w lavi*
*Pou pitit a ou yo ki malad*
*Ki kouche sou do . . . O!*


I come to your side. O! My dear Sun
I come to ask for your light
For your children who are in the hole where it's dark
I come to you [for] life
For your children are sick
And lying on their backs . . . Oh!


"Then the sun, all smiles, answered her by singing about his contentment at having made the wicked cloud disappear.

*Ale nan bwa*
*Ale chache fèy-yo-wè*

*Ale chache fèy-yo- wè*
*Ale chache fè yo wè limyè*

Go into the forest
Go look for leaves of power
Go look for leaves of power
Go look for leaves, they'll see the light.

"'There are no more trees, the waters have carried them off,' the woman replied, anxious to return home to inquire about her children.

"On the way back, people lowered their heads when they saw her. She understood then that she no longer had children. But a little girl had survived who'd had the presence of mind to cling to the mapou roots at the moment when she saw the avalanche of water coming down. The waters had carried away the cinders of the fire from the past that were under the mapou, though it had not erased the spot or the memory. The woman sighed, 'Lavalas has extinguished the spark of my cinders, I have nothing more to do. My story has ended. I must leave.'

"'Don't leave me, *man*, another story will be found,' the child sobbed.

"'You will write it, my child, As for me, I am exhausted. I must go away.'

"The woman bore her pain bravely because she was a fighting woman. For ten years she fought against the stinking waters. She decided to pray without eating anything until the country was completely freed from the rest of the avalanche of water that was still stagnating and causing epidemics. She prayed every day, and her body lost weight until it became a skeleton, and then a shadow. Then the child, in view of her *man*'s fading away, said, 'Don't leave me like this, *man*. Go back to King Sun to ask him to help you once more, just as you did on the day the avalanche of water began to descend on us. You are a fighting woman, a woman who, whether she wins or loses, knows how to control events and maintain her equilibrium. I believe in you, *man*. You do not have the right to leave resigned like this.'

"One morning, she got up and called the child, "Come with me. I can't walk by myself any longer. Hold my hand. I am going to see King Sun again.' 'Don't forget to take an offering this time!' the child exclaimed. 'What gift could I take him? I don't have anything.' 'Me, *man*, consecrate me to King Sun.'

"She obeyed the innocent child and prayed to the Sun. He was very happy to see her again as well as the child she introduced to him. He advised her: 'Go assemble all the strong young people and tell them to form a big konbit in order to channel the wandering waters of the flood that will later serve to water the dechouke terrain. You will see your country flower again as in former times. Trees will once again bear fruit. You will reconstruct your country according to your wishes and it will be even more beautiful than before.'"

I had completely forgotten this story. Aunt Tansia had told it to me through a woman's voice one morning in January 1989, while I was in Nan Dòmi. I listened to it joyfully. I retold it to a friend, Régine Laroche, who was visiting me that day. She asked me to record it for her on an audio cassette. I did so with pleasure.

"Mimerose, you must write it down, it's absolutely necessary. . . ."

I brushed her off. "Perhaps some day; I'll think about it."

"It's necessary to do it now," she advised. "There is no future guarantee, do you understand? Who knows what the future. . . ."

"You are right," I said to her, thinking about Aunt Tansia. I recalled the time when I begged Aunt Tansia to teach me how to read the future in the cards. She mocked me and said, "*Ou ta renmen fè bòkò-divinò, ti madanm*? (Would you like to become a fortune teller, little miss?)"

"Oh no, that's not my intention."

"But you are asking me to help you."

"You are teasing. I only wanted to verify whether there was any truth in it. At bottom, I know that cards are a game of chance."

"To know how to deal the cards or not is not the most important thing. What is important is to have Je. There is neither future nor past. Things are consequences, some things consequences of others."

"What place do you assign to prophecy, Aunt?"

"There is no prophecy that holds water. I don't give a damn about them!"

"The Bible speaks of prophecies. All religions speak about them. You cannot ignore them."

"What is prophecy?" she asked.

"Prophecy, according to the *Petit Larousse* dictionary, is 'the prediction of a future event.'"

"Well, I am not a prophet, even though I can read in your eyes and *see* that you will have a little boy very shortly, and one day you will weep over the loss of a child." I was one month pregnant and didn't know it.

"How do you know that?"

"*Paske mwen gen Je, mwen wèy*. (Because I have Je. I see it.)"

"What else do you see?"

"That you are afraid."

"Of what?"

"Of suffering. Because you stay wedded to the double dimension of good/evil. Because you are a hedonist, you love everything that can gratify your senses. That is why you are afraid of conflict."

"How do you know that?"

"Because I see it, I know it."

I knew that she was speaking the truth. But that didn't keep me from wanting to hear from her own mouth that she believed in the gift of prophecy.

"This is what prophets do: They predict the future," I retorted, to tease her.

"Well, I repeat that there is no future, there is only the kounye a-la-a. The future is the projection of our thought in time. Now, time is our invention. It is not real. It is a pretext to justify our laziness and our illusions. Do not put off until tomorrow what you can do today. Otherwise, you lose your opportunity."

"You told me once that it was necessary to proceed slowly in order to arrive unerringly, you remember, don't you? Isn't there a contradiction between that and what you have just said?"

"To proceed slowly is *pa èe tròp; pa bat kò-a ou. Sèlman, sonje leve bonnè wa wè leve a douvan jou* (No excess. Just make an effort to stay in a state of awareness and the mystery will be unveiled to you.) This is perspicacity. It is attention which sees everything. It is what helps us to act *an granmoun* (like an adult; impeccably.)"

"What must one do to proceed slowly? Because for me going slowly means wasting time."

"The discipline of Pinga-pye constitutes the ideal mode of being in order to exist in the present instant."

"What must I do to practice Pinga-pye?"

"Always hold to the path that leads to the heart of *M la-M pa-la.*"

"Are you confusing me? What does that mean? Aunt, you are really confusing me."

"The *M la*, is the 'I am'; the *M pa la*, is 'non-being.'"

"How do you define non-being?"

"It is the effacement of the kantamwa."

"How can one come to erase one's existence? I cannot imagine that."

"It is so simple, even too simple. 'Non-being' is the movement toward *toutouni* (nakedness, in the sense of formlessness)." Suddenly, she ordered, "Take off your clothes!"

I was going to follow her order. But with a movement of her hand, she stopped me and looked me straight in the eyes. Then I understood what she meant to tell me when she spoke of all my complexes and prejudices. For my mind, furnished with ready-made thoughts and ideas, was clothed with them. That was what blocked communication with the Invisible. Aunt Tansia was so sharp in her explanations that I asked myself whether she hadn't taken formal classes. How could she explain so many things with such facility if she hadn't had some kind of scholarly training? My seventeen years of studies (primary, secondary, university) did not mean anything next to her knowledge. I remarked on this to her.

"*Tande, pitit an mwen* (Listen, my child), it is very good to learn how to read and write, to have studied. Clearly, that makes it easier to communicate with other people, with other cultures through writings and readings. But that is not enough. It is also necessary to learn to read in the great book of life."

Knowing how to read, according to Aunt Tansia's explanations, was to possess Je. It was when I visited Lakou Palmine for the first time, at Lamontagne, that I reaped the first benefits from such a mode of teaching. I had been struck by these words: "The book of life contains innumerable pages. It is necessary to turn them over one after the other and perhaps, when one has not learned something well enough, it is necessary to return to the page that was not understood."

Lakou Palmine is one of the most beautiful places I have ever visited in the southern part of the country. It is situated a few kilometers from the town of Jacmel, on a beautiful hill that bears the name of Lamontagne. From the first hour I set foot on the soil of Lakou Palmine, I was transported by a sudden burst of joy. The color and odor of the earth made a strong impression on me. The least sound titillated my senses and drew my heart to the tips of my fingers. I was sensitive to everything as if I were a part of everything: I was everything and everything was me. I was a bundle of emotion. I laughed a lot. Man Tata had me visit the *Danti* and meet all the neighbors. I went everywhere with bare feet. The contact with the clay soil calmed my nerves, which were on edge after the voyage, which had lasted three hellish hours because of the bumpy road. I recall that people received us—Lòlò and the children accompanied me—to the sound of music from a rara band that danced the "warrior stick dance."

Man Tata, head of the lakou, told me: "Lakou Palmine constitutes an entire chapter in the history of Haitian Vodou. *Nou, se Ginen nou ye, nou pa mele! Vodou a gen de men, nou se yon dwèt nan men dwat-la.* (We, we are Ginen, we are not mixed! Vodou has two hands. We are a finger on its right hand.)"

"Was it there by order of the founder?"

"Yes, he was named Palmine. He returned to the country with a stone, which he had placed at the entrance to the lakou. *Sete yon sòt de Je.* (It was a way of seeing.)"

"Could he also see into the future?"

"*Tout kalite bagay*. (Absolutely everything.) He was as highly regarded as *Antoine-Nan-Gomie*.[84]"

"Who was he?"

"He was a great houngan, he was fran-Ginen. He genuinely possessed Je."

"Was he a prophet?"

"He was a man who knew how to read in the book of life. It held no secrets for him."

All the lakou-andèyo that I have been able to visit have a common feature, that of transmitting the importance of Je. According to them, a servant of Vodou who does not possess Je is an invalid servant. His magical force is thereby diminished. We found the same opinion among the inhabitants of a mandingo lakou which we visited in the north of Haiti, in one of the suburbs of the city of Cap-Haïtien.

This lakou, which was clearly different from the others we had seen before in the region, had also received a Ginen education by following the *Mori* (Vodou priest) Batèlmi. He brought a strong Muslim influence into the rituals and the rhythms that accompanied the purely Mandingo songs and dances. They called on Allah as they bent down, face to the ground, and during the sacrificial ceremonies Mori wore a large white tunic and a big scarf bound his head in the Muslim manner.

It was Gérard Barthélémy, my professor and thesis director, who first spoke to me about the existence of this lakou at a time when I was noting my difficulties in finding all the elements I needed in the end to support my research. He advised me to search further by directly exploring all types of lakou. I told him that I knew a lot but I always felt as if I were just beginning. He encouraged me to persist in my research.

"Don't be discouraged. If you come to write this thesis, you will be the first person to have carried out extensive research on the lakou. Go on with it, don't pause on the way. Even if it takes you many years."

I thanked him, but at that time I had lost all faith in myself.

---

84 Antoine-Nan-Gomie was a celebrated houngan highly regarded for his gift of clairvoyance.

I was going through the crisis all intellectuals face: the delay in handing over the thesis. Before we parted, he suddenly asked me, "Are you familiar with the several Mandingo lakou in the north?"

"No. I don't know any. I have never heard anything about Mandingos."

"Go visit them. I can give you an address. The head is called Mori Batèlmi. Go see him."

I thanked him again and suddenly felt quite excited by his revelation. I left to find Lòlò so that he could take care of all the preliminary arrangements: to look for all the information needed and leave first to visit our destinations. Lòlò was all enthusiasm when I told him the news, and he left for the north the next morning. He came back demoralized three days later and said to me, "I was not able to attend the service."

He went back in vain eight days later to the same places. That went on for three years. He used all means possible to obtain the favor of attending a ceremony. But engaged as we were in our music tours, we always lost our chance, whether we arrived too late or too soon.

Lòlò wasn't discouraged, however. He continued his visits until the day when he was finally able to win the friendship of the lakou's inhabitants. This time he returned completely amazed. His joy gave a boost to my flagging curiosity, because I was really discouraged at that time. He shook me out of my torpor by recounting his discoveries. Thus, one afternoon in the month of August we went to see Mori Batèlmi. Unfortunately, no service was planned. But Mori received us ceremoniously. "Why are you searching for Ginen?" he asked us in an authoritarian tone of voice. "*Isit nou se Ginen.* (Here we are Ginen.) In accord with the vow of Allah. All those who set foot here who are not Ginen will receive a shock that can be fatal." Then, addressing me, he said, "*Ki moun ou ye*? (Who are you?)"

"I am a researcher, a supplicant seeking understanding."

"You are a member of which lakou?"

"I am a solitary traveler," I told him. "I am not from a lakou. My Master departed without leaving me a place to rest."

"From whom did you receive your Ginen education?"

"From Tansia. Do you know her?"

"In Ginen we know everyone, even without having seen them physically. The Ginen principle is a universal principle, no matter where one comes from: from the Kongo, from Alladah, from the right or from the left. We recognize each other in the Spirit and by our practice. *Ginen pa Mazanza.*★ (Ginen is not Mazanza.)"

"*Ginen pa Bizango*," I added, to complete the saying of father Bien-Aimè.

"Mazanza and Bizango are part of the same tradition. Mazanza is hypocritical and cunning. One must possess Je in order to detect it. Because it approaches you like a Mater Dolorosa. Like a cat, it purrs and scratches its victim at the same time for no reason. Mazanza is naturally malicious."

I listened carefully to Mori's words. This information connected with that of the other sèvitè of lakou who give primordial importance to Je. Even the lakou *Bizango-andèyo* transmitted a message that was more profound than those of the towns.

At Léogane I visited another lakou Bizango. I was able to visit on a day when the service was organized by a family. The lakou sèvitè himself confided to us that it was a lakou Bizango and that we were to stand in the place he indicated in front of an orange tree. He explained to us that the lwa were very violent and that consequently they needed a lot of space for their movements.

At midnight, the sèvitè unsuccessfully called upon the lwa *Lisife* (Lucifer). But the chwal had him *mare* (tethered) somewhere because he was ashamed before the strangers who were there—he was a very handsome young man of twenty. He lived in a bourgeois neighborhood of Pétion-Ville. The sèvitè approached him and *foula* (blew) a liquid over his face. Suddenly, it was as if a lightning bolt had struck. Branches of trees were broken, a great noise coming from all directions filled the place. I could see everything from where I was. The young man who was possessed had put on a red tunic and ran from one part to another snorting through the nose, creating a wind that carried off everything in its path: plants, men and beasts. He uprooted a banana tree with one hand. It gave me goosebumps, but I didn't want to leave. It was a frightful spectacle, but I didn't want to miss it. The sèvitè told us later that the young man's great-grandfather was the founder of the lakou and that he descended directly from the Bizango tribe in Africa.[85]

"We are all Bizango, We are obliged to continue the tradition."

"Are you familiar with Ginen?"

"Yes, of course, but I do not know its pwen. I am strictly Bizango. The Bizango pwen is wholly different from that of Ginen. *Bizango ak Ginen. Yonn se bò kote palmis la, lòt la se bò kote papa Nò a.* (Bizango and Ginen. One is the tails side of coin with the palm tree; the other the side with 'Papa' Nord.[86]) Yet both of us have need of Je to be able to work."

"What does that mean?"

"Ginen and Bizango are two great schools, but they are different. Each one has its own perceptions."

"What are the perceptions of Bizango, can you tell me?"

"I can't teach you anything like that. Besides, you are not Bizango. When a person is not born Bizango, it is necessary to be initiated into Bizango practice before beginning to explore the Bizango world."

The sèvitè was a very calm man. He was very vigilant. Although he had a strong and authoritarian temperament he did not have the malicious air public opinion in general attributes to adepts of Bizango, imagining that they are simple assassins.

"*Moun tèt cho* (hot-headed people) can never manage anything. One needs patience for whatever one undertakes. Because *twò prese pa janm èe jou louvri* (too much hurry never makes the day open)."

The inhabitants of the lakou were so friendly that all my prejudices concerning Bizango fell away at once. They welcomed

---

85 The word Bizango may derive from the Bissango community that dwelled in the archipelago near the coast of Kakonda, between Sierra Leone and Cape Verde. Many of the first Africans in colonial Saint-Domingue were Bizango.

86 Pierre Nord Alexis was president of Haiti in 1902–08 and featured on coins minted at the time; the palm tree is a dominant feature of Haiti's national coat of arms.

us warmly. They prepared food for us, and when we wanted to reimburse them for their expenses they refused.

"Money is not the most important thing for us," an old woman said. "You are our guests, we are obligated to give you a bed, food and protection."

That struck a blow to my heart. There was a clear difference between the *Bizango-andèyo* and that of the town.

I recalled being in a lakou Bizango on the northeast side of Port-au-Prince. A friend, a member of the society, introduced us to the sèvitè. This person asked us for 100 gourdes at our first interview in exchange for information, which we handed over. Very pleased, he talked more than we asked him to, rambling about himself, his lwa, his numerous pwen, and the money he earned thanks to his cynicism.

"*Bakoulou-baka* is the Je of my badji. It helps me make a lot of money."

"Who is Bakoulou-baka?"

"It is a big lwa Bizango, a master in business. It teaches me to be crafty in drawing out money from hard sells."

He told us that he came from a lakou Kongo, but that people were jealous of him because of the importance of his gifts—even the people in his own family. That is why he was obliged to leave the family lakou to found his own lakou based on the Bizango pwen so as to protect himself from the evil designs of the other bòkò.

"Then," we asked, "you aren't Kongo anymore?"

"I am still Kongo and I am Bizango at the same time."

"Do the Kongo lwa and the Bizango lwa get along?"

"The lwa Kongo have no problem in working with the Bizango lwa."

"How is that possible? Isn't it said that the Kongo lwa are Ginen?"

"Not all of them. Sometimes, a Kongo lwa makes itself into Bizango. That is a mystery. Not all the Kongo lwa are Ginen."

"Ah, I see!" I said, astonished. "Is the lakou you founded organized with two families of lwa?"

"My lakou is founded on the pwen Bizango, but as for me, my practices are Kongo. I have a lwa Ginen who works with me, but it never comes during services. Usually, it only rides me when I go to my father's house. I became adapted to Bizango when I was very young after I was sick and was treated within a lakou Bizango. I suffered from malkadi and I couldn't learn anything at school. One of my mother's lwa came one day and revealed to us that my malady was caused by *Marinèt*★ (a female lwa). Then the lwa asked for me to be taken to a lakou Bizango so that the sèvitè could conduct a service for the lwa Bizango my mother had inherited from her grandmother. I was taken to a lakou Bizango in the Artibonite. After the service, I was cured. To *djanbwe* (make me stronger), the sèvitè sewed six gad on my forehead, my arms, legs and back. After that, I began to do extraordinary things. People set about envying me, accusing me of everything. This world is so wicked that it is always necessary to be wicked toward it, otherwise it is others who will be wicked toward you."

"Toward whom, the just person?" I asked.

"Toward everyone and especially toward those who do not love me. *Ayisyen mechan twòp!* (Haitians are too wicked)"

"One mustn't generalize there are also very good people."

"There are no 'very good people' on this earth."

"Aren't the Ginen good?"

"There are no longer any good Ginen. Now they are *Ginen-djòl, Ginen-mele* (hypocritical initiates)."

"Why do you say that?"

"Because even when someone calls himself Ginen, he kills, lies, cheats, steals, slanders. People here below are too busy seeking material goods to be Ginen. *Yo gen twòp lanbi. Yo bezwen gwo kay, bèl oto ak anpil grinòbak san redi.* (They have too much ambition. They dream of owning big houses, beautiful cars and plenty of money without making the least effort.)"

"To hear you talk, it seems that you are aware of the principles of Ginen teachings."

"My lwa Ginen tells me about many things that I cannot make use of. It is a lwa I inherited from my paternal side. It doesn't give me money; it refuses to let me get money. But I love it a lot. It is a good healer, but it never asks for money for its prescriptions. On the contrary, it takes my money and gives it to the poor." He laughed.

He became quiet and smiled mischievously, then he said, "Nevertheless, it is the one who protects me against danger and gives me good advice without asking for anything in return."

"Why doesn't it come down to your badji?"

"It is a lwa *tulututu* (pretentious). *Ginen pa mele ak Bizango.* (Ginen doesn't mix with Bizango.)"

"Why not?"

"*Ginen twò pwòp.* (Ginen is too clean.) Bizango has no problem. They are two entirely different tendencies. As for me, Bizango is my element. Only Bizango can stand up to this wicked world. *Ayisyen mechan twòp!* (Haitians are too wicked!) I want to be Bizango forever."

"What exactly have they done to you that you should have this fixed idea about everyone?"

"No one can do me wrong. I watch everyone. I don't trust anyone."

"Not even your relatives?"

"Not even them."

"If you don't trust anyone, how can you work with other people? Trust is the basis of progress."

"If I could get along without other people I would already have done so. But unfortunately, I cannot work completely alone. I am obliged to have people around me. But I am on the watch all the time, even before they might dare to think of dealing me a blow, I would have them all exterminated. If they attacked me, I would have them eaten up by *Marinèt manman lwa m* (Marinette, the mother of my band of lwa)."

"Have you caused anyone to be 'eaten up'?"

"To tell you the truth, I have put quite a few in the *ti pilon* (the little wooden pestle) of manman Marinette."

"Haven't their families caused you trouble afterwards?"

"What family could cause me trouble? Me, I'm strong." Then he began to laugh loudly and let out a cry expressive of disgust.

"Why did you have them *pile*★ (killed)?"

"I don't remember. Guilty or not, with me there's no chance of escape."

"What does innocence mean to you?"

"There are no innocents."

"Not even a baby?"

He didn't answer my question, but he pointed with his finger to a small coffin in the next room. I shuddered with disgust, exasperated by the day's events. His frankness disarmed me completely. I stopped asking him questions.

I saw him one other time, when he was officiating. The ceremony was macabre. It reminded me of Dracula movies. There were coffins everywhere of different sizes. A guilty person was tied to the poto mitan. He was going to be punished—cut up perhaps.

"Why is he tied up?" I asked the friend who had taken us there.

"He disobeyed the rules of the lakou."

"What exactly did he do?"

"He smoked while the ceremony was being prepared."

"Is it bad to smoke during the ceremonies?"

"The act of smoking is not bad in itself, but a Bizango ceremony is very delicate. It is necessary to enter the temple in a sound state. *Fòk ou veyatif anpil.* (One must focus one's whole attention.) If not, the lwa may feel offended and ask for the life of some adept as reparation."

"Why? Shouldn't the lwa, as I see it, protect the adept?"

"The lwa Bizango is irritable. Our world is a world of perpetual judgment, every fault is severely punished."

When I saw the sèvitè P, who is also a Bizango living in Croix-des-Bouquets—a suburb of Port-au-Prince—in a very beautiful lakou, I asked him for an explanation of the scene we had witnessed in the lakou C.S.

"That is a *pwen achte* (magic power which has been bought). It is complicated. It requires a great expense of energy. When one is born Bizango, one is no longer free."

"I don't see any coffins in your badji," I remarked, recalling the words of man Choune, who had warned me not to take any animals as gifts to this kind of lakou, because I would risk being made to eat them if I dared to do it.

"In our services our lwa drink a lot of blood. We are obliged to make large expenditures to satisfy them. That is because we are obliged to buy many animals. Our gad and our pwen are also very expensive, but that helps us cover the expenses of our annual ceremonies."

"Have you caused anyone to be killed?" I always had this worrisome idea in my head that the Bizango are nothing but motherless assassins.

"No, never. I could do it easily but I don't want my lwa to acquire this habit. My father forbade it. It is the rule of this lakou. However, I ought to tell you that once I was going to do it. I made an arrangement with another bòkò for him to do it in my place, but we spoiled the game."

"How did that come about?" I asked him.

"I got two daughters of a neighbor pregnant. The neighbor brought me before justice. I was humiliated in the eyes of the whole town. I wanted revenge. I was young at the time and felt offended. However, I was wrong. The planned blow did not take place. Then everything turned against me. I had to organize a great ceremony for all the lwa in order to pacify them. If not, I would be a dead man."

"Why? How could that happen to a sèvitè?"

"Because in order to serve Bizango it is necessary to know how to protect yourself from your own lwa. If not, they swallow you up pitilessly for the slightest error."

"What kind of fault, for example?"

"When you propose to make a human blood offering to a lwa Bizango, you cannot renege on your promise. If you do, the lwa will turn against you. To appease it, you must either give him a being dear to you, or offer it the blood of its choice of animal."

"That is truly upsetting. It is slavery," I allowed myself to insinuate.

"Everyone is a slave of what he serves," he answered with a sigh.

These words reminded me of Aunt Tansia's point of view on Vodou services. I asked her once why she never organized a ceremonial festivity. She responded that she lived in a perpetual ceremony and that she was freed from that form of slavery.

"All the lakou organize celebrations, if only once a year. You never participate with the pretext of avoiding the chains of this form of slavery."

"I am *Adja-Ewe-Balendjo* (above these services)."

"You also avoid talking about Vodou. You never use the same terms as the other sèvitè. Where is the Vodou in what you do and what you teach me?"

"I only try to put you in perfect communication with Vodou. I have made you see things that you never saw before in your life. I have taught you other ways of comporting yourself and other ways that belong to the unknown world. Only one thing remains for my work to be complete."

"Are you referring to Janbe? You remind me of that a little too often. I don't like it at all when you speak to me about it. I am in pain each time. I don't want you to leave us."

"Be still, you don't know what you are saying. I would not wish to delay my liberation for anything in the world."

"You cannot provoke it just like that."

"If I could I would already have done so. If you only knew what a great need I have for liberty! If you knew how much I look forward to this state, you would experience more joy in seeing me attain it than you do in seeing me remain a prisoner in this dimension. I must leave."

"But where do you want to go? Where are you going?"

She didn't answer me, but she closed her eyes. "There are four truths in one. The first says: 'You are dust, you will return to dust.' The second doesn't contradict the first but rather completes it: 'You are water, you will return to water.' The third is a little mysterious, it says: 'You are fire, you will return to fire.' The fourth has all its force and extraordinary magic: 'You are air, you will return to air.'"

"These four truths are summed up in one: 'Remember that you are Spirit.' When I have settled all my debts with these four elements I will have risen above the loans they have made me during the length of my apprenticeship in this dimension. I will finally be free!"

CHAPTER 14

# You Must Be Perspicacious in Order to See
# *or* There Are Conditions for Seeing

### Fòk ou gen Je pou ou kapab wè

Clearly, I wanted to benefit from the advantages that Vodou offered me. I wanted to understand the mysteries of Je. I questioned certain adepts about Je, but they only gave me superficial explanations.

For Aunt Tansia the important thing was to know the methods and means of gaining access to each world, of going there and coming back without causing damage to her Ti Bonnanj. Now, one cannot do that unless one is really *chwazi* (literally, "chosen," having a mystic calling) and possesses Je. One can easily be caught in a trap.

"One must wait for the right time," she never stopped repeating. "Everyone gets a call, but in a different way. The important thing is to be ready at the right time. One must be prepared in order to recognize the call. A certain aptitude and discipline is required to be a doctor, lawyer, woodworker, carpenter or whatever, isn't that so? Cooking rice or corn requires knowledge. In order to achieve mastery of any science, you have to undergo a series of tests. It is an inevitable law. Such is the universal order."

One afternoon we had gone to Duro, a suburb a kilometer from Ounaminthe. In response to an invitation from Jeantilus, Aunt Tansia asked Lòlò and me to accompany her. We accepted happily.

Jeantilus, a man of bad character, a long face, light complexion, thin, very tall—almost six feet—was the tenant farmer of a big farm at Ti Laurier on the great plain of Maribaroux. Every year, in September, he held a ceremony to mark the end of the season's work. He met us at the main gate with a jug of water in one hand and a lit candle in the other. Addressing himself to Aunt Tansia and completely ignoring us, he said, by way of a greeting, "I have been waiting for you for one hour. I thought that Zann"—Aunt Tansia's servant—"would accompany you. Why didn't she come? I am sorry she's not here."

He made a gesture with his hand that I did not understand, then continued in a grumbling tone of voice: "The day before yesterday, there was a konbit to harvest a field of corn, but the *tare* (field workers) did not respect the closing time."

Without even answering him, Aunt Tansia took the jug in her hands and proceeded to the ritual of Jete, then with her hand greeted the other people present in the large courtyard. She said gaily, "*M di, lonè lasosyete!* (I say, honor to the society!)" It was a way of greeting strangers. And everyone answered, "*Respè pou ou.* (All respect is due to you.)"

The place retained the scent of cut grass, which I loved. The air was fresh. Everything was beautiful: the big mapou, palm trees, coconut trees, mango trees heavy with fruit, the large co-lonial boiler filled with water where little frogs swarmed and croaked, the sugar mill, the horses that whinnied, the birds that came in great numbers to peck at the kernels of corn fallen on the ground, the children—a dozen of them—who were playing hopscotch and laughing loudly. Jeantilus threatened them with a beating if they continued to disturb the elders.

"Jeantilus," Aunt Tansia said to him, "Let the children play. Don't spoil their fun. What is bothering you? Is it because you can't laugh any more? *Ou serye tankou pis epi figi ou pòtre ak yon jibis.* (You are as serious as a flea and you look like a clown.)"

The children had followed the conversation and burst out laughing. Everyone else did too. Jeantilus was ashamed and gri-maced, revealing his toothless gums—he laughed *jòn*, as we usu-ally say of the forced smile of someone who would like to appear amiable but does not feel that way. Then he hastened to put two chairs and a bench for us under a mango tree. One of the chairs was rickety. I quickly walked over to sit in it, when Aunt Tansia stopped me, grabbing my hand. "Don't do that. Don't ever choose anything bad."

"I did it for you. The best place should be for the *granmoun* and the children."

"Then you did it out of pity? Do you take me for an old coot?"

"No," I hastened to respond, "That isn't what I meant to say, I. . . ."

"Don't defend yourself. I'm not upset. But I would like to point out to you that one should never choose anything bad. To make a habit of this is to make oneself an advocate of mediocrity."

"What would you have done in my place?"

"I would have chosen to sit right on the ground, on the roots of a tree, a cushion of leaves, or even on a stone. There are always good places offered to us by nature, but very few know how to appreciate and profit from them. *Fòk yon moun gen Je pou li kapab konprann sa.* (Only someone who possesses Je can understand it.) Life is. . . ."

Silence ensued, and it was then that I noticed that the children had followed us and were listening to us. My glance crossed that of one of the youngest, a little girl of about five. She smiled and I returned her smile. She had big, clear, beautiful eyes, and she came over and took my hand. "Come sit down with me, look, there is room for both of us." She pointed her finger to show me a natural bench formed by two flame trees that were joined at the roots.

"Happy is the man who has the heart of a child! What marvelous things will be unveiled to him!" Aunt Tansia threw out by way of a *pwent* (hint) in my direction. I sighed, because I didn't know what to say or think. My glance questioned hers, which wanted to speak to me, but I couldn't decode her message.

The silence was almost complete and I paid attention when Jeantilus intervened, chanting and calling out:

> *Pa pouvwa Danbala ake Ayida Wèdo Ago! Agosi! Agola!!*
>   *Bondje Bon!*
> *Adja-hou! Adja-hou! Adja-hou!*

*Nan non Jimo-Marasa, Dosou, Dosa, Dogwue, Marasa kreyòl,*
*Marasa bwa,*
*Marasa Kongo, Marasa Lafrik Ginen, Zenzou, Zenzès Ago!*
*Agosi! Agola!*
*Nan non Azaka Mede, nèg Awouba-vodou, nèg Azaka-si,*
*Azakèo-la,*
*Azaka-Tònnè, Ministre, Kouzen Zaka et Kouzin o Swa!*
*Nan non 29 pwen Gran Bwa, 29 pwen Kalfou, 29 pwen Simi-*
*tyè, 29 pwen*
*Sen Sidou myèl k ap koumande lè 4 pwen kadino ak lemond*
*antye Swa!*
*Pa pouvwa Gran Bwa Ile, nèg Kouloubwa mennen, nèg Anpaka*
*pongwe,*
*nèg Madioman-T-ka, swa swa swa*

By the power of Danbala and Ayida Wèdo . . . Listen! Ago!
Agosi! Agola! [terms requesting permission to enter
the world of the lwa] God is good!
God be praised! God be praised! God be praised!
In the name of the Twins Marasa, Dosou, Dosa, Dogwe,
Marasa Kreyol
Marasa savage, Marasa Kongo, Marasa from African Guinea,
Zenzou, Zenzès . . . Listen! Listen! Ago! Agosi! Agola!
In the name of Azaka Mede, the black arouba Vodou,
Azaka-Thunder,
The Minister, Cousin Zaka, and the Cousine . . . Welcome!
In the name of the twenty-nine points of power of the
Gran Bwa, twenty-nine points of power of the cross-
roads, twenty-nine points of power of the cemeteries,
twenty-nine points of power of Saint Such-Sweet-
Honey who commands the four cardinal points and
the entire world . . . Welcome!
By the power of Gran Bwa Ile, the person of Koloubwa
Mennen, the person of Anpaka pongwe, the person of
Madioman-T-ka , welcome . . . welcome . . . welcome
. . . We ask you to help us.

Then he cried out loudly, "*Gran Bwa Ile! Mèt Gran Bwa, Mèt tout rakraje! Pa pouvwa-ou, Vin konsakre sa nou vin ofri ou la a!* (Gran Bwa Ile! Master of the Forests! With your power, come to consecrate our offering!)"

I closed my eyes. For a moment, I thought I saw a big bird glide by. I held my breath. A voice began to sing inside me. I opened my eyes again to see a fog that enveloped all of us and even without seeing *It*, I was able to feel the presence of a majestic personage. Then I said to myself, "Without doubt it is Gran Bwa Ile."

The ceremony ended at six p.m. Jeantilus deposited the offering at the foot of a mapou. Everyone bent over, striking their chests while crying out in unison, "*Swa!*" Jeantilus bent down, kissed the ground, "*M remèsie ou pou tout lè byenfè, chè manman . . . Adja-hou! Adja-hou! Adja-hou!* (I thank you for all your benefits, dear mother . . . God be praised! God be praised! God be praised!)"

We took leave of the assembled people, taking care to embrace everyone without exception and directing a courteous word to each one before we left.

On the way back, I asked Aunt Tansia to explain the reasons for this ceremony. She made me understand that mother nature has always been very generous with us and that in consequence we owe her a gesture of thanks. "This affirms the faith of *yon moun ki sèvi* (a person who serves the gods) and to secure the success of his projects."

I asked her again about the conditions suitable for being able to *see*. She said to me with a great deal of patience and calm, "In order to see, it is necessary to observe the rule rigorously. Discipline is the key to success. It is absolutely necessary to observe a certain discipline that consists in turning one's attention away from the visible world so as to turn it toward the Anyen. Turning away one's attention supposes the triple capacity of Pinga-pye, of *M la-M pa la*, and of *Tande* (attentive listening). Seeing is nothing other than the combined exercise of these three movements. Seeing expresses one's consciousness of the existence of the invisible world. The state of seeing, then, is when you are capable of registering what is before you while seeing what is happening in front and behind you, and to your right and left. *Se sa ki montre fòs/pouvwa lèspri.* (That is what demonstrates the force/power of the Spirit.) In the state of seeing, the invisible world undergoes a transformation, because the object of Je is to touch the Invisible, the site of ideas and causes, and even of the mysteries."

"In this case, Aunt, is seeing an intentional movement?"

"Yes. Seeing is to translate ideas into the logic of real life."

"But on what must one concentrate one's attention?"

"In the first place, the initiate must observe a strict discipline. Then one's attention, playing a double game, without losing its intellectual quality, will become the bridge linking the two worlds."

"Are you speaking of attention or of intention . . . ?"

"Both. Understand this well: Intention is the energy that has the power of traversing all the worlds. It is A-Legba who guards the doors."

She was silent for a moment, then began to sing:

> *A-legba . . . mache non!*
> *Kote ou bouke*
> *Vye legba, m a pote ou*
> *Kote ou bouke*
> *Papa Legba, m a kore ou*

> A-Legba says, walk, why don't you?
> Anywhere you're beaten-down,
> Old Legba, I'll carry you
> Anywhere you're beaten-down,
> Papa Legba, I'll strengthen your core.

I interrupted her, "Is Legba a deformation of A-Legba?"

"*Legba se mèt kalfou.* (Legba is the master of the crossroads.) He is order and discipline. He is the agent for indispensable information needed for the initiate to communicate with *Zany yo, ak fanmi-Lwa yo* (the angels and the families of lwa)."

She began to hum:

> *Legba nan baryè la*
> *Se li ki pote drapo*

*Se li k ap pare sole*
*Pou Lwa yo*

Legba is within the gate
It's he who carries the flag
It's he who blocks the sun
for the lwa.

That didn't answer my question. "But is there a difference between Legba and A-Legba?" I insisted.

"Yes and no, although there is a certain distinction between the two as they fulfill their roles. It's like the difference between the enforcer of discipline and the trainer/educator; there is a strong collaboration or at least a kind of close correlation between them, because they are both working toward the development of the chosen one. Do you understand this nuance? There is the color white and a shade of white, isn't that so?" Then she whispered in my ear, "You can call him Attibon Legba or Legba, he will always answer you."

"I think I understand. And attention? What is that?"

"*Ago!* Attention is awareness on alert. It is the result of perfect and vital communication between Selidò and Sèmèdò, when *Fa*★ (the oracle) is the very principle of understanding."

"*Anmwe*★! (Help!) These names mean nothing to me . . . You are confusing me. I don't like that."

"I haven't said anything you can't understand. Consider the language and your culture." Then, changing her tone brusquely, she said in a low voice, "*Manje si ou vle . . . manje sa ou vle . . . manje jan ou vle. . . .* (Eat if you wish . . . eat what you like . . . eat when you like. . . .)" This was her way of saying that consciousness is an abundant and free nourishment. "The meal is served, my beauty! Your power of ingestion and your capacity to digest concern only you. I am teaching you not to give you pleasure or to pass the time, it is my sèvis Ginen. Such is the rule that I have received from Ginen an. I myself only have the power to transmit one bit of understanding. I'm doing it, that's all."

"Who is Fa? Would you explain it to me a little, if you please. I don't know where I am. My spirit has need of an explanation."

"*Se pa lespri a ou ki pa konprann, men se kabòch tèt a ou.* (It's not your spirit that doesn't understand, it's your hard head.) Fa is the oracle."

She sang:

*Fa, o! Fa, o!*
*Anwo lanmè an e!*

*Anwo lanmè m ap navige*

Fa, Oh! Fa, Oh!
On the sea

I sail on the sea

"Fa is the oracle. *Nan Ginen tande!* In a way, it is silent consciousness," she continued.

"Is it intuition, then? "I asked.

She nodded and I sighed with satisfaction. I felt light. For once, I was right. She was very crafty. She had an amusing way of concentrating my attention. Then she took up the conversation again with a different timbre of voice. She began to speak slowly, articulating each word: "*Nou toujou ap mache anwo dlo, Bondje fè baton a A-Legba la, pou sèvi nou Zavironn.* (We are still walking on water; God makes A-Legba his staff to serve as our oar.)" This was a hint to tell me that she had the patience to teach me even when it seemed difficult. That reassured me. I said to myself, *I must make an effort not to tire her too much.*

Aunt Tansia convinced me then that the cult of the ancestors is the key to all the magic of Vodou and the true answer for the development of Je. "The cult of the ancestors holds the authority to lift up the veil of legends and of divination, the revelation of the inside and outside of things, the connections between the known world and the unknown world, the mysteries of the lwa open only to initiates.

"The cult of ancestors is a cult of possession. The initiate is the vehicle through which the ancestors transmit messages for the group. Thus one must venerate and fear them. They are the elements that constitute the visible and the invisible world. They are the divine entities that constitute the Vodou pantheon. They participate in the existence of things. Through the trances of the initiate they speak, sing, dance, listen to complaints, solve thorny problems, resolve difficulties, treat maladies, and reconcile the worst enemies. They influence family affairs, political and economic questions, etc. The individual is nourished by his ancestors who are 'models for the comportment of the living.' Ginen is a science that is transferred directly and personally. In Ginen everything is harmonized; it is the place where one will return to be united with the ancestors. In a word, the cult of ancestors is the secret of immortality.

"Clairvoyance is a faculty of Ti Bonnanj. In order to *see*, it is necessary to go beyond appearance and therefore to a place where one can maintain oneself and keep guard. That is the place of *Loko-Miwa*,\* the master of the phenomena of visions and of ecstasy. This master is the vehicle which transmits the mirror where the Ti Bonnanj contemplates the physical world and the Gwo Bonnanj, through kadav kò, to the immaterial world. Once he is transported to this place, the initiate no longer heeds the exigencies of his physical body and he can communicate with the nannan-rèv of the assistants, the dead, and the ancestors. Once contact has been established, everything becomes transparent. Thus the past and the present have no secrets. This is the meaning of the veil of mysteries of Vodou. The seer can even read the thoughts of the assistants, see through walls, see through the dark, and leave for places he has never been. Everything becomes transparent because the spirit has eyes to see."

One evening Aunt Tansia visited us when it was not quite six p.m. I noticed a coffee pot and a packet of leaves in her hands. She asked me to make a fire with the wood charcoal I used at the time. She boiled some flowers of *toli*, poured the liquid into the coffee pot, and closed the mouth of the utensil with a plug made of leaves of white cotton. She let the liquid cool and told me to drink the potion. I did so with pleasure, because its taste was extraordinary. She recommended that I rest sitting down for a rather long time, almost a half hour. Meanwhile, she patiently explained to me that the Zany serve as intermediaries between the heavens and the earth. "All of space," she never ceased re-peating, "is filled with these beings invisible to our eyes. They can enter into communication with us and transmit their will thanks to the nannan."

She blindfolded me and asked me to *see*. Obviously, I saw nothing but blackness. I told her so, she laughed and patted me on the back. Then she lifted the blindfold and gave me a packet of leaves, which she had steeped in a liquid whose scent re-minded me of Florida Water.[87] Then she advised me to tie it to my forehead with the blindfold. I obeyed her. She sat beside me, lit a candle, and began to recite a long prayer.

Finally, she asked me to stretch out on my back. "Get rid of all forms of thought. You must be able to face everything you see," she whispered in my ear. A few minutes later, when I was resting, looking at the ceiling of the house, I saw a spark of light and I heard a sound coming from the spark. I wanted to lift my head to see it better, but I noticed that my head was heavy and I began to make out a strange scene: a little house on top of which was an enormous snake, many-colored, like a beautiful rainbow. The snake had a human head and a ring attached to its nose. It looked me straight in the eyes and, speaking to me in my mind, told me that it was one of my alliés, and had appeared on earth one million years ago. It invited me to see hundreds of years of activities, by presenting my genealogical tree. My family, it said, was merely its receptacle, thus it could ride me. Strangely, I did not experience the pathological fear I usually felt when I saw a reptile. Suddenly, the door of the small house opened and I entered. There were snakes everywhere. They were singing and I surprised myself by singing with them: "*Dan, O Dan! Dan, m se koulèv la e Dan, m se zangi O Dan! mwen la e* . . . (Dan, O Dan! Dan, I am the snake . . . Dan, I am the eel Oh! Dan, I am . . .)." I felt that I belonged to that place. Suddenly, I was aware of my deepest being; then I began to move about openly as they were doing. I went around the small house and climbed up to the roof. I saw a field and thousands of yellow butterflies that flew about and pollinated the flowers. In the distance I noticed a

---

87 Cologne used in Vodou rituals, it has both spiritual and practical effects.

white horse mounted by a man whose features I couldn't make out; instead of eyes there were fiery flames that shot out, reached me and burned my shoulders. It hurt. The man signaled to me, showing me a strange scene: a sea that changed color, green, blue indigo. There was a boat, and I didn't see the beach or the land. A man of color (a mulatto) who was very tall, with luminous red hair, got out of it.

He was handsome and his white clothing sparkled in the light. He walked across the space and advanced toward me with a measured pace. He stopped right in front of my head and has-tened to tie two infinite lines that looked like two transparent cords—one from the east and the other from the north. I raised my eyes to look at him, and our glances crossed. He asked me in a severe tone of voice, "Why have you called me? Why have you disturbed me?" I wanted to open my mouth to answer him, but no noise came out. He touched my forehead and disappeared.

At that very touch, my entire being caught on fire.

I felt pain in my lower body and I cried out, "*Anmwe!*" I was thirsty. I cried out again, I saw flashes and heard a thunder-clap's growl. In the glow of the flashes, I saw frightening scenes: beings without faces or arms, heads without bodies, enormous eyes, mammals with human heads, eels. All of a sudden, twenty-one luminous beings appeared. Then, one by one, they touched my navel while circling around my head. I experienced vertigo. I heard Aunt Tansia's voice, "*Masa-Wè*★[88]. . . !" she said in a strong voice. Suddenly, seven of them were extinguished. Ten clung to the palms of my hands and four to my shoulders. Then night fell. From far off, I heard a very sweet female voice singing. I could not understand the words. The melancholy notes of the song touched something in me: the depth of my consciousness. I sang with her: "*Mwen pa genyen manman, mwen pa genyen papa, O!* (I have no mother or father, oh!)")

When I awoke from these visions it was ten p.m. I was so tired I could not get up. I wanted to sleep, but Aunt Tansia's voice interrupted me: "Don't sleep . . . Stay with us . . . Speak to us, tell us something." I was indifferent to her words. I wanted to follow

---

88 Transfer of one mystery to another. A magical transfer.

my instincts. Repose seemed sweeter than anything. Besides, I couldn't gather enough strength to say anything at all. She lifted my head up and urged me to drink, "*Se yon ti dite* (it's a little bit of tea)," she said. I opened my mouth and she poured in the liquid, but I no longer had a swallowing reflex. She rested my head on her knees and began to massage the back of my neck. At the first touch of her hands, I sneezed, and then she gave me a drink that I was able to swallow.

After that I fell into a deep sleep, not waking until the next day in the afternoon. Aunt Tansia visited us. She again had me drink tea from the flowers of *toli*, but this time a cup full with a bit of *rapadou* (raw brown sugar).

I recounted my visions to her. She didn't interpret them right away, but she made me consider this, "There are images that are only echoes, my daughter."

"Do you mean reflections?" I said, as if to correct her.

"Echo . . . o . . . o . . ."

"*Ki kote sa ekri*? (Where is that written?)"

I wanted to know the basis for the reference that Aunt Tansia relied on. But she put her hands on my lips. Her gesture intimated that I should be quiet in order to be able to listen more carefully.

"I have not studied this," she said. "*Se Ginen-an aprann mwen tout bagay*. (It's Ginen-an that teaches me all things.) There are images that represent the end of a story. It is in this sense that I say to you that they are echoes, for in the time it takes to perceive them, they fade away."

I understood afterwards that she wanted to refer to my dreams about the snake. She tried to make me understand that I was on the point of conquering my fear and reconciling myself with the snake, who is one of my closest alliés. My other alliés such as the man with flaming eyes, the white horse, and the man in the boat with red hair, had intervened in order to help me get over my fear. "The alliés are the principal forces that help the initiate. They are gad, who with the Mèt tèt protect the initiate. One must not be afraid of them. On the contrary, one ought to reclaim their presence all the time, call on them by humming the tune of their song of power. One must also *chofe* (warm) them. However, one can only perceive them in Nan Dòmi. Each human being has at least two of them in his service. They can appear under their hidden forms.

"You know, *Je kapon anpil. Je se gad a kò a. L ap veye pou li pa pèdi li* (Je is a coward. Je ['the eye'] is the guardian of the body. It watches over the body because it doesn't want it to be lost.) *Men sonje byen, je ou wont la se ladan y ou kriye.* (But remember well, the shame of the eye is that it weeps.)"

That was a way of encouraging me. Peals of laughter followed her reflection. I laughed heartily, as often happened to me in Aunt Tansia's company.

"Then, if I understand this," I asked her, "seeing is being in a trance?"

"Yes. Seeing is being in a trance, and it brings joy. It must be said that there are different kinds of trances. There are some that are very deep, in which the initiate could spend a month and even more outside himself. This is the trance that the medium or chwal experiences. There is a trance conducive to inspiration familiar to writers, poets, painters and artists in general. There is the trance of dreamers enabling the seeing and hearing of spirits in which the initiate acts lucidly while at the same time his spirit is communicating with other spirits. The trance of ecstasy is one in which one travels to faraway lands, but in a state of consciousness."

"If there is joy, there is pleasure, and the individual *I* is necessarily present. . . ."

"Only in the role of witness."

"How can one experience joy without being conscious?"

"The initiate, in the midst of his transformation is in a state of complete beatitude. During the trance, he experiences a sense of wonder mixed with fear in view of the mysterious worlds he encounters. The initiate is an independent explorer of the universe. His voyages resemble dreams, but dreams experienced in a wakened state. To enter Nan Dòmi is to have the capacity to see what others do not perceive. The joy felt by the seer is a gentle emotion. It brings peace. It is like a mail service. It sends the news to Sèmèdò while the chosen one is in Nan Dòmi. The joy of the seer does not come from the discovery of two parallel worlds—one where his individual *I* expresses itself and where the other, his integral being, begins to vibrate. Rather, it comes from the pleasure of having found the point of conjunction between the two worlds and of having been able to maintain itself there. This point is found at the site of Anyen where joy goes back and forth incessantly and gradually between the Gwo Bonnanj and the nannan-rèv. It is in this place where one pays, in spite of oneself, the price of one's total disintegration. Seeing constitutes an extraordinary power, but there is another, still more extraordinary power—which is that of seeing the risks of Seeing."

## CHAPTER 15

# Having Cold Eyes
## *or* **the Fear of the Unknown**

### *Je kapon*

Aunt Tansia sighed and began a long discourse on clairvoyance. I remained crouched at her feet, looking at her attentively as if I could draw more information and benefit from greater knowledge from her eyes in this position than if I sat somewhere else. She cast a fleeting glance in my direction from time to time as she spoke.

"Seeing is very important. Everyone wants to know the future. That is why certain people consult diviners with the intention of having an idea of the future. There are people who received the gift of clairvoyance at the time of birth. But there are others who have developed it through initiation and others still who buy the corresponding pwen.

"When does the initiate become truly conscious of his power of Je?"

"When he leaves the Djèvo, at the moment when he directs a greeting to *Sen Nikola, Sen Solèy, Wa de Jistis* (Saint Nicholas, Saint Sun, King of Justice)." She lifted her hand in the air as she pronounced the name of St. Nicholas, King of Justice, and made a sign on her lips with the thumb of her left hand. "The initiate," she went on to say, "is like the newborn who by breathing air in his lungs at the same time receives the baptism of the air. Sen Solèy is the ray that cleaves through the darkness and opens the door of consciousness to the initiate. Thus, the initiate can no longer step back."

"Is this commitment definitive? I think that the gift of clairvoyance imposes too many demands. Among other questions, Aunt, do all initiates possess Je?"

"That must be so. Yet, there is also a notion of relativity in the invisible world. No one can know another person's degree of understanding. *Men dwat pa konnen zafèr a men gòch.* (The right hand does not know what the left hand is doing.)"

"There is something I want to ask you. My older sister Jocelyne told me that there is a myth according to which those who read the future in cups of black coffee die blind."

"This mode of clairvoyance must be handled in a certain way."

"Are there several ways of seeing?"

"Of course, there are infinite of ways of seeing. You know that the gift of clairvoyance is to be capable of sight. One sees when one is capable of seeing what happens behind oneself without turning the head while at the same time looking at what is happening in front of one. In other words, to see is to turn to past scenes, it is to be capable of reading the present and the past."

"There is something I do not understand. I ask why God has not granted Je to everyone? That would have made things easier."

"That does not concern God. If someone wants to open his Je, he only has to work his second attention. Vodou asks no one to search it out. Each person is born free to do as he likes. As for me, I only want to show you the educational aspect of Vodou."

Completely astonished by her response, I wanted to question her further. But she cut me off and said to me in a dry tone of voice, "*Pa fè tèt a ou travay twòp. Tèt a ou dur pitit an mwen.* (Don't make your head work too much. Your head is very hard, my child.)"

I was impatient. I thought that the obligation to learn all these stories was superfluous. I saw no connection between them and the development of Je. I began to doubt my abilities. I said this to Aunt Tansia.

"The reason you can't see is because you have not used the entry pass. You must exert yourself. The body has its own knowledge and its own memory. That is why every good education demands of the initiate the necessary strength to master his *kantamwa*. Only then can he reach the place of Anyen and recover his natural spontaneity. If not, he will never reach the place of Seeing, which is guarded by *Loko-Miwa*. The risks of seeing are very high. The secret of Je is that of *being able* to lose, give, take again, lose again. There is a price to pay. *Pitit an mwen, Hm! Si ou pa travay pou ou gen Je a ou, OòBatala p ap resevwa ou nan lekòl a li.* (Hmm, my child! If you don't work on getting your Je, O'Batala won't accept you into his school.)"

"I don't like these conditions. I feel ill at ease. Do you mean to say that there is a sacrifice to be made?"

"In a sense, yes."

"I should like to assure myself of one thing."

"Which one is it?" Aunt Tansia asked me with a certain irony.

"After so many sacrifices what will I be left with?"

"The trance. Before entering into a trance, the personal *I* must necessarily cease to be preoccupied with itself, and it must economize enough energy to lift the veil, which is what permits the initiate to contemplate the holy place!"

I trembled in my innermost being because the word "sacrifice" had long had a disagreeable connotation for me. The image of Jesus Christ on Calvary always came to mind, and I automatically felt a sort of cramping of my spine. Aunt Tansia sensed my uneasiness. She got up and came over to me. She lifted my blouse and struck my back many blows. I coughed nervously. She took her little marine-blue phial filled with tobacco from her pocket and she said to me, "*Pran yon ti priz, non.* (Take a little snuff, why don't you.)"

She stuffed it into my nostrils. I sneezed a first time, and she said aloud and in a grave tone of voice, "So *djèmè!* (I swear!)"; a second time, and she said, "*Ake Badji an m, m plen!* (Full of charm in my temple!)" I sneezed a third time, and she said, "*Agaou di: Si Bondje vle, lavi ap long o! na gen tan.* (Agaou says: If God wills it, life will be long! We shall have time.)"

Then she bent down and traced a design on the ground: a circle enclosing a triangle that enclosed another circle. She put her red headscarf on it. I started in astonishment, as if in response to a kind of signal that something was going to happen, when I saw the headscarf that she only used on rare occasions. Once it was when she had spoken to me about Ogou, god of fire and war, and another time when she gave me an explanation concerning the work of Erzulie Dantòr. When she was finished, she invited me to erase the first circle with my left foot. At the precise moment I put my foot on the design, I felt a shaking coming up from the ground that made me sway from right to left. Then I began to spin like a top without being able to stop. It was like an intoxication, but I was able to glimpse a scene: a man clothed in a red shirt and black pants standing up on a brazier. I was even able to distinguish a jumble of strange forms next to him—knives that stretched upward like serpents and intertwined. Then suddenly the man turned into a bat and ordered me to sit on the brazier. I refused to obey. He took on human form again and grasped me by the hand to take me there by force. I resisted again and used all my strength so as not to be led there against my will. Then he raised a dagger to threaten me. I stepped back unsteadily. He took out a cord from the pocket of his pants and threw it in my direction. I stepped back again. Suddenly, I noticed that we were located on a patch of ground that could only hold three people at most. I wanted to cry out, *Help!* But I couldn't articulate the words.

Breathless and dripping with cold sweat, I trembled, wanting to vomit. I held out my hands to Aunt Tansia in a sign of distress. She took them. I leaned on her, and I was ready to vomit. "*Vire Je a ou lanvèr* (Turn your eyes backwards)," she ordered. I obeyed her, and suddenly I saw the earth open up and close upon the man and the brazier. Water gushed from all directions, sprinkling my face, arms and feet without wetting my clothes. A few minutes later, I lost the rest of the vision and was relieved. Then I let myself lie down on the ground, on the design. Aunt

Tansia raised my head and slipped the red scarf under it. I looked at her. . . . I didn't have any thoughts in my head. Tears fell down my cheeks. Suddenly, I felt a coolness envelop me. I closed my eyes. Aunt Tansia did not disturb me. I turned over on my stomach and laid my face on the ground. I smelled the odor of the soil. I rubbed my face on it and caressed it with my hands. I felt that my whole body belonged to it. I was in harmony with it. I felt gratitude, which became more intense as I heard myself speak to it as if to a human being:

*I want to thank you dear Mother!*
*Bless you, helpful Mother*
*Oh! How I love you!*
*I love your scent. . . .*
*Help me to exhale it*
*In the particles*
*Of dust that form*
*Your temple, my flesh*
*Make me sense it in the air I breathe*
*At every moment*
*Teach me to vibrate to your rhythm*
*I have such need of you!*

Aunt Tansia went away without saying a word, leaving me in my state of bliss.

## CHAPTER 16

# Laziness *or* Indecision

## *Je fenyan*

I saw Aunt Tansia again two days later. She resumed the conversation as if it had not been interrupted: "The duty of the initiate is to maintain continuous attention. That means that he must obey the rule."

"However, there is a code," I replied.

To help me understand, she explained that the first movement of the initiate is to be able to impose silence on himself; to hold back time and arrest the world of appearance by an eye gesture. "Gestures and movements are two ways of giving form to the expression of the soul. The eye is the mirror of the soul. The soul itself is nourished by thoughts. The air transmits the movements of thought. It is the tool that the Gwo Bonnanj uses to transport thought in the body. Thought itself takes on form through speech. Speech is made of images and words. In crossing the line that separates the two worlds, the Visible and the Invisible, speech metamorphoses into sound that becomes images. The image is the materialization of speech."

She was silent for a moment and then asked me, "Would you tell me what books convey on the subject of speech?"

"I learned that speech is the expression of thought in words."

"Very good, but it's necessary to add that it can create everything just as it can destroy everything."

"What do you mean?"

"This requires a great deal of attention. The universe is

composed of notes and sounds. The harmony of notes signifies the harmony of all the elements found in the universe. If one does not recognize this truth, one can no longer see the elements as they really are. For notes are a constituent part of the universe. The word possesses an unimaginable power. With a word one glorifies someone and with another word one can destroy his reputation. The word has the power to displace a body from its original position. All bodies finding themselves in a similar environment and who feel threatened put themselves on the defensive. Thus notes become discordant and dissonance replaces euphony. Everything that exists in the material world already exists in the spiritual world."

"Why do you insist on 'already'?"

It must be said that I was avid for knowledge. I recorded everything on a cassette and copied it in a notebook with the aim of digging deeper into the content point by point. I felt that that's where my salvation lay. Aunt Tansia went on without bothering about me.

"To begin with, I must inform you that the couple *Sobo/ Badè*★[89] occupies an important place in space. *Yonn se van, lòt la se Tonnèloray. Ki vle di paròl pa ka pale san Sobo/Badè.* (One is the thunder clap—in the sense of sound—and the other is the wind. This means that no word can be uttered without Sobo/Badè.)"

"Explain this to me. . . ."

"I'm telling you that there is no speech without air and sound."

"Do you mean the lwa Sobo and Badè? What do these lwa have to do with the air, sound, wind and speech?"

"What impertinence! You twist everything. You talk like the foreigner who understands nothing about Haitian culture and who, not seeking to understand, tries to analyze data which he doesn't have. *Sobo/Badè se mistè.* (Sobo/Badè, are mysteries.) They have a great influence on the dimension Earth/Sky. Whether one likes it or not, the Zany have connections with everything that is done in this dimension. Why are you trying

---

89 Sobo is the great judge of the temple, master of rain. Badè is the god who governs the wind.

to trivialize the role of Sobo/Badè? My child, the objective of Vodou is to convey a universal message, destined for all people without exceptions for race or culture. You ought to be touched in your thoughts, in your sentiments and in your judgments."

"I'm not trying to trivialize anything. It's just that I thought that the chapter on the question of the lwa is written simply for Haitians and that the interest in the lwa only concerns Haitians. Aunt, do you agree that Sobo and Badè are among the lwa who only interest a very small number of Haitians?"

"You are right, in part. In effect, it is up to Haitians to understand the concepts of their culture. *Menm si chak pèp konprann yon bagay dapre kilti pa li, men gen bagay ki menm pou tout pèp. Gen yon provèb ki di: Chak chen niche kòk a li jan li konnen, men se menm jan tout chen pise.* (Even when each person understands something in terms of his culture, there are still things that are the same for all people. There is a proverb that says: Each dog has its own way of licking its cock, but all dogs piss the same way.)"

This is a proverb that may be translated in this context: Each people has its own culture and its own philosophy, but the human race has one sole reality. Each people is free to organize its way of life, to interpret and express the power of its knowledge according to its capacity for understanding.

"*Se poutèt sa, pesonn pa kapab anpeche m kwè pawòl nanchon Ginen ki di ke: souf lavi se nan men Legba li ye, lè ak van nan men a Sobo ake Badè, ki se de frè jimo ki mache kòt a kòt san yo pa janm deparye. Se grenn Je Badè ki sèvi mirwa pou Sobo.* (This is why no one can keep me from believing this statement of *nanchon Ginen*,[90] which says that if the breath of life is instilled by Legba, the wind and sound are channeled by the twins Sobo and Badè whose force is never weakened. The eyes of Badè are Sobo's mirror.)"

What I am able to translate and sum up from this after getting more precise information later is that she was saying: The air is the mirror of sound.

"Who is Badè?" I asked. I posed the question to her because I knew perfectly well that Badè existed in the past. He was an important figure in the history of the Fon, a tribe from the re-

90 Assembly of Spirits (lwa, Mysteries, Zany) who make up the Ginen rite.

gion of Dahomey who vanquished the *Gedevis* (or Gedes) and then took them prisoner.

"My child, you come up with ideas because you read too many books. History has been recounted to you in a certain way. *Kite m di ou yon bagay, tande byen sa m ap di ou la: listwa rakonte ke Badè se te yon wa, se vre. Men anvan wa Badè te fèt, Badè te deja la, wi. Tankou Lespri a Kris te la anvan Jezi.* (Let me tell you something—listen well to what I say to you now: History tells that Badè was a king, it's true. But before King Badè was born, Badè was already there. Just as the Christ existed before Jesus.) There is the rule, my child."

"Aunt, you speak like a scholar."

"*Se ou menm ki save. . . .* (You are the scholar. . . .)"

"What is the difference?" I replied.

Aunt Tansia began to laugh quietly; then she said to me, "*Mwen menm, se eksperyans kinan m ki ban mwen, alòske ou menm se liv ki aprann ou.* (As for me, I learn from experience while you, you learn from books, and that's the difference.)"

"I agree that the approaches are different, but isn't it said that all roads lead to Rome?"

"I don't agree." Aunt Tansia burst out in sonorous laughter and gathered up her skirt before sitting down on a step.

"*Kite m chita* (Let me sit down)," she said.

At that, point the conversation changed and took another turn.

"I'm going to comment on something for your sake," she said. "It is necessary to get out of this world. It destroys you. You waste your energy. It is necessary to liberate yourself. You've been taught things that have caused your dullness, your slowness in understanding Ginen. Remember that this world in which we live is not the only one. There are others, an infinity of worlds. You must begin to explore them, you have the right to do so."

It was truly difficult for me to live as Aunt Tansia asked me to do. I humbly confessed it to her. "I know, Aunt, but I am obliged to prepare for my future in this world. If not, I will be a dependent all my life. I would not like to beg for my bread. Poverty horrifies me."

"Really? Hmm. Do you intend to become well-off in preparing for your future? Do you even know how to do it? You always insist on this kind of superstition: the future. *Nan Ginen pa gen pi douvan men sèlman Jodi-a.* (In Ginen, there is no future, only the present moment.)"

"Since childhood I have heard nothing but this sermon, '*Pitit, prepare lavni ou!* (Child, prepare for your future!)' My parents reminded us all the time that the greatest wealth they were giving us was a good education to ward off the harmful blows the future might have in store. They sacrificed to send us to the best schools. They wanted us to be among the most brilliant. My mother never stopped telling me, 'The greatest mercy is to have a good head and a virtuous soul. The world doesn't hand out gifts, life is a battleground, it's necessary to be armed, that is, to be prepared to win.'"

"Very good, very good. You have learned the lesson well. Then you are prepared to fight against life?"

"No, Aunt, to earn my living."

"But who are you going to fight against?"

"Against everything that would prevent me from living well. Nothing is easy in this world. We live in a world. . . ."

She interrupted me with a big smile and asked, "Can you show me the world where you live? Touch it. . . ."

With a rapid gesture I touched the hem of her skirt. "Ah! This is the world where you live?"

"A part of its presence," I replied.

"Ha, ha! You are teaching me new things. I would like you to explain it to me a little. Go on, my child, I'm listening. . . ."

I waited a long time, deep in my thoughts. I didn't know what to say, I was confused.

I surprised myself by saying, "This world is a veritable theatrical scene. . . ."

"That is true, but who are the actors?" Aunt Tansia asked me.

"We are, Aunt."

"But why did you touch the hem of my skirt, what role does it play in all that?"

"It plays a role like make-up, like a backdrop."

"Who are the principal players?"

"All of us who are a form of life, we. . . ."

"I am not of this world," she said to me.

"What? I don't understand. You eat and you drink, you make *pi* and *pou* (you piss and you have bowel movements), you wash and dress, you laugh and cry."

"I am not of this world. I tell you again: I have nothing to explain."

"What you say makes me think of a phrase from the Bible, the one that says: 'I am not of this world.'"

She looked me straight in the eyes and said calmly, "This phrase is written on my skin, in my flesh, in my spirit, in my soul, in my dream body. *Nan Ginen tande: m pa nan monn sa, se lonbray an m sèlman k ap pase la. Adja-hou!* (In truth: I am not of this world, it is only my shadow that is passing through. God be praised!)"

## CHAPTER 17

# Watch Your Feet
## *or* Constant Attention

*Pinga-pye*

*Marengwen ping-a pye-an mwen*
*Pinga-pye an mwen, pinga!*

Marengwen, pay attention to my feet
Pay attention to my feet, attention!

This is what Aunt Tansia was humming. "The *marengwen* rhythm," she told me, "is a funereal rhythm. This song is a warning meant to caution the lazy initiate of the danger lying in wait for him because of his negligence."

Her warning put me on the defensive. "An attentive initiate cannot eat the bread of laziness," I replied. "There are so many tasks planned in advance to carry out. Nevertheless, certain things could escape his vigilance, in spite of himself, and that is why it wouldn't be fair to blame him."

"But I am not talking about blame. I only want to make you understand that an initiate is a pilgrim, my child, he has no right to let himself become a *kan-nannan* (do-nothing), a *wololoy* (lackadaisical fellow), or *en san grenn* (a coward with no balls). He has no place to rest his head. He is in constant combat. He is a warrior."

"What exactly are you talking about?"

"I only want to draw your attention to the Pinga-pye that

one cannot attain without first entering into the Anyen state, which one always has a tendency to confuse with the *manfouben* (negligent) state."

Aunt Tansia liked to use mythological references from Vodou to help me understand certain concepts. Her vocabulary was rich and she never failed to use coarse words, which shocked me. She did it on purpose. It was her way of demystifying taboos. It didn't prevent me from liking her style of teaching.

On the ground she traced a triangle which I recognized as a vèvè. "It is the boat of Agwe-t-Awoyo," she told me, "the master of the great salt waters. It is capable of transporting us from one point to another or of helping us to change our perceptions. However, to get there, the initiate must stand completely naked (divested of all make-up and artifice) on the site of Anyen, and, above all, once the state is reached he must not linger. If not . . . he is going to catch cold."

By "cold" she meant "indifference."

"There is no danger of death because the Gwo Bonnanj stands guard over his position. He has his own habits, which remind the traveler of the conditions of other places. He knows, of course, that Anyen is situated at the junction between *Faire* and *Non-Faire*, that is, between the *kantamwa* and the Pinga-pye."

"Still, is there a danger somewhere?" I asked.

"The traveler sometimes risks getting mixed up, confusing the scenes he has viewed and therefore reacting in a neurotic way."

"How does one touch Anyen without causing harm to the Gwo Bonnanj, and how does one recover one's normal state?"

"By harmonizing his breath with the *Emi*."

I had never heard the word before. "Emi?"

"It is the universal breath administered by A-Legba."

"Aunt, doesn't the initiate risk losing himself in the Unknown by touching Anyen?"

"This is the risk of Seeing, my child. But there is no great danger due to the fact that Gwo Bonnanj always watches, he is solidly placed in his position."

I noticed then that I was very nervous. I asked her, "How does one return to the normal state?" I expected an answer about returning to a normal state after sleeping. But she didn't respond. I asked the question again. I breathed deeply and asked her, "How does one leave Anyen?"

She took my hand and made a *krake* (a hard sound, bending the fingers over the palm of the hand) bending my fingers one by one, which stopped me.

"One makes the same movement as one made to enter there, but in reverse . . . ," she answered.

"No! No! No!" I heard myself cry out. Aunt, *w ap pase m nan betiz* (you are making me sound ridiculous). How does one muster the energy to carry out such an exploit! It is impossible, inhuman! In order to be able to reach the supposed site of Anyen, doesn't one have to consent to lose everything?"

"The recuperation of energy is automatic, she explained to me, owing to the very fact of having touched Anyen, which is the original state where energy is boundless: In returning to the Je klè, the Gwo Bonnanj, filled up with energy, has the power to execute unimaginable exploits, I assure you."

"How can the Gwo Bonnanj find the means to revivify itself when it is completely ignorant of what it has been engaged in? To my mind, repose would be the only way of recuperating energy."

"You are right that repose is the best remedy against fatigue. *Men, kannari pa sous.* (But the jar of water is not the source.)" In other words, she was saying, one should never be satisfied with simple explanations but go farther to find their origins.

"You are teaching me many things, but I'm not truly convinced."

"I am only giving you explanations. There is a big gap between theory and practice. Up to now, you have lived in the world of the imagination and thought. *Se kan w a wè, w a va konprann. Se kan w pran, w konnen. . . .* (When you see, you will understand, when you hold it in your hand, you will know. . . .)"

"Is this a warning?"

"Yes, in a way."

"In that case, where is the liberty of the initiate?"

"It is here or there. . . ."

"Explain that to me, I don't understand."

"One has only to search for it and one seizes it right away. Liberty lets itself be taken by whoever searches for it. It is a question of will."

"I have searched for it for a long time. In truth, it is the only thing I really need. I would like to live it without ever going back."

"Begin by showing respect for all forms of life."

"That is too vague. I would like to know how to preserve liberty once and for all."

"*Fè tèt kole ak tout sa ki gen lavi.* (It is necessary to hold fast to all living beings.)"

"I have tried, but I never succeed in grasping liberty."

"What are the reasons that have prevented you from doing so?"

"I don't know. But I desire it with all my soul."

"With all your spirit," she corrected me. "The soul knows only the dream."

"Meaning?"

"That the spirit eternally searches for liberty. The spirit is nostalgic for it ever since its insertion into matter. That is because the human being is always thirsty to have things explained and to understand, even after acquiring a lot of knowledge. Now, my child, *Ago! Pinga-pye a ou!* (Attention! Watch out for your foot!)" Be vigilant, she meant.

"I thought that I was going to find liberty by practicing the methods that permit me to acquire Je."

"To seek to see is the quest for liberty. Taking the road that leads to seeing is a movement that stimulates the need for liberty. Choosing to follow this road is already a step toward liberty."

"There are many things to learn in order to come to see."

"Don't knock your head against a wall. There is nothing to learn by heart. Seeing is to know how to discern what one did not see previously. That is all."

"How long will it take to get there?"

"It is true that time plays an important role in the apprenticeship, because the initiate needs a period of time to sustain the effort of his spirit. But he must be prompt and faultless on every occasion."

"All this is a bit confusing to me; you have said that the initiate doesn't have time."

"Time plays a supporting role. In effect, the initiate does not have time."

"Can the initiate discern his own time?"

"Certainly. However, no one can either express it for someone else or measure the time he lacks. Each initiate is unique. In the spiritual world, everything is relative."

"In that case, there is no guarantee that one will arrive."

"Patience is the only guarantee."

"I can't wait. I've been waiting a long time, everything seems uncertain."

"I don't know what you are waiting for."

"To have a lot of authority *nan Ginen-an* (in the Unknown) and a lot of power."

"You haven't been cured of your mania to draw everything into your world of the intellect. *Twou Ginen an fon* (the gulf of Ginen is deep), the route is long and narrow, you must be capable of waiting and then you must have the energy to wait."

"Things are not as easy as I thought."

"How many times must I tell you that every thought is not necessarily true?"

"I would like for everything to happen now. I sense that things are about to escape me. I have the feeling that I am losing something that I thought I had gained."

"It is caused by fear."

"I have not paid attention."

"Fear is underhanded. It is hidden in the courtyard of Pinga-pye, you know? It hides in the smallest recesses of our emotions. One always has the impression that misfortune is close at hand."

"But isn't it a kind of emotion?"

"Of course, but it is also a form of energy. It can be conquered."

"I would like to know how to dissolve it entirely."

"In order to cause it to disintegrate one must move away from the site of *M la-M pa la*. Nevertheless, *Ago!* You need it. Fear is the best stimulant to push us beyond our strength. A man recounted to me his exploits during the American occupation, how he was able to lift a big rock in order to hide under it for more than an hour for fear of being arrested by an American soldier who was chasing him. He was able to deceive the soldier's vigilance by letting out a strange cry, inspired by fear. At the time, that is, during the American occupation, *danse Vodou*★ (Vodou ceremonies) were forbidden throughout the republic, except on weekends. His family, in rebellion against this rule, had organized a service for the *Zany-pwotektè* (guardian angels or protective angels) of the family and of the lakou-Bitasyon. When the ceremony was nearly over, a lwa, who had been participating in the ceremony with them, sang a song advising them to be on guard against an intruder who was going to come there to *mete twoublay* (cause trouble). The lwa had not finished his song when suddenly the voice of a stranger was heard ordering them to open the door. The grandmother answered him, '*M lakay an mwen, m lib pou m kapab fè sa mwen vle.* (I am in my home, I am free to do as I wish.)' '*Non, madanm ou pa lib, madanm, lalwa defann moun danse Vodou pou la senmèn.* (You are not free, Madam. There is a law that forbids Vodou ceremonies on weekdays),' the stranger responded in a heavy American accent. '*Lwa kinan ou la pa kapab anpeche Lwa kinan nou yo vin danse nan tèt an nou.* (Your laws (lwa) do not have the power to prevent our Lwa from dancing in us.)' '*Si ou pa sispann bagay la madanm, m ap oblije arete ou.* (If you don't stop, I will be obliged to arrest you.)' Silence. But the ceremony continued. '*Louvri pòt, madanm.* (Open the door, Madame.)' Continued silence. But the ceremony went on. '*Si ou pa louvri pòt, madam, m ap anfòse li, epi m ap mete tout moun nan prizon.* (If you don't open the door, Madame, I will be obliged to push it in and then I will put you all in prison.)' '*Lènmi yo sou nou!* (The enemies are at our door!)' the lwa exclaimed before leaving the head of its chwal. '*Tout moun vin sere anba rad an m'!* (Everyone come hide under my dress!)' the old woman said as she lifted up her skirt. Everyone hastened to do as the grandmother said, except for a young man who was sleeping in a corner of the room and, unfortunately, did not hear her. The soldier again ordered the occupants of the small cottage to open the damned door for him, '*Louvwi!* (Open up!)' Silence. And the soldier pushed in the bamboo door, which crumpled before his rage. When he entered he found nothing but the sleeping young man he awoke by kicking with his boot. '*Kote tout moun ki fè bwi toutalè a*? (Where are the people who were making noise just now?)' he asked the sleeper. The young man, stupefied at seeing a foreigner, let out a frightened cry. In the grips of fear, he went out a window, which he opened easily before the soldier had time to handcuff him. But the soldier located him quickly with the aid of a powerful flashlight. Tracked like an animal, the fugitive turned around, going to the right, then to the left. The only way out was a big rock. He lifted it and hid under it. The soldier ordered him to surrender and walked around the rock, thinking the young man was hiding behind it. He tried to push the rock, then walked around it one more time with the intention of trapping the clever fellow. But he didn't see him anywhere. He could not imagine that the escapee was only a few meters from him lying flat under the big rock."

"That's extraordinary, Aunt, I love this story."

"I wanted to explain to you that fear always makes its appearance at the moment when one becomes conscious of one's limits. Now in this case, the Ti Bonnanj taking the place of Pinga-pye acts out of a sense of urgency and pushes the Gwo Bonnanj to act also under the impulse of the *Pa-gen-tan* (more time), of the *Rive-nan-bout* (reaching one's limits)."

"It is a very edifying story," I added.

"There is another story told to me by the victim herself, who was my good friend. Her name was Altagrâce Julmus."

"Tell it to me, Aunt. I love stories."

And she did:

"A Haitian-Dominican family lived in Santiago de los Caballeros. Altagrâce, of Haitian origin, had married a Dominican named Emilio Jiménez. The couple had two children: a daughter, Emilia—my godchild—who had very light skin, fine features and silky hair; and José, who was bronzed and looked like his mother. José married Muñeca Rodríguez, a woman of great beauty of the type called *indio* by Dominicans because her features somewhat recalled those of the Maya. An only child was born of their union. The couple named her Altagracia. This child was the pride of the entire family. She was graceful, intelligent, sensitive, and more than beautiful. One would have taken her for a princess. At eighteen she was already working as a *kontrolèz* (supervisor) in one of the big hotels in the city. The millionaires who came there to spend their vacations noticed how beautiful she was and did not fail to praise her. A German *bizisman* (businessman) staying there was smitten and planned to marry her despite her young age and her dark skin—at that time, racism was intense. He even took her to visit the United States, Cuba and Trinidad. He showered her with presents. Unfortunately, he suffered an attack of apoplexy and died suddenly. Altagracia bore her grief with dignity and vowed not to sleep with another man. She placed herself at the service of the family and, with her income, bought a beautiful house where the whole family resided. There were six of them.

"Her grandmother, Altagrâce, was her best friend. Every evening, before she went to her room, she spent time with her, the two of them alone, to chat about everything and nothing. Altagrâce in turn adored her grandchild. She told her stories about the past. She told me that it was the best way to attach her to Haitian culture. Altagracia learned to speak Kreyòl without an accent, to dance the Petwo, the Yanvalou, the Kongo, the Ibo, the Ngo and the Mayi. She danced like a Haitian peasant woman *anba tonèl* (under the arbor). She could also recite the *lapriyè dyo* (prayers addressed to the lwa, saints and the *Djehoun*) and could prepare certain special dishes such as the *kokodjè* (puree of pigeon peas with cashew nuts, a dish much appreciated by people in the north), and *duri kole*. The grandmother transmitted all her Haitian knowledge to her granddaughter. One day, by accident, Altagrâce lost her sight after a terrible kick from the donkey that was taking her to the Acul des Pins, *nan bitasyon fanmi a li* (dwelling, a mystic site from which each Haitian family draws its energy). After that she did not leave Santiago again until the day she had to flee to save herself from the massacre of Haitians perpetrated on Dominican territory and ordered by the president, Rafael Leonidas Trujillo. On the eve of the massacre, Altagracia had a nightmare: She saw herself on the edge of the Jean de Nantes River transformed into a river of blood.

She leaned over to see better and heard a voice coming from the water: 'Altagracia! Take off your sandals and run. Flee far from this horror!' She woke up with her heart beating wildly. The next morning she ran into her grandmother's room to tell her the dream. She met her father, José, in the dining room and told him about her vision. 'You are tired,' he said to her. 'How can a river be transformed into a river of blood? Don't worry. Blood represents victory, for everything red is a sign of glory.' '*En En* (No no) Joselito,' replied Altagrâce, who was listening to the conversation from her room—after she went blind, she had keen hearing. 'I believe instead that it's a sign of misfortune, it gives me goosebumps. I am afraid, I smell the odor of blood. A lot of blood is going to run over this land.' She made the sign of the cross and said: 'Grace grant us mercy!'

One week later when he returned from work, José told his mother that one of his friends, who was a military police-man in the Dominican Army, had advised him to warn all his Haitian friends who were living in the Dominican Republic to leave the country as soon as possible, because there had been a falling out between President Trujillo and the Haitian president. The affair was serious. In the course of that very night Trujillo's crusade began. You could hear the sound of gunfire everywhere. Altagrâce called her daughter Emilia and asked her to take her to Haiti. She remembered Altagracia's vision: 'If I stay I will be killed, I sense it. *Pitit sa gen bon Je, wi. Se li ki pran Je a manman an mwen* (This child has good Je, yes. She inherited it from my mother.)' Altagracia went to find her aunt to figure out how to protect the life of her *gran manman*. For more than an hour, the entire family conferred without being able to find a solution. In the end, they all decided to flee. Altagracia ran to the bed of her mother, Muñeca, to tell her. Muñeca, seeing the look of defeat on her daughter's face, asked her, 'What is wrong with you, my child, you have nothing to fear.' Altagracia responded, 'We must all leave now, *madrecita*.' Must I leave too?' 'Everyone must, *madre*. Don't ask questions. We are in danger of dying.' 'Leave without me, I'm not afraid to stay here, I'm Dominican. I don't want to go to Haiti.'

"She rejected the idea of going with them for fear of being

arrested and suffering the same fate as they if she was discovered. She said that to the others who cried out in chorus, '¿Solidaridad? (Solidarity?)' 'Yo no puedo porque la policía me matará si yo voy con Altagrâce (I can't because the police will kill me if I go with Altagrâce.)' '¡Bueno! (Well!)' said Altagracia. Then she decided to take her grandmother by herself to Acul des Pins. She helped her to get dressed and they both left in haste and without baggage. On the way they met a military policeman who stopped them. 'Halt! Who are you?' 'Dominican citizens,' Altagracia answered. 'Where are you going?' the policeman asked. 'To my sister's house. She is having labor pains. I'm taking the midwife with me.' 'But you are black. Repeat after me, perejil.' It was a trap to distinguish Dominicans from Haitians [who could not easily trill the Spanish "r"]. Altagracia repeated perejil faultlessly. '¡Perfecto! Ahora la vieja (Perfect! Now the old woman),' said the soldier. 'Es muda (She is mute),' Altagracia said, before her grandmother could speak, for her Kreyòl accent would have betrayed her origin.

"The policeman let them pass without further questions. They walked for a long time before they reached the border. At the moment they crossed the line separating the two countries, they heard horrible cries. Altagrâce pressed her granddaughter's hand and asked, 'Where are we?' 'Nou amba gwo pyebwa anakayit la. (We are under the great tree, the anakayit.) The mapous are on our left.' 'Find us a hiding place. I am tired. I need to rest a bit. After a half hour of rest, we will set out again. Ti Cia [Altagracia's nickname], promise me to go back to find the others in the Dominican Republic.' Altagracia pressed her hand in response. Once the half hour was over, she said, 'Go back now to your country, ma nina (my child). I can go along the road alone, I will doubtless find someone on Vallières Street [one of the main streets in Ouanaminthe] who will be kind enough to take me to Acul des Pins.' 'No, granmanman, I will not leave you.'

"She had scarcely stopped speaking when a group of policemen armed with rifles, pikes, lances and big knives reached the edge of the river, leading prisoners to the riverbank and cutting their throats right there. There were young children among them. The mothers cried, sobbing loudly, and begging in desperation, '*Souple* (I beg you), don't kill us. . . .' 'Kill me first!' a pregnant woman asked, not wanting to witness the murder of the three- or four-year-old daughter she was carrying in her arms. The gendarme snatched the child from her arms and stabbed her before the eyes of her mother, who in turn grabbed the knife from the murderer's hands and plunged it deep into his stomach. The other policemen beat the woman with their rifle butts before finishing her off by stabbing her in the womb with a bayonet thrust.

"Altagracia witnessed this genocide from her hiding place. She watched in horror the murderous movements of the soldiers thirsty for innocent blood. She also trembled with grief. At a certain moment, unable to contain herself in the face of so much cruelty, she cried out. 'Gang of assassins!' A gendarme turned around, aimed his rifle in their direction, and fired. Altagracia let out a cry and tried to run to escape death. Altagrâce took her by the hand, '*Pa bouje* (Don't move),' she said to her. But her whole body was trembling. She was afraid. Another policeman ran toward their hiding place. Altagrâce, sensing the danger, had time to say to her granddaughter, 'Press against me and don't be afraid of anything.' She repeated three times, '*Nannan kpra kpra O!* (Eternal Nannan!)' and performed the necessary gesture. At that very moment they found themselves perched on a branch in the mapou, entwined in each other's arms. The gendarme came up and, not finding anyone there, in a rage, shouted insults: '*¡Haitianos malditos, diablos! ¡Feos, coño! ¡Caramba!* (Damned filthy Haitian devils! Shit!)' He circled the trees several times in vain, then he hastened to rejoin his band to carry on their dreadful task.'"

This story made me hold my breath, as if I were watching a horror film. My body shook, and my eyes welled up with tears. "My God, Aunt Tansia! They escaped death miraculously. . . ."

"Their faith saved them."

"How were they able to climb up the tree in so little time?"

"*Altagrâce te granmoun, wi. Li te sèvi fran epi li pa t piti.* (Altâgrace was a wise woman, yes. She served sincerely and her power was not small.)"

"Do you mean that they had a pwen?"

"They were held up by *Lentansyon*★ (will power)."

251

I hung on her words to understand better the meaning of the story's message. She went on without even looking at me. "*Le Bon konprann ak Lentansyon se de kokenn raliman.* (*Le Bon konprann* and *Lentansyon* are two centers of coordination.) Each one is nourished with its own essence. Reason with pride and the will with humility.

"*Yon moun ki sèvi ta dwe rive gen kontwòl tèt a li. Li pa fèt pou l ape fè grandizè. Kè a li dwe toujou rete nan labèsman. Men an menm tan, fòk li rive marye lentansyon a li ak bon konprann a li.* (A person who serves must come to control his own mind. He was not created to aggrandize himself. His heart should always stay in a state of humility. But at the same time, he has to marry his intention to his understanding.) If not, he will remain a *mofreze* from the mystical point of view. For the secret of life is to achieve one's own wholeness. In other words: Living is an achievement of the will."

"The life force is the daughter of humility. It is a glue that binds the different consciousnesses together. Each consciousness is a ray of light. The initiate is obligated to watch over them so that no one of them dominates the others, and to remain in Pinga-pye. In other words, he must be equal to himself. Pride weakens the force of will because it wants to be right all the time. As a consequence it weakens the life force. It provides itself with tools— arguments—in order to dismantle what it can't justify. However, lentansyon can render possible what reason judges impossible.

"Lentansyon can transport us into an infinity of worlds. It erupts into the Gwo Bonnanj by the forcefulness of perception when the latter has been able to harmonize all the consciousnesses of the double. That permits the initiate to enter into the unknown world and leave it without a hitch, that is, without incident.

"We conserve all the experiences of the will in our bodies—the eyes, feet, hands, nose, ears, spine, heart, womb, navel, sex, buttocks, etc. That is why the body has its own consciousness that reason does not know.

Again she explained, "Lentansyon is the unity of all the sentiments in an ensemble of rays of light. It is light. The secret of the dream body is at the very heart of this bundle. The initiate must be able to disperse it or concentrate it; that is, increase its intensity."

## CHAPTER 18

# Witness of the *Nannan-rèv*

By way of edification I would like to evoke the memory of a mysterious event I experienced while I was on a musical tour with Boukman Eksperyans on the east coast of the United States—more precisely, in Philadelphia. It was the first time that Lòlò and I went together into Nan Dòmi.

After our concert and the post-show party, we went to our hotel room. After staying up a long time to listen to the news on CNN, and after talking about our performance, we turned off the light and began the ritual of silence that we were in the habit of observing every night. After a few minutes, I sank into total silence, almost into sleep, when I suddenly heard a sound that seemed to come from very far off. It attracted me, but I couldn't figure out why. I closed my eyes. I concentrated all my thoughts on the sound. I discerned a drumbeat in a rhythm that reminded me of Petwo rhythm. Very soon the sound permeated my being. I continued to follow it. I searched my mind to find where it came from. As I did so, I proceeded toward a dark thoroughfare ending in a place where I saw a woman armed with a big knife in her right hand. She was clothed in a red dress with a collar of black lace, the skirt drawn up to her waist. On her bare leg, I saw a knife held in place by a garter. There was also a younger man dressed in a black costume with a red scarf on his head. He was leading a steer on a tight rope. The woman was singing, and her voice was enchanting. Suddenly, she turned and saw me. She performed a *chika* step (a dance accompanying the

Maringwen rhythm in the north of Haiti, or the Banda[91]). I saw the man cover the steer's back with a red tunic. Then the scene I was witnessing changed suddenly: The man continued to hold the animal with the rope, and began to rub his forehead against its horns. The beast quickly lifted its front legs and crossed them as a man might have done, then kneeled like a trained circus animal. The woman, still singing, climbed onto the back of the steer, which was again standing on four legs, and then she sat on its horns. She was very agitated, her whole body convulsing. In a quick movement, she lifted the knife and stabbed herself in the stomach. Blood gushed from her eyes. The knife pierced her body and I saw the man draw it out of her back with a quick movement.

I jerked, and asked Lòlò if he had seen or heard anything.

"I hear a song. It is very beautiful," he answered.

"I would like to learn it. I'm going to try," I said to him.

At the very moment I began to hum the first notes, I felt a strong breath, right next to me. I was seized with fear. I turned to tell Lòlò, when suddenly I saw a threatening hand holding a knife above my head. I automatically lifted my arm to protect my face and cried out. Something abruptly stirred in my navel. I heard Lòlò's voice call my name. We hooked arms and took flight. Then I felt a falling sensation at the level of my womb. I trembled. I opened my eyes and after a moment of stupor, I realized that we had come back to the ground in front of the door to the bathroom, holding each other in a tight embrace, out of breath and sweaty—although I couldn't remember how we had come to be able to fly together. We remained in that position for about five minutes. Then suddenly the room was invaded by an invisible presence. It was not through intuition or the result of induction but quite simply through that consciousness, that evidence that has no connection with reason, that knew I that there was a *yon moun* (one person, in the sense of intelligence) that had followed us. Having seen two rocks that Lòlò had mysteriously found in

---

91 The Maringwen is a highly staccato rhythm played on a string instrument, with a rest after three measures. The Banda has the same rhythm, but is played on a Vodou battery composed of two congo drums: the manman (mother) that marks the counterpoint, and the Kata rhythm that is played on the boula couché (hand drum).

his pocket during a Vodou dance under the peristyle at Lakou Souvnans, it began to fight with us to take them back. But Lòlò defended himself energetically, shouting ferociously. It drowned us in an overpowering odor. It was like an essence. I knew that it had the power to reduce us to almost nothing. It tried several times to suffocate us. Lòlò made a movement like a cat stalking its prey, then with great nimbleness threw himself on the bed. He made another gesture with his hand that I didn't understand and from his pants pocket drew out the bag—one I had sewed for that purpose—which contained the rocks. He let out another horrible cry and stuffed the bag under his pillow. Then slowly the *moun* retreated and left the room. With a movement of my head I signaled Lòlò to switch places with me. He understood and we went back to bed. I looked at the clock. It was three a.m.

It was nine a.m. when I woke up. I felt exhausted and anxious. I sat on the edge of the bed waiting for Lòlò to wake up. He had scarcely opened his eyes when I began to question him, asking him to give me a detailed account of the events of the previous night. Aunt Tansia had always counseled us to describe to each other all our experiences in Nan Dòmi. "That will help you to retain the details," she explained. The details in her view should serve as reference points which would enrich our real understanding.

Lòlò told me what follows, not without emotion: "I heard a song, then a sound, and I followed them. I ended up in a place that opened upon a vast space. I reached a kind of clearing where something like a ceremony was unfolding. From a distance, I perceived a group of individuals. Among them there was a dark mass that almost had the appearance of a human form. Suddenly the dark mass began to advance in my direction and I saw two enormous red eyes charging toward me. I heard you cry out. I had time to shout your name. I grasped your arm and we flew together. Then we landed in front of the bathroom door. I experienced the biggest shock of my life when I realized that we had been followed. For a moment I was afraid but I quickly got over it by crying out. I was beside myself when I sensed the presence of *yon moun* in the room. It had seen the rocks and wanted them. It hated me. It threatened to kill me if I didn't give them to it. I refused. I cried out to repel its attacks. I fought it with all my strength. It tried to dilute us by spreading an odor all around us. But we were stronger. At that moment I had the feeling that I could make it disintegrate and that was what I was going to do. I began to chase it around the room to overcome or capture it, but it got away in time."

While Lòlò was talking, I had a sensory experience. It was a sensation analogous to what I felt when I had to make a decision: The eyelid of my left eye began to tremble uncontrollably. My shoulders also. I thought about Aunt Tansia, who told us many times: "When one makes a choice, the body knows it. The left side of the body contracts for a bad choice. The eye is very receptive. It grasps at anything."

"We are going to have to cleanse our *zafè* (belongings) before leaving the room," I suggested to Lòlò. I meant that we had to exorcise our fears by rubbing sage leaves, steeped in tepid water, on our bodies, our clothes, our suitcases, our shoes— everything we owned.

"You are right. I agree. It has soiled everything. And if we don't do it, it will be able to keep on following us to do us harm."

I understood very well what Lòlò was feeling. We found the experience—apart from the flight together—terrifying. We realized that we had been in Nan Dòmi and that what we had seen was not an *ordinary dream*. We had gone together to the place, guided by the sound and the song. I concluded that the scene we had witnessed was real. A series of thoughts assailed me, such as that the *moun* might have been able to take not only the rocks but also our lives. Lòlò's cries were crucial. They were the weapons that had placed us outside the *moun*'s reach. My role was that of a trigger to find the way and to be able to fly.

I am clearly not in a position to say exactly what level Lòlò reached from the mystic point of view. But speaking as an initiate, I must recognize that he was unpredictable. Now, Aunt Tansia had always reminded us that a good warrior is unpredictable. "Don't deploy your forces before you measure the strength of the enemy," she used to say. "*Ou k ap konnen sa ou pral fè, men ou p ap janm konnen sa ou pral pran.* (You know what you are going to do to your enemy, but you don't know what is in store for you.)"

Lòlò's comportment that night convinced me that he had enough personal power to know how to act and to benefit from his actions. When I analyzed the experience of that night, I was struck by his determination and I deduced that he was gifted with an infallible strength and that I was fortunate to be in the company of a warrior who was so determined. I drew a lesson from this experience: I learned that our intimacy went beyond the marital bond.

His comportment that night surprised me. I had never seen him before from that perspective. That aspect of his personality was unknown to me. He had always given me the impression of being an emotional and offhanded kind of person. When we first met, I thought he was a loudmouth. I thought so because, since he was a man of the popular theater—a musician, a man of action, engaged with Haitian society—he was always prepared to make attention-grabbing appearances in the media, whether criticizing Haitian politicians or talking about Vodou. But after a year of life together, I revised my judgments. I saw him instead as a shy man, because he never spoke about his personal experiences. I knew him as a fervent adept, respecting the calendar, never missing Vodou celebrations. Before I went, he would visit the lakou we had noted on our agenda and got along easily with the people there. He often went back alone. He always had the kindness to give me a detailed account of the ceremonies he had attended. But never a word about what he had done or lived through personally.

That morning, with great frankness, he told me about other terrifying encounters he had experienced despite his young age. One night, for example, toward midnight, when he was returning from a nightclub—he loved to dance—a band of *champwèl* (literally, hairless pigs, a secret society whose members are said to be able to change form at will, for example into animals) he encountered at a crossroads, not far from his paternal home, blew something onto him. The next morning he awoke sick and feverish. His father nursed him. We spent several hours talking. He ended by getting up and saying, "Last night we suffered a rather severe attack. I might even say a mortal attack."

"Were you afraid?" I asked him jokingly.

"I was furious. If you had seen me you would have realized that my allié and I were a single being." He changed the subject quickly and said in a low voice, "*M pa pitimi san gadò.* (I am not an orphan; I feel well-protected.)"

A thought suddenly came to mind: the flight of Beke over the Plaza of Arms at Ouanaminthe, before midnight Mass on December 24, 1980. Her cry had shaken loose some perceptions in me. It is clear that these memories have significance, but I would rather not linger over explanations now, because at a certain point it will be necessary for me to go back and include some descriptions.

The sound and the song of our dream produced the same effects—that is, they shook loose some perceptions in me. The scenes—the woman, the man, the knife, the images, the red and black colors, the blood—aroused strong emotions in me. It was so intense that I became aware again of ordinary danger, quite simply because I had placed everything within a frame of reference: the Bizango world. I had the feeling that I was at the point of lifting the veil off something that I already knew and that was being transformed into a vision. I knew that when we feel the menace of danger over our heads, *nou dedouble* (we split in two). After this experience, I adopted the song of Agaou for my fetish song, that is, my warrior song:

> *Agaou! Pito m vole*
> *Pase djab la manje m*

> Agaou! I'd rather fly away
> Than that the devil should eat me.

That night I *saw*. But I committed a considerable act of stupidity, that of taking too much time to look and sort out what I was in the process of seeing. Aunt Tansia always warned us that in Nan Dòmi one must look without asking for reasons. Otherwise, the mirror becomes clouded and one might become emptied of all one's energy. "In Nan Dòmi, reason has no place," Aunt Tansia repeatedly explained to us. "Fortunately," she said, "when there is awareness of the danger menacing the physical body, Lentansyon always bursts out and takes control of the situation."

That night I was transported on the wings of the *will*. I experienced it through my own methods, with my body. My reason knows that it cannot explain or comprehend but only testify that a parallel world exists and that it knows nothing of the nature of that world. Reason can only bear witness to the effects of the *will*.

## CHAPTER 19

# The Farewell Ceremony

"How did you come in?" I asked her, perplexed.

"We didn't see you come in," Lòlò said to her. "Did you become invisible?"

"I came in through the front door. If you didn't see me, it's because you weren't paying attention."

"On the contrary," Lòlò said, "we were very attentive. We were waiting for you."

"Where were you?" I asked her.

"I am always with you, believe me," she replied. "You were talking about me, isn't that so? I'm going to ask you to pay attention now."

This time it wasn't hard for me to concentrate. Already, the fact that I could not understand how she had been able to pass by us without our seeing her had put me on alert. At the beginning, I thought that she must have come in through the back door, or that she had hidden somewhere. But hers was a small, one-room house with two doors. One of the doors had been barricaded with wire for a year; the other was nothing but an open frame. There were no curtains. The décor of the room in which she lived was more than modest. There was nothing but a bed, a large jug on the right, three chairs, three spoons, three tumblers, three cups on a table, and a cupboard. Her belongings consisted of two straw bags, a big straw hat, three petticoats, three *kòse* (blouses of lace or cotton), three long dresses of raw cotton, and a pair of sandals *batalenbe* (leather and tire rubber sewn together). She also had a small marine-blue jar for tobacco and a big pipe that she named *kalimèt-de-mon-kèr* (peace pipe of my heart) as well as a stick made of cedar wood.

That day it was as if my eyes were opened. Like those of a newborn baby my eyes were suddenly opened to a fantastic world full of magic and unimaginable effects. Everything had new meaning for me in this house. She had us drink a good cup of basil tea. It was our preparation for the ceremony that was about to begin. She lit a candle and placed it on the ground in the middle of the room. Next to the candle she put a *pòt dlo* in which a twig of *bale wouze* was soaking. She beat her chest saying, "*So djèmè twa fwa, nan Ginen tande. Adja-hou! Adja-hou!* (Three times in truth! I take Guinea as witness. God be praised! God be praised!)" She sprinkled us and then began a long discourse on Haitian Vodou. She had us note that Haitian Vodou derived from African Vodun but that it was even richer because it had appropriated the shamanic magic of the natives—Taino, Arawaks, Caribs—and of Christianity. She added that it was important to distinguish between Haitian Vodou and Vodun, which seemed paradoxical, considering that one is derived from the other. But if one succeeds in piercing the mystery of Vodou, which by definition means Spirit or Mystery, one grasps the nuance. When one says "Haitian Vodou" one knows automatically that one is speaking of the mysteries of the Haitian people or of their culture; of everything that describes their language, their way of walking, preparing food, dressing, making love and communicating with the unknown world. It is to speak of their philosophy of life in general. She also insisted on the fact that every people posesses its own culture as a guarantee of its survival. A people manifests itself through its culture. It is called kay mistè. It is also called lakou. The culture of a people is its own house, which it has built thanks to a well-defined social consensus and whose fundamental structure is known only to that people.

"For Haitian culture," she explained, "we point to the structure of the kay mistè or kay mistè-Bitasyon. It is built on *sèt poto* (seven pillars) of which the poto mitan is the central point. These seven pillars support the roof of the kay mistè-Vodou whose material consists of the *san en nanchon* (one hundred one nations) or the *vente en nanchon* (twenty-one nations). These seven pillars are magically bound together by the *twa wòch dife* indispensable for cooking *Manje ti moun yo* (a dish prepared for the lwa marassa). It is that which permits communication between the two worlds—the Known and the Unknown."

She took her time to develop these concepts and to speak to us about their meaning. When she finished, I remarked that I had understood everything—for once—and that from then on I was in control of the question. My consciousness was expanded, and I finally understood that Haitian Vodou was my life's foundation. I had also discovered that to know Vodou was to know myself. That recognition led to the recognition that my entire being was imbued with it, and that therefore I must live this philosophy with the objective of realizing the totality of my being. In order to achieve that, I must carefully bind together all the pieces detached from myself that I had stupidly lost after suffering the negative effects of my inferiority complex vis-à-vis other cultures. It was time to cure myself of my infirmity.

Using cornmeal, she dexterously traced three designs on the ground. Then she walked around them holding three lit candles above her head with one hand. When she stopped, a gentle breeze blew through the room. She put one candle at the heart of the first design, which now strangely resembled a butterfly. She sang, "*Papa Loko, se ou menm ki ban m Ason sa. . . .* (Papa Loko it is you who gave me the Ason . . .)." She bent down and kissed the design.

When she finished, she turned, stopping at each of the four cardinal points. Then she stopped before the second design. It was like a star with five points but looked human. She sang, standing on one leg. I recognized the song:

> *Pwen sa se pwen manman mwen,*
> *Pwen sa se pwen papa mwen,*
> *Sa yo ka fè mwen,*
> *Ma pr ay nan Gran Bwa,*
> *Ma pr ay chache fèy o.*

*Si m pa ka pote,*
*M a woule.*


This pwen is the pwen of my mother
This pwen is the pwen of my father
What can they do [to me]
I'm going into the Great Forest
I'm going to look for leaves


If I can't carry [the weight]
I'll roll it.


The third design represented a recumbent eight with other signs to the right. She kissed it. I didn't speak. I followed all her moves and gestures and listened. I was astonished and soothed by songs that were new to me. The room was full of light and sounds. For a moment, she became quiet, opened her arms and pronounced an incantation that I shall never forget because she taught it to me later:


*A-Legba! Se ou menm ki bay souf lavi-a,*
*Ou menm se Mèt-kalfou,*
*Mèt-lide ki soutni lentansyon*
*Se Ou ki louvri-fèmen tout pòt*
*Louvri pòt Sa-nou-pa-wè-a*
*Pou nou kapab wè lwa an nou yo*
*Pou nou kapab pale ake yo.*


A-Legba. It's you who gives the breath of life
Yourself who is the Master of the Crossroads
Master of the idea that supports intention
It's you who opens and closes all doors
Open the door to What We Don't See
So that we can see our lwa
So that we can speak with them.


She was silent for an instant and then began to move around the designs, sprinkling them with water from the jug and the twig of *bale wouze*. At the same time, she sang, "*Mache, non! Kote ou bouke, vye A-Legba m a pote w.* (Let's go then! Where you are tired, I, old A-Legba, will carry you.) "We repeated all these incantations after her. While we were singing, I saw the room fill up. There were many people everywhere at the same time as the room was illuminated with a strange and inexplicable light. She called each one of us by his *vanyan* name★ (literally, "valiant name," a special name bestowed at initiation). When my turn came, she approached me and made me turn around passing under her left arm.

Aunt Tansia opened some bottles of *kola nèkta* (a carbonated drink popular in Haiti), and offered us bonbons *lanmidon* (sugared cookies made of manioc flour) and bread. Everyone had his fill. The celebration was truly beautiful! But she ended it brusquely.

"This celebration must be held again. You will be responsible for it," she told me before we left.

"Will I ever know how to do it?"

"Intention alone will be enough for you."

That is how my last conversation with Aunt Tansia ended.

She made Janbe a month later. In the meantime, she did not once open her mouth to speak to me of anything. During our final encounters, we spent the time looking at each other without saying a word. It is not that I didn't have anything more to ask her, but rather that I didn't want to upset her with my eternal pleading, "Don't leave me, Aunt Tansia."

# Epilogue

On December 4, 1994, I informed Lòlò of my intention to write a book. I had my first notes on the teachings of Aunt Tansia that dated from more than eighteen years earlier. I wanted to transmit them onto the printed page so that I could burn the pile of papers and cassettes that I had guarded jealously until then without good reason.

"You are going to leave your mark through this book," Lòlò said to me.

"No, on the contrary, instead I am going to erase it."

"What a funny way to do it!"

"Everyone has his own tactic for tracking himself down," I heard myself answer Lòlò.

I surprised myself. I thought I had forgotten certain practices.

On December 7, 1994, a torrential rain beat down on the entire region. The water came down the hills and overflowed ravines and sewers. An avalanche of water, such as I had not seen for a long time, filled the streets like a great river. It passed through the house. My notes, cassettes, tape recorder, fax and radio-telephone floated in the water. All the instruments I used to communicate with the world were *nan dlo*. All my efforts and my dream of writing a book were also *nan dlo*. At that precise moment I experienced tangible proof of the truth that Aunt Tansia had taught me, "Only water can disappear things without a trace." It was as if I had been cut in two by misfortune. But a voice deep inside told me that all was not lost. I was convinced that I had learned things that the water could not carry off or erase.

This experience taught me how to distinguish between temporal knowledge, accumulated in the intellect, and consciousness. I was able to draw the line of demarcation between the temporal and the eternal domains. I was able to gather the wet pages. I dried them in the sun. Fortunately, they were written in pencil. Little by little, though it was difficult, I deciphered them. I knew that all that amounted to a premonition. Aunt Tansia's predictions about the day when I would lose my notes and my tape recorder came to mind: "You are too dependent on these things. You must know that what has not been born on high—in the unknown world—cannot survive here below. *Nan Ginen tande!*" She had wanted to draw my attention to the hardening in me caused by my logical thought, the origin of my obstinacy in wanting to conserve important teachings in the memory of a perishable machine instead of integrating them into my own memory. "You always push aside the most important things. You refuse to live them and gain consciousness of them yourself."

I spent ten days in retreat. I fashioned a new identity for myself. I moved everything in the whole house. I rearranged the space where I was living.

In January 1995, when I began to write this book, I had a vision. It was my last. I saw a snake come into the living room and climb the poto mitan that I had placed at the center of the house. I tried to make the snake come down by sprinkling it with water, and I lit a candle to frighten it. Suddenly, it was no longer a snake but rather a man whose features seemed blurred. It was a white man who held out his hand to me in greeting. I stretched out my right hand to respond to his gesture and he took my hand gently and drew me to him, holding me firmly. A strange thing happened. I saw our two hands blend into one, then our two bodies. I found myself grasping the poto mitan, looking at Lòlò and the children down below, seated at its base, their eyes lifted up to me. I don't know how long that lasted. All I know is that I woke up with a song on my lips, "*Kore, kore, nou kore. . . .*"

Lòlò and the children were standing before me.

"A lwa possessed you. It revealed many things to me. I'll tell you about it later. Go lie down; you seem tired," Lòlò said.

I shook my head in protest, because I knew that I was not tired but, on the contrary, filled with energy. I spent the night deciphering my notes and writing. That night I wrote more than fifty pages at once. It was a feat I was never capable of after that day. I began my text with acknowledgments, and right at the bottom of the page I wrote a strange and meaningful sentence: "*Se Nan dòmi m te ye*" (I was in Nan Dòmi).

That will be the title of my book, I said to myself.

# Lexicon

**Abobo!**: a cry uttered in greeting a lwa Rada, meaning "Welcome!", "Amen!", "Hallelujah!"

**Adja**: an initiate in the depths of the water or in Nan Dòmi (see anba dlo; Nan Dòmi); the title given to an initiate who has reached the highest level.

**Adja-hou!**: God be praised!

**Agaou**: A male lwa who is a healer.

**Ago!**: Attention!

**Agwe-t-Awoyo**: God of the sea and oceans.

**Allié**: a luminous, vibrant being; alliés are beings who inhabit the crevices in the earth, exchanging knowledge and know-how with human beings.

**Anakayit**: a big tree belonging to the same family as the ceiba, and the baobab from Africa.

**Anba dlo**: in the depths of the water, or in the mysteries of the water. Refers to a kind of initiation into the Ginen mysteries.

**Andèyo**: the countryside.

**Anmwe!**: Help!

**Anyen**: a concept that defines the central void.

**Asogwe**: a "kouche" or initiate, that is, one who has followed the teaching of a line of priests in a Vodou convent.

**Ason**: a sacred object received after initiation upon leaving the Vodou convent.

**Attibon Legba**: *see* Legba or A-Legba.

**Ayitien**: ancient inhabitant of the island of Ayiti, now written as "Haiti," which means "high land" or "mountainous place."

**Badè**: god who governs the wind.

**Badji** or **sobadji**: office, the private temple of the Vodou priest.

**Bale wouze**: a sacred plant used to bless altars and the tables where food is arranged for the lwa.

**Bitasyon**: family patrimony where the tree altars are located, where the powers are transmitted from one generation to another.

**Bizango**: a Vodou sect, a type of secret society. It is also a state of consciousness.

**Bòkò** or **Bòkòr**: a Vodou priest.

**Bondje-manman-mwen!**: Holy Mother!

**Bon-konprann**: reason.

**Bouboun**: pubis.

**Brav**: the Good Being, one of the Mysteries who bestow the Ason.

**Cacos**: At the time of the U.S. occupation (1915–1934) cacos referred to rebel Haitian peasant armies whose leader, Charlemagne Péralte, was assassinated in 1919.

**Chante pwent**: satirical song. During Carnival (a popular celebration preceding Lent) all the musical groups (rara, bande a pied, rasin') compose such songs.

**Chwal**: a medium. In the language of Vodou, the chwal (horse) serves as a channel through whom the spirits of the ancestors and forces come down from the unknown world and possess.

**Clairin**: distilled, unrefined rum.

**Danbala** and **Ayida Wèdo**: mystery of creation, symbolized by two snakes that represent duality, harmony, consciousness; the egg placed between the snakes symbolizes the Word.

**Danse Vodou**: Vodou ceremonies.

**Danti**: elder.

**Dantòr**: one of the surnames of Erzulie (a female lwa).

**Dechouke**: to uproot.

**Dekou**: phase of the new moon.

**Demanbre**: portion of the terrain of an undivided lakou. It represents a kind of savings account of the group.

**Diri kole ak pwa**: rice and beans (Haitian national dish).

**Djakout**: straw bag carried by country people.

**Djehoun**: mystery of the Word.

**Djetò a**: soul inherited from the ancestor.

**Djèvo**: Vodou convent.

**Dlo**: water.

**Double**: *see* Nannan.

**Eskize konesans**: without knowing.

**Fa**: the Oracle. A lwa whose divinatory tradition stems from the town of Ife in Nigeria. This system of divination shapes human destiny and is interpreted by a priest of Fa.

**Fanmi Ginen**: a family of initiates belonging to the same discipline (Ginen).

**Filyè lespri**: link of communication with the Spirit.

**Fons**: people from the Dahomey region who vanquished the Gedevis (or Gedes) whom they had taken prisoner.

**Fran-Ginen**: an initiate into authentic Ginen.

**Fritay**: fried food.

**Frite**: freeloader.

**Gad**: protector of lives and goods.

**Galipòt**: member of a secret society.

**Gede**: African tribe—ancient inhabitants of Dahomey—conquered by the Fon and transported to Saint-Domingue during the colonial period. Lwa Gede: Mysteries of the cemeteries, family of lwa who rule the world of the dead.

**Ginen**: literally "Guinea"; principle that supports and directs every Vodou teaching. It is also a state. In order to have the right to enter into it, the initiate must transform his being.

**Ginen-an**: the Unknowable; the Unreachable; the Spirit; the Invisible.

**Gobe**: to eat gluttonously.

**Gonmen**: to trap.

**Gran Bwa**: lwa who inhabits the forest. One of the three mysteries bestowers of the Ason.

**Grandèt**: a respectable personage.

**Granmoun**: a grown person, adult; old person; someone who has had many experiences in the magical-spiritual domain.

**Griyo**: grilled pork.

**Gwo Bonnanj**: intellect or physical body, according to the context. Its other names are: Landwat (Place), Sèmèdò.

**Houmfò**: Vodou temple.

**Houngan**: Vodou priest, divine, healer.

**Isit-la**: the here and now.

**Janbe**: to traverse the unknown world.

**Je**: supernatural power of clairvoyance. The gift of clairvoyance.

**Je klè**: open-eyed, or possessing consciousness. A concept that defines the first level of attention; the faculty of seeing and distinguishing material, physical and visible things.

**Jete**: ritual to attract and greet the arrival of a lwa.

**Jete dlo**: literally, to cast water; libation; water cast ritually on the ground; ritual to attract and greet the arrival of a lwa.

**Jodi a**: today.

**Kabicha**: light sleep.

**Kadav kò**: physical body.

**Kaka griyo**: leftovers of grilled pork.

**Kakòn-je-bourik**: fruit of a certain plant. When it is dried in the sun, it oddly resembles the eye of a donkey.

**Kalfou**: croosroads; spirit who stands at the crossroads.

**Kantamwa**: personal I: ego. Another sense: boastfulness, bragging.

**Kay**: house/dwelling.

**Kay mistè**: house or main room reserved for Vodou ceremonies, in the center of which are the Pe (the altars). It is in a way a databank for all the elements composing the magical-spiritual structures of the lakou.

**Koko Ginen**: an oleaginous tropical plant. Its fruit produces a sacred oil with which one prepares the wicks that are lighted in certain ceremonies; or in anointing the temples, forehead and the back of the neck of the initiate, and in massaging the ill.

**Konbit**: type of collective work.

**Konnen**: connoisseur, seeker, savant.

**Kore**: highest degree of consciousness.

**Kounye a-la-a**: concept that means the present moment; that which cannot be seized.

**Kwiy**: half a calabash.

**Lachòy**: sage.

**Lakou**: site of many-dimensional living where an extended family shares all aspects of life.

**Lakou-andèyo**: lakou in the countryside.

**Lakou Ginen**: lakou founded upon the Ginen principle.

**Lakou lavil**: lakou situated in towns (for example, Lakou Blain in Bel-Air at Port-au-Prince) or very near towns.

**Lakou-Bitasyon**: several dwellings opening onto a single courtyard.

**Lanmidon**: manioc flour used in the preparation of pudding, kasav (cookie made of manioc flour), gruel and sauces.

**Lanperè**: literally, "the Emperor," a title given to the second in charge at a lakou.

**Lavalas**: avalanche.

**Lave-tèt**: Vodou initiation ritual.

**Layo**: winnowing tray or basket.

**Legba**, or **Attibon Legba**, or **A-Legba**: a male lwa filling the role of guardian of the crossroads, of doors and of barriers.

**Lentansyon**: the will.

**Limen**: the ritual of lighted candles designed to attract beneficial effects from the lwa, Zany, and Mistè.

**Lwa**: in theory, a divinized ancestor who derives his personal power from his life on earth. The lwa is a valued family asset. An enlightened spiritual being.

**Loko-Miwa**: Vodou divinity, master of the phenomena of vision and ecstasy.

**Lougarou**: sorcerer.

**Ma**: water pond where certain lwa live.

**Mabi**: a drink made of fermented cane syrup and the juice of sour oranges.

**Maldyòk**: word derived from Italian *malocchio* which means evil eye; pieces of porcelain of all colors used to guard against calamities and bad luck. These pieces are attached to clothing with a safety pin (three or four pieces of different colors together).

**Malkadi**: epilepsy.

**Mambo**: Vodou priestess.

**Man**: term of respect used for elderly women, diminutive of *maman*.

**Mapou**: big tree belonging to the same family as the baobabs of Africa.

**Marinèt** in Kreyòl, or **Marinette**: name of a female lwa.

**Masa-Wè**: transport of one mystery to the other. A magical transfer.

**Mazanza**: secret society. A kind of magical power. It is also a state of consciousness.

**Mèt Dega**: spoilsport who disrupts ceremonies.

**Mèt tèt**: literally the "master of the head"; the lwa chosen during initiation which the adept has agreed to serve.

**Mistè**: literally, "mystery," can refer to a guardian lwa, the lwa itself, or something that is a mystery, in the general sense of the word.

**M la–M pa la**: a concept that defines the state of interior silence.

**Mofreze**: infirm.

**Monte Anwo**: a concept that defines ecstasy.

**Mori**: a priest belonging to the Mandingo society in the north of Haiti.

**Moun**: human being, intelligence.

**Moun Ginen**: initiate who follows the Ginen principle.

**Moun òdinè**: an ordinary person, common mortal.

**Mouton zenzen**: kind of legume, a plant that bestows power, with a bitter taste.

**Nago**: rhythm scanned in three weak beats and one strong beat. The Anago or Yoruba are an African tribe inhabiting southern Nigeria and the southeast of Benin, a part of Togo and of Ghana.

**Nan Dòmi**: a concept that defines the second level of attention. One enters into a state that permits one to see abstract things unknown until then. A lucid dream state.

**Nan Ginen**: the unknown, or the unknown world.

**Nan Ginen tande!**: So be it!

**Nanchon**: nation.

**Nannan**: an astral body. Another name: double.

**Nannan Boulouklou** or **Naa Bukuu**: divinity who represents the first female principle.

**Nannan-rèv**: dream body.

**Nèg Ginen**: name of the founder of Lakou Souvnans.

**O'Batala**: the assembly of biological ancestors who constitute the priestly body and transmit the wisdom of the past.

**Ogou**: lwa of fire, of iron, of blood and of war. The many Ogou lwa are onsidered among the most powerful lwa.

**Ogou Feray**: lwa of armies and war whose element is fire.

**Omi-Nannan**: sacred water.

**Palma-kristi**: castor oil.

**Papa Loko**: Master of the Vodou temple, conservator of tradition, he is in principle the treasurer of the databank [paraphernalia] of the temple's ceremonial chamber.

**Pase pa filyè**: literally, "passing through the channel of the spirit"; a concept that refers to creating a channel of communication.

**Pe**: from the Yoruba word *peji*, which means "altar." It is also the verb "to be silent."

**Pen manchèt**: long loaf of wheat bread.

**Petwo**: a category of Vodou divinities. A dance rhythm.

**Pile**: to trample. In the pejorative sense: to kill.

**Pinga-pye**: literally, "watch out for your feet"; a concept that defines the state which is above the first and the second level of attention. It is the state of awakening, the taking control of energies, a state of concentration that reinforces the strength of the initiate.

**Pitit an mwen**: my child.

**Poban**: small jar.

**Pòt**: pot; a large jar, a Haitian measurement equivalent to a liter.

**Pòtay-mistè**: name given to the points of opening along the physical body.

**Poto**: pillar, post.

**Poto mitan**: middle pillar, principal axis in the center of the Vodou peristyle, symbolizing the encounter of two worlds: the spiritual world and the material, physical one (sky and earth).

**Pratik**: merchant who delivers his or her products, or a storekeeper one frequents regularly.

**Pwen**: magical power.

**Pyebwa sèvi**: a certain belief that there are trees that are great initiates and are therefore inhabited by lwa: they serve as altars.

**Rada**, or **Arada**: a category of Vodou divinities. A dance rhythm.

**Reklame**: to reclaim. To be chosen by a lwa, Zany or Mystery.

**Replasman bòn**: ceremony in which material and spiritual limits are laid out before certain lwa in a well-determined space.

**Sakit**: small bag.

**San en nanchon**: literally "one hundred nations." A concept that defines the assembly of the mysteries and nations that form the Haitian Vodou pantheon.

**Sele**: to sit astride, ride. A state experienced by a medium [the "horse" is straddled].

**Sèvi**: to serve. A concept signifying that one is a Vodou adept.

**Sèvis**: Vodou ceremonies.

**Sèvis Ginen**: ritual pertaining to the last stage of initiation.

**Sèvitè**: spiritual and temporal head, the principal person responsible for the lakou.

**So djèmè twa fwa**: an oath that means "In truth three times."

**Sobo**: the grand judge of the Vodou temple, master of rain.

**Syam**: cream-colored, untreated cotton.

**Tafyatè**: drinking companions who imbibe from the same jug and who demonstrate complicitous movements, characteristic of them alone.

**Tako**: bird of prey about the size of a large blackbird.

**Tanbou kata**: second drum in the Vodou drum battery.

**Tchatcha**: maracas; percussion instrument made from an emptied gourd.

**Ti Bonnanj**: the spiritual body, a part of God. Its other names: Lanvè, Selidò.

**Ti moun**: child.

**Tisisin'**: tasting.

**Toli**: a bush with clusters of small, white, gamopetalous flowers, hallucinogenic, belonging to the family Oleaceae.

**Toutouni**: literally "completely nude," a concept that means "formless."

**Twa gout dlo**: concept that defines the authority of the initiate.

**Twa pawòl**: concept that defines the union of thought, word and act. Name of a plant (*Allophylus occidentalis*), whose leaf is composed of three parts. Cures are said to be impossible without this plant, which guarantees protection from the Father, the Son and the Holy Ghost.

**Twa wòch dife**: concept that defines the architectural plan of the kay mistè, signifying the three fundamental rules that support the mysteries of Vodou. A triune formula that produces miracles. (*See also* Wòch dife.)

**Vèvè**: complex designs traced on the ground like so many maps to indicate to the spirits where to go.

**Vire rad lanvè**: expression that signifies "putting oneself in another state."

**Vodou:** spirit, mystery.

**Wòch dife**: stones that produce fire when rubbed together.

**Woule vant**: belly dance.

**Zaka**, or **Azaka Mede**: a guardian spirit of Haitian agriculture. Other names: Minister Azaka, Kouzen.

**Zany**, or **Zanj**: angel.

**Zèb gore**: a kind of very hardy dwarf herb.

Mimerose "Manzè" Beaubrun was born in Ouanaminthe, in Haiti's Northeast Department. She studied ethnology at university in Port-au-Prince, and earned a degree in Social and Cultural Anthropology. She is the co-author of *Livre ouvert sur le développement endogène d'Haïti*, and *Enquête sur les productions culturelles dans le Nord'Est*. Her professional experience includes research in the field of music throughout Haiti.

Beaubrun is also the lead singer and co-founder of the musical group Boukman Eksperyans. In 2002, she was named an Ambassador for Peace and Development by the United Nations, in honor of her efforts to promote unity through music that transcends cultural barriers. In her own words: "We are one spirit and a plurality of cultures. Our mission is to encourage every human being to feel the need and the urgency to contribute, with respect and peace, to the creation of a new world."